*Best wishes in your journey to
live the life you love with the
love of your life.*

Remember to <u>Be</u> <u>The</u> <u>Chooser</u>!

CONSCIOUS DATING

CONSCIOUS DATING

Finding
The Love
Of Your
Life In
Today's
World

David Steele

RCN Press
a division of Relationship Coaching Network
P.O. Box 111783, Campbell, CA 95011
www.RCNpress.com

646.77
STEELE, D

All credits appear on pages 339-341. Every effort has been made to trace the ownership of all copyrighted material included in this volume. Any errors that may have occurred are inadvertent and will be corrected in subsequent editions, provided notification is sent to publisher.

All personal vignettes, anecdotes, and stories are from my life, the lives of my clients, or people I interviewed. However, names and identifying details have been altered to preserve their privacy.

Conscious Dating: *Finding the Love of Your Life in Today's World*

Conscious Dating® is a registered trademark of Relationship Coaching Institute and may not be used without permission.

First Edition

Printed in the United States of America.

Published by RCN Press
a division of Relationship Coaching Network
P.O. Box 111783, Campbell, CA 95011
www.RelationshipCoachingNetwork.org
www.RCNpress.com

Library of Congress Cataloging-in-Publication Data

Steele, David, A.
    Conscious Dating: Finding the Love of Your Love in Today's World / David Steele-
1st. ed.
                        p.   cm.
1. Mate selection 2. Love 3. Dating 4. Relationships I. Title

ISBN 0-9755005-5-4

Library of Congress Control Number: 2005906353

Acknowledgments

*T*HIS BOOK HAS taken eight years to complete, and would not be possible without the support of these wonderful people:

Rachel Sarah, who helped bring this book to life by interviewing conscious singles and telling their stories so engagingly, as well as helping me keep forward momentum going with this project while I juggled my commitments.

My dream team: Editor Melanie Rigney; Designers Cathi Stevenson and Judi Lake; Publicist Penny Sansevieri. Each is a talented professional who "got" what makes this book special, believed in this project, and gave me her best.

Garry Cooper and Cindy Barrilleaux, who were instrumental in helping me take a mess of ideas and concepts and shape them into the book as it is today.

My coaches, Phil Humbert, Jim Donovan, and Burt Dubin, who inspired me to believe in myself and the larger vision for this project, while keeping me on track and grounded with their wisdom and experience.

Marvin Cohen, my friend and business partner who was there at the beginning of the journey that resulted in this book, and who influenced many of the concepts and paradigms that make *Conscious Dating* truly unique.

Ed Shea and Hedy Schleifer, who have taught me much about relationship coaching and embody the best of what it means to be a relationship coach with their impeccable coaching skills, unconditional love for their clients, and total commitment to their profession.

The staff of Relationship Coaching Institute, whose professionalism and dedication have supported me and made it possible to create a worldwide organization dedicated to promoting successful relationships for singles and couples: Brenda Zeller, Linda Marshall, Lynne Michelson, Colleen DeCew, Jeff Herring, and Laurie Cameron.

The students and graduates of Relationship Coaching Institute. Our unique community of relationship coaches has been instrumental in testing and developing the principles in this book as well as supplying ample feedback, ideas, and case examples.

And last but not least, my life partner, Maggie Harris. Our relationship coincided with the development of this book and provided the crucible for me to personally test the principles of *Conscious Dating* with honesty and authenticity. ✄

*This book is dedicated to my children and stepchildren,
who continually inspire me and drive my purpose for my work:*

Alaina Steele

Victor Steele

Eric Steele

Michelle Harris & Casey Zolezzi

Daniel Harris

Joy Harris

Table of Contents

Introduction

IN TODAY'S SOCIETY, we all want the same thing, whether we are single or married, young or old, gay or straight: to love and to be loved. The great majority of us desire a fulfilling life partnership. As social beings, we need intimacy and connection with a community of friends and family, and a committed relationship that meets our emotional, physical, and spiritual needs. As our world grows increasingly complex, personal relationships—the building blocks of our society—seem to suffer. We want to be happy and fulfilled in our most important relationships, but don't seem to know how.

The rules for dating and mating have changed, and up until now you may have been discovering the new rules by trial and error. The good news is that in today's world you are able to live the life that you choose. I hope this book helps you make conscious, wise, and effective relationship choices. Moreover, I sincerely hope you will "find the love of your life and the life that you love."

Regrettably, one holdover from the past is a misperception that singles are selfish, failures, inadequate, immature, unwanted, and/or unlovable. When that misperception merges with our impatience and desire for immediate gratification—an unfortunate characteristic of today's culture—many singles believe that the path to happiness lies in getting into a relationship as quickly as possible. Typically, after heartbreak and failure, many singles feel confused about how to make relationships work. Thus, you may hesitate to trust yourself and others. Consciously or unconsciously, you may fear commitment. Unsatisfying and painful relationship experiences breed discouragement and defensiveness. This intensifies a fear of intimacy and creates barriers to having the relationship you really want.

You are not alone. Today, there are more single people than ever before: 101 million singles in the United States, which means 46 percent of the adult population. Since 85 percent of adults marry, it is clear that the great majority of people prefer to be in a committed relationship.[1]

Most singles today want to find their life partner, but are scared and confused, afraid of failure and perplexed about how to succeed. There is a whole growth industry providing solutions for singles, much of which is shallow, exploitive, and worthless. Our high divorce rate suggests that this process is ineffective. As a result, people are increasingly aware of the importance of making good relationship choices, of realizing that infatuation, hope, promises, and good intentions will not help them find and keep the love of their life. Singles like you seem ready and eager to learn how to have conscious, intentional, and successful committed relationships.

In *Conscious Dating*, I hope to help you find your Life Partner efficiently and effectively. However, the quickest route to happiness is not necessarily the best route. I will give you a road map to avoid mirages, dead ends, potholes, and swamps so that you are able to go where you genuinely want and need to be.

Finding the love of your life in today's world means being the pioneer of your destiny. When it comes to relationship choices, there are no guarantees or predictable outcomes, despite romantic promises and fantasies. *Conscious Dating* can help you have the life and relationship that you want by showing you how to make intentional, conscious choices. In these chapters you will learn more about who you really are and how to get what you want in your life. You have many choices. You are not bound by the traditions of the past. You are free to choose the life and relationships that you *really* want.

MY STORY
Like you, I've learned about life and relationships from personal experience—first, the wrong lessons and eventually, the right ones. Growing up in a single-parent family, there was no one to show me how to get what I wanted and needed in my life and relationships. I had to learn by trial and error.

One of my first serious relationships led to marriage. My wife and I had married young and unconsciously. There was a lot of tension in our relationship, but I believed that love could conquer all, and if we just worked hard enough we could "make" the relationship work. Not so. It was a hard and devastating lesson, learning the reality of relationships. In 1990, after ten years of marriage, the birth of our daughter, and years of unsuccessful marriage counseling, we divorced. It was the same year I started my private practice as a marriage and family therapist. How ironic.

In 1997, I had been a helping professional for almost two decades, including seven years of full-time private practice. When I decided to become a therapist, I fantasized about being a superhero that, on his own, could lower our country's divorce rate. But through all those years, my work did not seem to be making couples happier or more stable. And, at age forty, my personal life was not looking very positive either.

I'd been running a yellow pages ad offering professional help for "couples in crisis." Couples were continually coming to me seeking support. But rather than saving their marriages, half or more of my clients were still ending up in divorce court. I was burning out.

Today, I look back and wonder, half-jokingly, why I didn't advertise to help "happy couples" or "easy couples." Instead, I was seeing angry and bitter couples on the verge of breaking up. Often, I was the second call they made after first consulting a divorce lawyer. For a long time I felt responsible for saving their marriages, and if I couldn't, it was just a matter of my needing more training and experience. Over time, I discovered that the average success rate for other marriage and family therapists was no better than mine. I was somewhat comforted by these statistics, but dissatisfied at the same time.

I was in no hurry to remarry. A few years after my divorce, I had started dating a woman who had worked with me at a local counseling clinic. She was fun and attractive and pursued me persistently. We decided to live together. It turned out to be a passionate push-and-pull relationship with lots of chaos and broken promises. In May 1995, I had moved out, determined to regain my sanity and never see her again. Four months later, after some lengthy and intense discussions, I moved back in. That October, we married. She was very eager to have children, but we ran into fertility problems due to her age (she was forty-three) and started costly in vitro fertilization (IVF) treatments.

Under tremendous financial pressure, my entrepreneurial side got creative. I was looking around for ways to expand my practice. One morning in 1997 at the monthly meeting of my men's organization, Robert, an acquaintance who was a vitamin salesman, announced that he was training to become a life coach and was seeking practice clients.

A "life coach"? I thought, "Hey, he's going to charge people for helping them with their lives—that's what I do! Is this a gimmick for practicing without a license?" When I asked him what coaching was about, he smiled and told me that a life or personal coach is someone who helps people achieve their goals and live fulfilling lives. At first, I felt threatened that someone without a graduate degree or a license was seeking to help people be happy and charging them hundreds of dollars to do so!

However, intrigued with the idea of personal or life coaching, I researched the profession of coaching on the Internet and discovered a whole new helping profession had been growing right under my nose. Robert offered to coach me for practice at no charge, so I decided to give it a try.

We started with weekly phone conversations. His approach was awkward at first, obviously reading from a list of prepared "coaching" questions. He was trying really hard and I went along. I worked with him on my dilemma about my career, my passion for helping people have successful relationships, and my burnout as a couples therapist. Within a few weeks, I had a breakthrough idea for a new direction for my practice and a whole new vision for my career.

Moreover, this experience piqued my curiosity, and I decided to check out exactly what coaching was all about.

I signed up for training with a large, established professional coaching organization. Its paradigm for helping people sounded familiar to me, given my counseling background, yet seemed very new at the same time. For example, in one exercise I was partnered with another participant and was told to listen and ask questions for five minutes without giving advice or feedback. I could ask questions, but not respond as an expert by telling him what to do or sharing my perspective. This approach to supporting someone was a challenge for the therapist in me! But it was a great exercise in learning how to be present with my client and frame powerful questions that empowered the client to be the expert on his/her life.

I thought: "What if I applied a coaching approach to help my clients in their relationships?" I researched models for relationship coaching, but could find no standard; everyone seemed to be doing his/her own thing. Still, I was impressed by what I had learned and experienced, and I thought seriously about transitioning my practice to relationship coaching.

As part of my introduction to the coaching approach to creating successful relationships, I decided to review and reread a number of the current self-help books on relationships. What I discovered was an oversimplified approach: "Do this" or "Don't do this." Yes, relationship self-help books could help couples improve their relationship and singles find a partner in the short term, but not necessarily help find a life partner or create a sustainable lifelong relationship. It was then I decided I wanted to create a comprehensive model for relationship coaching.

At the same time, I was dreading going to my office every day. I knew I was burning out because I was at the point that I couldn't stand working with my clients anymore. While I had made the decision to work with couples experiencing difficult challenges and was dedicated to keeping them together, I was frustrated with getting so few positive results.

But my discovery of coaching opened up new possibilities and gave me a new direction. One day, I was thinking about the different stages we go through to create a successful life partnership, and I had an epiphany: singles become couples! THAT WAS IT! As a therapist, it had never occurred to me to work with singles. Moreover, I thought that if I started coaching singles and they became couples, I could continue to support them through coaching.

I decided to launch a weekly group in my area to help singles: a "Friday Night Social" in which singles could meet, socialize, and learn about relationships. We talked about how singles could prepare for a committed relationship and set themselves up for success. We outgrew our first space in just three weeks!

In working with singles, I saw a lot of well-educated middle-aged men who worked in the technology industry and who had little clue about how to have a good relationship. I helped them learn basic dating skills, like asking a woman out, and supported them to be more assertive. I met many women who felt they were past their prime, too old, or too overweight. I helped them become more positive and less desperate. It seemed that most singles needed to overcome fears, become more authentic with others, and focus on the big picture of their life and not be in such a desperate hurry to find a relationship.

In January 1998, my wife and I had twin boys. Shortly thereafter, I discovered that she had been addicted to prescription medication for quite some time. I knew there were a lot more medications in the house, but I had assumed they were related to her IVF treatments. She reluctantly went into rehab, relapsed, and went to rehab again multiple times. Finally, the welfare of two beautiful baby boys was at stake. We divorced after two years of denial, conflict, and broken promises.

Certainly in my own life I had made enough relationship choices that didn't work out and learned about unsolvable problems the hard way. As a new relationship coach, my hope was to make the path for others less arduous.

As I expanded my relationship coaching practice, the Friday night singles socials grew more popular. Around this time, I also discovered that many other coaches were holding seminars by telephone to reach wider audiences, so I put together a variety of teleclasses for singles on dating, communication, and other topics. While conducting classes over the telephone was new and awkward at first, I was thrilled at how many people called in from all over the world, and found this new way of teaching to be a lot of fun.

My excitement at the success of my relationship coaching ventures led me to dream big. What if relationship coaching grew so expansively that it resembled McDonald's? Just as easy as it is to find a hamburger anywhere in the world, you could step out your door or pick up your phone and receive solid support with your relationships. How different our world would be! I envisioned how our society would be different if helping professionals from every facet—whether they were therapists, social workers, psychologists, or personal coaches—got together as a unified force to help singles and couples to have successful relationships.

As I entered into this new millennium, I branched further into the world of professional coaching and developed the niche of relationship coaching. At the same time, I had another huge responsibility: caring for my two-year-old twin boys. As their mother continued to battle her addiction to prescription drugs, I needed to adjust my schedule to work more from home and less in the office. (Today she is doing very well, and though we didn't work as a couple, we're good friends and coparents.) Meanwhile, our divorce was finalized and I had legal custody of my sons. With the breakup of my second marriage, having painfully learned about unsolvable relationship problems the hard way, I felt further inspired to help singles prepare for relationships in which they could set themselves up for success.

During this time, I was seeking someone to help me lead the weekly Friday night singles groups so I could spend more time at home. My relationship coaching practice attracted Marvin Cohen, a local graduate student and executive coach who left the corporate world to become a therapist. Marvin started attending the social each week, even though he was not single! He impressed me with his commitment to becoming a therapist and coach and with his like-mindedness about helping singles and couples from a coaching perspective. Within a few months, I offered Marvin a partnership and asked him to step in to lead most Friday nights. This freed up more of my time for my family and to further develop relationship coaching programs while continuing my private practice. Occasionally, I filled in for him on Friday nights as a leader or gave a presentation as guest speaker.

One night, a divorced mother of two showed up at our Friday night social. Her name was Maggie and she'd read a letter to the editor I had written to the local paper in response to an article about the scarcity of single men relative to single women in the area. Intrigued, she had called Marvin and decided to check out our singles group. This was her first time at a singles event since her divorce a few years earlier. Maggie did not catch my eye that night because I was focused on leading the group. I also believed it would be unprofessional of me to date women who were participants of my programs, even if they weren't my "clients," so I wasn't "looking."

As time went on, Maggie decided to take the Conscious Dating Relationship Success Training for Singles program (RESTS) that I had created and that Marvin was teaching. After the eight-week course, Maggie decided she was ready to attract a life partner, so she placed her profile on Match.com. She described herself as a forty-four-year-old warm-hearted woman, spiritual seeker, mom, social worker, and amateur musician.

Maggie was very specific about what was essential to her: giving and receiving love, her family and community, her work in the world, music, and the natural world. She wrote, "I seek a life partner to share the joy, fun, bumps in the road, and waking dreams in which there is so much for us to learn and discover. I would like to believe that my partner and I could mirror the lightness and darkness in each other and promote the evolution of other and self." Unfortunately, Maggie got very little response to her profile.

In the meantime, I had posted my own profile on Match.com as I felt it might be easier for me to initially connect with women online. Being single again was awkward for me, as I now had a high profile as a "relationship guru" for singles in my area. My headline was, "Romantic Single Dad." My user name was "3DMan," which meant that I was three-dimensional in my life as a family man, a businessman, and a relationship-oriented person. I described myself as a forty-three-year-old father who liked to sail, hike, run, and bike. I also specified that I had young twin boys and an older daughter.

Over the next six months, I went out with about ten women I met online. In person, I found them to be very personable, but there was very little chemistry. We also did not have much in common. I could not imagine myself being in a relationship with any of them. I soon began to think that this Internet dating method just wasn't for me. It took a lot of time to correspond by e-mail, and all my leads seemed to turn into dead ends. I was ready to give up and stay single for the rest of my life.

One day, out of sheer frustration, I changed my profile and made it much more specific, even demanding, knowing it might result in zero responses. For one, I wanted to meet a woman who was a helping professional like me. (I discovered I had very little in common with women who worked in high tech.) I wanted her to share my life's mission of helping to make the world a better place. Among other things, I wrote that I wanted to meet someone who: loved kids, was relationship-oriented, enjoyed being with family and community, was physically active and enjoyed nature adventures, was spiritual but not religious, spoke her truth with high integrity, was responsible and addiction-free, tolerated and appreciated differences, communicated well, owned her projections, and was ready and available for a committed relationship. I put it all out there and was not going to settle for less!

After three months, I had no responses and was sure I had scared everyone away. I surrendered to the idea that I might be single for the rest of my life. I let go of my attachment to finding my life partner and decided that I would enjoy my life, friends, family, and work as a single person.

Then, one evening, there was an e-mail from Maggie in my inbox. It turned out that we had both been on Match.com all this time; however, our search criteria had missed each other. Maggie had specified men who were her age or older (I was a year younger) and I had specified women who were at least five-foot-two (she is five-foot, one and a half). So, our profiles had never matched up. Out of frustration due to low response to her ad, Maggie changed her criteria and widened her search. When she lowered her age bracket by a couple of years, she discovered me.

We exchanged a few e-mails in which I found out that Maggie was a social worker and had a twelve-year-old son and a ten-year-old daughter. (My daughter was also twelve, and my boys were two.) Maggie was pleased to discover I was the founder of the singles program she attended. She remembered me from that Friday night social. We decided to meet in person (again!).

It was December 3, 2000, and Maggie waited until we got together in person to tell me that it was her birthday. We went on a long walk during which I asked her some tough, straight questions about her past. It was important to me that she (or any partner) have the ability to handle my directness, and Maggie was caught a little off guard. She seemed uncomfortable when I asked her about her ex-husband, and I took this as a sign that she might not quite be past her divorce. However, she later explained that she was struggling to talk about him in a positive light rather than speaking about him harshly.

During this first meeting, there were no big sparks; yet we liked each other and conversed easily. I liked that Maggie spoke to me as David, rather than projecting her experiences onto me because I was a therapist. Unlike many others, she did not seem in awe of or uncomfortable about my credentials; she was a fellow helping professional and related to me as another human being. I really liked that Maggie seemed a very real and genuine woman. I experienced her as nurturing and loving, and appreciated how she listened to me with such care.

Maggie and I continued to e-mail, talk on the phone, and get together in person. Because she had taken my training for singles, she was familiar with the process of "conscious dating" and comfortable talking to me openly and honestly. Neither of us bought into romantic illusions. We asked each other very direct questions related to our requirements and needs for a life partner. As the months passed, we were both amazed at our alignment. We were developing a deep appreciation of each other and our mutual connection and attraction grew.

Both of us had read *Intellectual Foreplay: Questions for Lovers and Lovers-to-Be* by Eve Eschner Hogan, a book of questions and exercises for getting to know yourself and your partner on a deeper level. We developed an enjoyable routine of talking on the telephone in the evening and taking turns asking each other questions from the book. It was refreshing to see that the more we consciously explored each other's realities, the more excited we were about being together. Even more, I felt that for the very first time, I was using for myself all the relationship concepts and tools I'd developed in my work.

One weekend a few months after we met, I backpacked alone in the Santa Cruz Mountains. Away from Maggie, I missed our routine phone calls to check in and ask questions from *Intellectual Foreplay.* So, in the dark, I hiked by flashlight to a pay phone near the campground and called Maggie. She was pleasantly surprised and impressed that I had called her from my camping trip. I didn't have my copy of *Intellectual Foreplay* with me, but when it was my turn, I made up my own questions for her and we kept our ritual.

Eventually, Maggie and I started to get together with our kids, too. As the months passed, we made the decision to date exclusively. Our main conflict, however, was time. Between our work and our children, how could we carve out enough time to be together?

One evening about six months after Maggie and I had met, I asked how she felt about the idea of our moving in together. I knew it was a radical step, but it would certainly give us more quality time together! Maggie was very surprised. She had been raised to believe that you shouldn't move in with a man until you had been dating him for at least a year.

At the same time, Maggie was also impatient to have more time with me, and we were very clear that we were creating a solid long-term relationship. I invited her to move in with me, but we decided that my house was too small for two adults and five children. Conscious of a tremendous commitment we were making to blend our lives, finances, and families, and excited about the direction of our relationship, we went house hunting.

In August 2001, after nine months of dating and two months of house hunting, we fell in love with a home that happened to be in the same neighborhood where my ex-wife and I had lived before our divorce. My daughter was still living there and would now be able to easily walk between her mom's and dad's houses! The house was smaller than we preferred, but we couldn't afford a larger one. So we decided to buy it and build an addition. Today, the three older kids have their own rooms—the twins share—and I have a comfortable office space overlooking our backyard.

Maggie now works as a Licensed Clinical Social Worker, dividing her time between her private practice and working for a large HMO, and I continue to build the Relationship Coaching Network, which comprises three programs: Conscious Dating for singles, Partners in Life for couples, and the Relationship Coaching Institute to train helping professionals.

Today, Maggie and I spend less time together than we'd like. However, we're very committed and feel strongly about making our blended family work. We consciously cocreate our relationship and are open about our issues and needs. Sometimes, I need to be more cautious about how I say or do things so as not to hurt her feelings; other times, Maggie needs to work on communicating her needs directly and making her boundaries clearer.

Having found a soul mate in each other, we plan to marry, but we're in no hurry to set a date. I appreciate our relationship blessings and challenges, and I gratefully believe that she's the best thing that has ever happened to me!

During my personal journey and professional work, I learned that being single is truly an opportunity to create the life that you really want. My hope is that this book will help you seize your own opportunity to prepare for and find the love of your life and the life that you love.

ABOUT THIS BOOK

In this book you will discover how to avoid the many pitfalls and traps that can hold you back in your journey to find your life partner. You will learn effective principles, tools, and information you can use to find the life and relationship that you really want.

Conscious Dating will introduce you to many innovative concepts and tools to help you make conscious, sustainable relationship choices. The first four chapters address "The Mystery of Relationships," "What Do We Really Want" in relationships, "Why 'Dating' Doesn't Work," and "The Opportunity of Being Single."

The remainder of the book is organized around the Ten Principles of Conscious Dating. Following an explanation of each principle, you will find tools, exercises, encouragement, and concrete tips for applying each principle to life and relationships.

The final two chapters cover how to develop a "Conscious Dating Plan" to find a life partner, and how to use a relationship's "pre-commitment" stage to determine if the relationship is a good long-term choice.

Within each chapter, you will find the stories of real singles who have implemented these dating practices in their own lives. As you follow their relationship journeys and learn the principles and tools for conscious dating, I hope you too will gain clarity about who you are and how you can get what you really want in your life and relationships.

Being single is truly an opportunity. Today, a whole new world begins. You are the pioneer of your own life. Let's begin our journey together. ✄

The Mystery of Relationships

The media today pay very close attention to singles, offering plenty of advice about how to find the perfect partner. This is no accident: there are more single adults today than ever before in history. While today's singles are more aware than ever about how important it is to make careful relationship choices, it can be confusing and frustrating to be flooded with "guidance" that's often shallow or exploitative. In this chapter, we'll discuss some common questions you might have about why so many relationships fail and why dating seems so challenging.

THE RULES HAVE CHANGED

Every media outlet today seems to be rushing to offer singles the latest solutions to finding and keeping that perfect partner. *Glamour* features "How to Come Back from the Brink," about couples on the verge of divorce who turned their relationship around. eHarmony.com has patented a matchmaking formula to bring singles together in successful relationships. Nerve.com, an online magazine exploring sexuality and culture, is promoting "The Future of Marriage" issue with experts answering all your relationship questions.

We have a powerful need and desire for a successful life partnership. But we grope around in the dark, using trial and error to try to make them work, often learning our lessons the hard way. We have all made relationship choices that led to feelings of confusion and hopelessness. When we are single, we want to be in a relationship. When we are in an unfulfilling relationship, it is often very difficult to accept the status quo and we want to move on. I believe that we all want to be happy. We're just not sure how.

I initially entered the psychology field to understand and help people in relationships. I wanted couples to be happy together. Yet, during most of my years as a therapist, relationships remained a mystery to me. I wondered, for instance, why so many couples allowed their marriages to become so severely troubled before doing something about it. I also questioned why some couples called a divorce lawyer before calling a therapist. I shook my head at the divorce rate, considering the fact that there are over 350,000 licensed mental health professionals in the United States.[1]

We have a powerful need and desire

for a successful life partnership, which drives us into

and out of relationships.

Angela
Raleigh, North Carolina

Angela, a forty-year-old single mother, was more than mystified with her recent relationship. She was feeling just plain lost. Angela's boyfriend of two years had just split town believing, like Moses, that God was calling him to the desert, literally!

Last Friday, Matt, her boyfriend, had called and said he urgently needed to talk with her. He was never the urgent type, so her heart pounded when she opened the door at 10 p.m. in her cotton nightgown. She'd asked him to whisper, not sure if her son was still up.

2

"I've been packing all day," Matt said. "My time in Raleigh is through."

"Packing?" Angela said, dumbfounded. "I don't understand—"

"I wanted to tell you before," Matt said, "but I didn't think you'd understand."

"Understand? No, I don't understand!"

"Please, Angela," Matt said. "Let me explain."

He went on to tell her that a few days earlier, when he had gone camping alone in the mountains, he woke up under the stars and had a vision. "God commanded me to go to Arizona. He says I'll receive further communication when I get there."

Mark
San Francisco, California

The ink was barely dry on Mark's divorce papers when he started to date again. Thirty-five-year-old Mark felt that he'd already spent the last two years of his unhappy marriage grieving and bickering, and was ready to move on. The divorce papers were signed and he had his daughters—ages ten and twelve—every other weekend. This gave the successful marketing manager lots of free time for his new life as a bachelor.

Word seemed to travel quickly that he was single. Socializing with friends for drinks every night also sped up the process of getting out there as a new single. In a short time, his bureau at home was decorated with a number of women's phone numbers written on cocktail napkins.

Women were drawn to his financial wealth, as he was to their good looks. But recently, he had a wake-up call when his twelve-

3

year-old daughter told him point-blank: "Dad, women are like Kleenex to you. You use them and throw them away." That one comment has sent Mark into a period of deep self-reflection.

Cathy
Denver, Colorado

Cathy, age thirty-eight, was grieving the end of her ten-year codependent marriage. Cathy was devastated that she and her husband were splitting up. In a bold move to regain her self-confidence, Cathy signed up for my Conscious Dating Relationship Success Training for Singles (RESTS) class. She'd been battling depression for years and was now reaching out to connect with a more supportive community.

I recommended a book to her—Rebuilding: When Your Relationship Ends. The author, Bruce Fisher, compared the healing process after a divorce to climbing a mountain composed of nineteen different "rebuilding blocks." Fisher says it takes time and effort to get past the emotional pain; finishing the climb is what counts, not how long it takes.

Over time, Cathy would let the words sink in. She realized she couldn't expect herself to wake up happy and different tomorrow; this was going to take time, maybe a long time. But she was committed to her journey to rediscover herself and find her life partner.

Seth
New York City

Seth hopped onto the train to downtown Manhattan for his midday lunch date. At 2 p.m., he would take the train back to work. At 6 p.m., he would meet his dinner date in midtown.

To an outsider, this thirty-year-old gay man's dating life might seem hectic and frenzied. But he was on a mission to find the love of his life. After five years of living in Manhattan, Seth had had enough of the Greenwich Village gay bar circuit.

When he first moved to the city from suburban New Jersey, he was only looking for sex. He had a long string of one-night stands, mostly with muscular white men who were attracted to his "exotic" appearance. (Seth was a clean-cut, five-foot-six first-generation American of Korean descent.) Seth did not want to be anyone's "boy toy" again. He knew that hooking up with guys was easy; the challenging part was staying together.

After his last breakup a few months earlier—the first time he'd lived with another man—Seth came up with a plan for finding his next and, hopefully, last relationship. He placed numerous ads online in search for "a monogamous, honest, intelligent, spiritual, financially responsible partner." Now he was going out on two or three dates a day (lunch, dinner, drinks)—yes, it was a feat! Dating was his assignment, and his life partner was his "degree."

Dorothy
Houston, Texas

It seemed like one of the craziest things Dorothy had ever done in her life. The weekend after she had dropped by the video dating office, Dorothy, age fifty-five, sat down to call her potential matches. Each time she reached a man's voice mail, she took a deep breath, trying her best to listen to his greeting, and then said in her friendliest, most outgoing voice, "Hi! This is Dorothy! I got your number from—"

Dorothy had been divorced for two decades. She'd been in and out of short-term relationships, but longed to get married again. Joining a video dating service for the first time in her life was a very bold move! But when the service sent her ten possible matches, her fear turned to excitement.

ANYTHING GOES

As I stated in the Introduction, there are 101 million singles in the United States, which is 46 percent of the adult population. Twenty five percent of all households are single occupants, compared with 17 percent in 1970. And the marriage rate is at its lowest in thirty years.[2] I see many singles traveling to a vague destination without a map or compass. They seem unsure of where they are going and feel off-track without knowing why. I like to refer to our society as the Anything Goes Culture. Today, we have an infinite number of choices and, as a relationship coach, I love this! Change brings about personal growth and evolution. But it can also be overwhelming. Without the security of tradition to lean on, singles are often left groping around in the dark.

- **101 million singles in the United States, 46 percent of the adult population**

- **25 percent of all households are single occupants**

- **Marriage rate is at its lowest in thirty years**

- **For every marriage, there is about one divorce**

- **More than 85 percent of all adults marry at least once**

- **The majority of first-born children are now conceived by, or born to, unmarried parents**

With our new freedom of choice come growing pains. As a father, I've seen my children learn about behavior and consequences. A lamp breaks, for example, and a child naively thinks he or she can lie and get away with it. Children often think magically, and are in denial of reality. However, many adults also are still learning about consequences. We have unprotected sex and get pregnant. Or we jump into a relationship after dating for two weeks and then wonder why it doesn't work out.

Recently, I was discussing these issues with another relationship coach and he said to me, "We've been raised on movies and TV shows to believe that it's all about the romance and climactic moments. Despite popular 'reality' shows, because of the cameras, we never really see the reality of everyday life. It's not about going out into the world and finding that perfect partner. We need to see that we, as individuals, are a part of the big puzzle. This fairy-tale image ignores our responsibility for our choices and adds to our confusion about our relationships."

It's our responsibility to be conscious

about where we are in life

if we are to find our own happiness.

In our culture we are goal-oriented and consumer-driven. We want what we want, when we want it. Many of us are concerned with looking good and obtaining certain material things, and we believe that's what will make us happy. But even when we get all those things, we are not happy and we don't understand why. Similarly, in relationships, we pair up and expect to be happy. Once again, we need to understand that it's our responsibility to be conscious about where we are in life if we are to find our own happiness.

Moreover, for many of us, our role models—our parents—are divorced, and there is divorce all around us. For every marriage today, there is about one divorce. More than 85 percent of all adults marry at least once. The majority of first-born children are now conceived by or born to unmarried parents. And there are more single people today than ever in history.[3] When I study these statistics, I find it amazing that so many people are doing this committed relationship thing at all.

And yet, they are. Couples everywhere continue to make their vows. And as I write this, despite political resistance, same-sex couples are tying the knot legally for the first time in history. While many view gay marriage as radical, I see it differently. Gay couples want the same thing everyone else wants—lifelong commitment and family—so they are actually making very traditional choices. What's amazing to me is that even though we have so many lifestyle alternatives today, we all seem to share a common goal—a fulfilling life partnership.

* * *

At the gym, Angela cranked up the speed dial on the treadmill, imagining that she was the one running away from Matt. "Go, go, go!" she repeated to her herself, beads of sweat dripping down the sides of her face. "He's such a spoiled brat. He doesn't know how good he had it with me."

Her back was wet. She hurried, as if she were late for her own plane.

Matt had been her first long-term relationship since her divorce ten years earlier. Angela knew that divorcing before age thirty was not uncommon. She'd just read a story in the morning's paper about the so-called "starter marriage," a phenomenon happening in every demographic of society, in which a union lasts just a few years and ends before children arrive. The article said the most common time for a marriage to end in divorce was in the first five years.

Angela and Matt had celebrated her fortieth birthday the previous month with a weekend getaway to a beach house at Cape

Lookout. Matt had always treated her like a princess. Every Saturday, after her son's father picked him up, she and Matt dashed off to a local bed and breakfast, drank mimosas at brunch, and picked up box seats for the symphony in the evening. Matt had been living off an inheritance for the past few years since his father had died. Angela's salary as a social worker had never afforded her much room to splurge, so weekends out of town with Matt were a treat.

Angela's salary as a social worker had never afforded her much room to splurge, so weekends out of town with Matt were a treat.

Still, she was never sure how he spent his days, exactly. Whenever she asked, Matt rambled on about playing bridge, watching basketball, or going fishing. He didn't have many close friends. Matt often talked about moving in together someday and how he wanted to be a role model for her son.

"God, I'm such a fool!" Angela thought. Then she laughed, wondering if she was talking to the same God who had spoken to Matt.

"Hey there," a deep voice resonated from beside her. "How's it going?"

Angela opened her eyes (not realizing they were closed) and turned to see Jerry jogging on the treadmill to her right. He was going much slower than she was.

"Fine," she lied, feeling resentful for the interruption in her thoughts. "And you?"

"What a nice surprise to see you here in the morning. Usually I see you working out after work."

"Yes," Angela replied, thinking that if she kept her answers short, he would leave her alone. She wasn't feeling very social.

Jerry was a tall, athletic, gray-haired man in his mid-forties. They usually ran into each other in the sauna following an after-work workout. Last week, they talked about her clogged kitchen sink. Jerry had suggested a way she could get all that gunk out of her pipes without calling a plumber. Although he was a nice guy and she was impressed by his plumbing knowledge, she didn't feel like talking to him right now. She focused her blue-gray eyes back on the treadmill screen and sped up her pace.

"Maybe I'll see you in the sauna," Jerry said, stepping off the treadmill onto the rug next to her.

"Yeah, maybe." She didn't want to meet him in the sauna today, so she decided to wait until he left, even if it meant being late for work. Upset about Matt, she spent this "waiting" time sadly reflecting on yet another failed relationship.

* * *

PAST, PRESENT, AND FUTURE

Until recent generations, men and women dated, married, had families, and rarely divorced. Not long ago, there were clear rules for relationships—in which couples did not focus on personal fulfillment or happiness—and stayed together "till death do us part."

Then our society changed. I think that the biggest change impacting relationships is that we've developed a need to be "happy." This is a dramatic shift from past generations who were quite satisfied surviving and achieving some measure of comfort and security for themselves and their family.

The need for happiness sounds very simple and innocent, but it's the primary reason for failed relationships today. As a consequence, we have consistently high incidences of divorce, single-parent families, mental and physical health problems, juvenile delinquency, welfare, and so on. While we seek to be happy in relationships, we don't seem to know how.

But how did all the rules change, exactly? During the '60s, we saw a tremendous shift in the roles of men and women in our society. As we started to question our tasks in the household and workplace, technology was changing rapidly too. Women now had access to birth control, which meant that sex could be for recreation, not just procreation. In 1973, abortion was legalized and the stigma of divorce was disappearing. With the rise of feminism, women had so many more choices. This dramatically changed the rules and, for better or worse, the dance of courtship changed too.

A couple of generations back, it was the man who asked the woman out on a date and paid the bill. Today, there is no set protocol. The most common response I hear from single women when I ask them who should pay for the date is "We'll go dutch." Moreover, most women are going to drive themselves to a first date, rather than wait by the door to be picked up. Today's woman does not want to be beholden to a man. Sometimes I witness that women feel uncomfortable with this new and powerful role. Other times, it is men who are feeling insecure or intimidated, unsure about how to relate to assertive and strong females.

Having no set rules in dating can be confusing. While many single women prefer to split the bill on a first date, I've heard many stories about women who "test" the man by waiting for him to first offer to pay—even though, in the end, she'll insist on splitting it. And I've heard that some men will "test" a woman on the first date, say, by unlocking the car door on her side and opening it for her, and then waiting to see if she reaches across and unlocks his door. It seems as if both men and women want to be reassured that if they're going to give, they're also going to receive.

The fact that families look different today has also changed the dance of courtship. Now it's common to have two-career households—in which the woman sometimes earns more than the man—so the role of provider is up for grabs. Many are putting off marriage and childbearing until later in life, focusing more on career and self first. Then, when couples do finally get together, they might hear the woman's biological clock ticking. Or, after the babies arrive, they might have a hard time dealing with the loss of autonomy. Moreover, now that gays and lesbians are mostly out of the closet and in the mainstream, they are creating their own dance of courtship.

In general, I think that we are smarter nowadays, and perhaps more cynical. We fear commitment today more than we did in the past. We no longer believe that tying the knot equals a happily-ever-after fairy tale.

To be sure, there are many cultures around the world that follow the conservative traditions of past generations, in which men and women have very defined roles in a family. This is further proven by the popularity of radio talk show hosts such as Dr. Laura Schlessinger and Rush Limbaugh and by groups such as the Promise Keepers. Leaders such as President George W. Bush are attempting to bring back life-long monogamy with programs to promote healthy marriage.

These groups seem to be clashing with the predictions of some futurists who say that Americans will marry at least four times and have extramarital affairs. One futurist bases her predictions on trends showing women becoming more financially independent, with marriage and childbearing becoming more "delinked," "serial monogamy" becoming more acceptable, and extramarital sexual affairs occurring more frequently and with less public outcry. She sees singles of the next century moving through at least four kinds of marriages, which are the following:[4]

FUTURIST VISION OF MARRIAGE

1. The Icebreaker Marriage

This has many similarities to the "starter marriage" that was mentioned above. The first union will be "the icebreaker marriage," in which couples learn how to live together and become sexually experienced. Icebreaker marriages are likely to last no more than five years. Once disillusionment sets in, couples will split up, as divorce will not carry any stigma.

2. The Parenting Marriage

The second marriage, known as "the parenting marriage," will last fifteen to twenty years. These couples will view raising children as their primary purpose, although child-rearing in the future will be in communal settings, not nuclear families.

3. The Self-Marriage

After the second marriage ends, couples may enter a third union, called a "self-marriage," in which partners pursue self-discovery and self-actualization.

FUTURIST VISION OF MARRIAGE
1. Icebreaker marriage
2. Parenting marriage
3. Self-marriage
4. Soul mate marriage

4. The Soul Mate Marriage

Finally, because people will be living until age 120, many couples will reach for a late-in-life "soul mate connection." In this fourth kind of marriage, couples will discover "marital bliss, shared spirituality, physical monogamy and equal partnership."

As the past and future bump into one another in today's world, singles seem to be focused on these five critical questions:

1. How can I find my life partner?
2. Where do I meet compatible singles?

3. Why, in spite of my best efforts and intentions, do my relationships seem to fail?

4. Why do relationships seem to be so natural and easy for some, and so challenging for others?

5. Why do so many people claim that marriage and family are their highest priorities, and then act indifferent—or even hostile—to those closest to them?

It's an interesting phenomenon that even though we are not following any set of rules, in the end, most of us want to be in a committed relationship. Linda J. Waite and Maggie Gallagher, researchers who have conducted hundreds of studies and surveys, concluded that most young Americans want marriage but at the same time fear it. In their book, *The Case for Marriage: Why Married People Are Happier, Healthier, and Better Off Financially*, they state that marriage is more than just a sheet of paper. Marriage is an "insurance policy" that more often than not brings couples long lives, good health, fat bank accounts, and personal happiness.[5]

Marriage is an "insurance policy"

that more often than not brings couples long lives,

good health, fat bank accounts,

and personal happiness.

—Waite and Gallagher

Yet with this freedom of choice, I see so many singles leaping into relationships without using good judgment. They make choices based on impulse without much conscious thought. What's astounding to me is that when we enter a committed relationship, we do not intend to fail. We truly believe this is going to be for life. I entered each of my first two marriages with 100 percent commitment. I did not envision myself getting divorced. What motivated me to specialize in working with couples were the serious and traumatic consequences of divorce. Getting together is a natural drive. We are social beings, and getting together with a partner is a strong instinct. In spite of the fear of many singles of being alone forever, relationships happen naturally. We're going to get together anyway. The trick is staying together.

* * *

Angela was a social worker in early intervention and prevention services. At work, she was relieved to focus on something other than Matt and his sudden departure. At lunch, Angela had plans to meet her friend Gretchen at the cafeteria downstairs. They had been friends since college and worked two blocks away from each other. When Angela trudged into the cafeteria, her face was sullen.

"Come here, Honey," Gretchen said. "You look like a wreck."

"Oh, thanks for the compliment," Angela said, half-jokingly. She talked for ten minutes nonstop, telling Gretchen about Matt's urgent call about his "order from God." She gazed out the window. "Maybe he's out in the Arizona desert right now, speaking with God."

Gretchen looked into her eyes: "Honey, you're the one who's just been saved."

* * *

Like Angela, most of us need and want a committed relationship. However, the divorce rate is not going down, and the marriage rate is not going up. I asked a roundtable of relationship coaches what they considered to be the biggest challenges facing singles today. There is still such a stigma about being single in our society, and a prime motivation for me as a relationship coach is to overcome this.

The coaches came up with a long list of challenges, including:

1. Not knowing what you're looking for; having unclear expectations

2. Having a long "grocery list" and looking for the one person to match it

3. Living in fear that you will repeat past experiences

4. Not healing before starting a new relationship

5. For women, feeling that their biological clock is running out

6. For men, fearing to start a family and stay committed

7. Lowering of standards by older singles, or giving up or settling because they're afraid they will always be alone

8. Knowing where to meet other singles with whom you might be compatible

9. Too busy to date or cultivate a relationship

10. Discouragement of not finding someone that meets your expectations

11. Expectations for sex

12. Cynicism

13. Getting involved too quickly

14. Not knowing where to meet suitable partners

15. "There are no good men, no good women" mentality

16. Pressure from family or peers to be coupled

17. Not having the skills to create a successful relationship

18. Fear of failure

19. Fear of rejection

20. Fear of commitment

21. Shyness

22. Seems easier to stay single

23. Exhaustion—children, careers, hobbies consume your energy

24. Determining when to introduce children

Today's singles carry around many fears. For those of us who grew up surrounded by confusing relationships—like bickering parents who ended up divorcing—it can be challenging to envision a successful relationship. Many of us have been affected so deeply by our pasts that we carry around negative attitudes about relationships. Many singles are feeling frustrated, discouraged, and cynical about relationships. Yet our biggest goal in life remains to love and be loved by a life partner. ✄

CONSCIOUS DATING PLAN EXERCISE NO. 1:

Please refer to Chapter 15 to write your answers.

Are you ready to date?

1. Have you been hurt in a relationship? How does being hurt affect your being single?

2. Do you believe that happiness in a relationship is really possible? (In subsequent chapters, you will see how your beliefs affect your life decisions.)

3. Do you believe that your next relationship can really be your last? (In subsequent chapters, you will look at how your beliefs affect your life choices.)

4. What do you think a fulfilling life partnership would look like?

What Do We Really Want?

We all want to love and be loved. But what does this actually mean? A committed relationship is more than a biological drive to ensure the survival of species. I will show the many real benefits to being in a loving and committed relationship.

STARTING OVER

Cathy, age thirty-eight, was grieving the end of her ten-year codependent marriage. She had been battling depression for years, and was now reaching out to experience a more supportive community. Cathy was devastated that she and her husband were splitting up.

Cathy decided to leave Denver, where she'd spent the past fifteen years. At the same time, she was worried that maybe she was running away from all her anger and grief. Still, she wanted a radical change to lift her out of her sadness. She just wanted to start over again. Cathy was already making some bold changes. For one, she called her father and had a heart-to-heart talk in which she told him how bad things really were in her marriage. She told her father the truth: that her ex had refused to see a therapist or attend Alcoholics Anonymous meetings. Her father, a recovering alcoholic himself, was very supportive. He asked Cathy to move back home for a while. She felt grateful.

In the meantime, Cathy was working hard in her RESTS class. She spent every night for one week working on a collage that illustrated how she envisioned her life. Since she was about to embark on a big change—leaving her job and home, moving back in with her father—creating a picture of what she wanted in her life seemed like a good idea. Cathy sat on her floor with numerous magazines about travel, family, and adventure. She cut out about fifty pictures and glued them onto a poster board. There were beaches, families eating together, children laughing, flowers, and couples dancing and kissing. After hanging the collage on her living room wall, Cathy stood back and admired it. Maybe, just maybe, she would love again.

After hanging the collage

on her living room wall, Cathy stood

back and admired it. Maybe,

just maybe, she would love again.

WANTING A SOUL MATE

No matter how old we are, we all want to love and be loved. A recent national survey conducted by the Gallup Organization stated that 94 percent of young adults said that finding a "soul mate" was one of their highest goals. There was a discussion about this survey on one of the discussion lists I subscribe to. Shannon, an articulate eighteen-year-old about to graduate from high school, was writing about her anxieties about the future. "Unlike our parents and grandparents, my generation hasn't worried about suffering through the Great Depression or surviving Vietnam," she said. "Instead, we've grown up fearing AIDS, divorce, and school shootings."[1]

Shannon's parents, like many of her friends' parents, were divorced. She could think of only three friends whose mothers and fathers were still together. In third grade, Shannon had attended a support group for children of divorced families. I asked her about it. "My counselor seemed very old, with too much eye makeup and crooked-ly applied orange lipstick," she told me. "The last thing I wanted to do was sit in her office with ten other kids, discussing my private family life. At our first meeting, the counselor had us repeat this phrase: 'It is not my fault that my parents got a divorce.' The thought that the divorce had been my fault had never crossed my mind."

When I get married, I will never entertain

the idea of divorce. Never.

If I have to wait until

I'm eighty to find the right person, I will.

Marriage is not like going steady—it's forever.

"I know that for my parents, divorce was best," she added. "But I also know that when I get married, I will never entertain the idea of divorce. Never. If I have to wait until I'm eighty to find the right person, I will. Marriage is not like going steady—it's forever. I hope the rest of my generation feels the same way."

Shannon's certainty about relationships struck me. She's not alone. In 2005, two nationally prominent family experts—David Popenoe, a professor and former dean at Rutgers University, and Barbara Dafoe Whitehead, an author and social critic—published their annual "State of Our Unions" report, saying that 82 percent of girls and 70 percent of boys stated that having a good marriage and family life was "extremely important" to them.[2] In 2001, these two researchers had published a Gallup survey on young adults in their twenties that found that most singles today are looking for a spouse who will be their soul mate for life. Some of the highlights from the report—called "Who Wants to Marry a Soul Mate?"—include:

- Ninety-four percent of never-married singles agree that "when you marry, you want your spouse to be your soul mate, first and foremost."

- A large majority of young adults (82 percent) agree it is unwise for a woman to rely on marriage for financial security.

- Over 80 percent of women agree it is more important to them to have a husband who can communicate about his deepest feelings than to have a husband who makes a good living.

- A high percentage of young adults (86 percent) agree that marriage is hard work and a full-time job.

- Close to nine out of ten (88 percent) agree that the divorce rate is too high, and 47 percent say that the laws should be changed so that divorces are more difficult to get.

"When you marry you want your spouse to be your soul mate, first and foremost."

The Gallup survey highlighted the hopes of young people, but what's really going on with today's couples? Nearly nine in ten people expect to marry sometime in their lives, but about half of first marriages end in divorce according to a report released in 2002 by the Commerce Department's Census Bureau. The same month that the Census Bureau released its report—the first comprehensive portrait of marriage and divorce in nearly ten years—*The Christian Science Monitor* ran an article headlined "America's on/off relationship with wedlock."[3]

Staff writer Laurent Belsie summed up the report in this way: "Americans revere wedlock. Nearly nine out of ten of them will tie the knot sometime in their lives, more than the citizens of most other countries. There's only one problem. Americans seem more enamored with the institution than with each other."

Indeed, the figures seemed to prove just that. Two-thirds of twenty-five- to twenty-nine-year-old women had married, but only 12 percent had been through a divorce. Using a mathematical model and the assumption that today's newly married couples would go through the same transitions as their predecessors, the Census Bureau projected that half of those marriages could fall apart.

"Those figures are really ballpark," cautioned Rose Kreider, coauthor of the report, in *The Christian Science Monitor*.

Still, Belsie concluded: "In the view of some experts, America's newest newlyweds, for all their idealism about finding a soul mate, often fall short on the glue that makes match-ups last."

Popenoe and Whitehead conclude that Americans haven't given up on marriage as a cherished ideal. Indeed, most continue to prize and value it as an important life goal, and the vast majority (an estimated 85 percent) will marry at least once in a lifetime.[4]

* * *

Angela, the divorced single mother whom you met in Chapter 1, was devastated after Matt split town. Every weekend, she came home to a dark and empty house. She turned on the oven to heat up a frozen dinner. One Friday, she sat down at the kitchen table and flipped through the bills. The only sound was the shuffling of papers. Her ex-husband had picked their son up from school.

Then she noticed that her answering machine was blinking. Maybe Matt had left a message saying this had all been a big mistake and he was flying back to Raleigh. She pushed the play button:

"Hi Honey! Wondered if you wanted to go out for dinner down-town, my treat—"

It was her friend Gretchen, who probably knew that Angela was moping around. But she didn't have the energy to drag herself out tonight. Maybe tomorrow.

Angela set up a tray in front of the TV, something she prohibited her son from doing. (They always ate dinner together in the dining room so they could talk.) She poured herself a beer and sat down with her dinner. Flipping through the channels, she passed a few sitcoms. Then she paused for a moment on a news special about grieving. She put down the remote.

The news anchor was interviewing a middle-aged male psychologist: "It's important to make time for the healing process. Too often, we are encouraged to be strong and keep it all inside."

The doctor raised his hands for effect: "This only serves to keep the former loved one on your mind and you frustrated."

Then the camera focused on a woman in her early forties, dressed in a blue suit: "After my ex-husband and I split up, I spent three years alone. When I finally started dating again, I thought I'd found the love of my life—"

Angela picked at her enchilada without looking, paying close attention to the TV. "Wow, that could be me!" she thought.

The woman on TV went on to say that after one year, her boyfriend suddenly dumped her. She vowed to remain single until the end of her life, gained twenty pounds, and spent nights and weekends alone at home. Then, for her birthday, a friend signed her up for a local self-help class on grieving and healing. Not wanting to hurt her friend's feelings, she reluctantly went. The first night, the class leader instructed everyone to write out a list detailing 100 things they wanted to do and to have in their lives.

Angela listened carefully, taking mental notes. After the show ended, she turned the TV off and got a notebook from her desk. She imagined that she had ten billion dollars and only ten years left to live. What would she want to do? What would she want to be? What would she want to have?

She imagined that she had ten billion dollars and only ten years left to live. What would she want to do? What would she want to be? What would she want to have?

At first, the list flowed easily: "I want to have a house with a large garden and a swimming pool. I want to have picnic dinners with my friends and family, with fresh grilled vegetables and lots of laughter. I want to learn how to swing dance. I want to feel loved and worthy and supported." An hour passed, and she had written down over fifty items. She was exhausted. She left her notebook open and went to bed.

The next morning, over coffee, Angela continued her list and easily got to one hundred items. She couldn't believe how easy it was to write about her dream life. It made her feel alive to imagine what she wanted instead of focusing on her broken heart.

* * *

THE MIRACLE OF CONNECTION

The desire for partnership is pervasive and universal. It reaches back to the origin of species and spans almost every culture and civilization. We all seek relationships to find love, happiness, security, healing. But what exactly is a "soul mate"? Is it the same as your life partner? Is it your husband or wife? Is it your significant other? In your own life, who and what exactly are you looking for?

Finding your soul mate is not about putting together two pieces of a puzzle. There is not just one possible match for everyone. You don't have to go out and find your one other, unique piece. There are many possible partners with whom you could have a loving and lasting relationship—as long as they are aligned with your requirements, wants, and needs. (You will read more about this in Chapter 5.) Finding your soul mate isn't just a romantic idea—it's a functional one. The chemistry between you is strong. You love this person and feel loved by him/her. You have a connection on every level—mental, emotional, physical, and spiritual.

Your soul mate can be the person

who's best suited to bring out (what can seem to be)

your worst nightmare.

One of my colleagues, Hedy Schleifer, who conducts workshops for couples worldwide, refers to being with your soul mate as "the miracle of connection." While we are often attracted to "incompatible" people, our differences actually create our best opportunities for connection. According to Hedy, your soul mate can be the person who's best suited to bring out (what can seem to be) your worst nightmare. While there's an alignment between you and your partner—he/she fits your goals and values—there's also enough difference so that this person encourages you to grow and evolve. We all want to be connected, but connecting can be challenging when life gets busy and our minds are so full of noise. Hedy—who has been married to her partner, Yumi, for over forty years—says that they spent many years preoccupied with their own individual thoughts and feelings. They had to learn how to be truly present for each other when there was tension or conflict. Hedy says the real miracle is that when we experience a conflict we have the ability to "leave the country we live in and walk over the narrow bridge to visit the other person... In this moment, we relax together and feel something that we were born to feel—completely connected and aligned with each other."[5]

In the midst of conflict, when one partner is actually able to hold the other partner in his/her experience with a completely open mind, "limbic resonance" results. "Limbic resonance" is a physical experience in which both nervous systems connect and relax together in a blissful state of essence that allows us to let go and transcend even our biggest differences. Isn't this the state we would all strive to experience consistently? Hedy assures us that when we learn and apply the tools to resolve conflict, we evolve into our true essential nature and can experience the connection and fulfillment in our relationships that we really want.

Happiness is limited, self-centered, and unconscious;

it is prone to boredom,

saturation, and satiation.

But fulfillment in a relationship is conscious and

unlimited, and can only be achieved

in connection with our partner.

Your limbic system can be your friend, but it can also be destructive. What's interesting is that this same limbic system that causes us to feel good can also cause us to feel threatened and make us feel that our partner is a threat, and then we argue. The very source of a lot of relationship pain and conflict is also the source of bliss.

That's why Hedy calls our limbic system "the old brain" (which controls our fight or flight response). Staying in conscious connection with our partner creates new neural pathways in the brain and enhances "object constancy" so we can experience love even when hurting or upset. We really can stay connected and give and receive love deeply, even during conflict.

I used to tell singles that we all want to be happy in a fulfilled partnership. Then Hedy pointed out that "happiness" and "fulfillment" are different: happiness is limited, self-centered, and unconscious; it is prone to boredom, saturation, and satiation. But fulfillment is conscious and unlimited, and can only be achieved in connection with our partner.

We want to be independent, yet we don't want

to be alone. We want to avoid pain,

yet we compel ourselves to find someone

with whom we can be vulnerable.

LOVE AND SURVIVAL

In her book *Anatomy of Love: A Natural History of Mating, Marriage and Why We Stray*, Helen Fisher, Ph.D., points out that "marriage is a cultural universal; it predominates in every society in the world. Over 90 percent of all American men and women marry; modern census records go back to the mid-1800s."[6] Yet, why do we marry? And moreover, why do we get divorced and then remarry? We seem to have a powerful need and desire for coupling that drives us into and out of relationships.

We want to be independent, yet we don't want to be alone. We want to avoid pain, yet we compel ourselves to find someone with whom we can be vulnerable. Are committed relationships simply a biological drive to ensure the survival of the species? I don't think so. As humans, we pride ourselves in rising above our primitive instincts and biological programming. So, what do we really want? Certainly, the young adults interviewed in the Gallup poll knew that finding a soul mate was very important in their future.

Still, we have no good relationship model to follow. While marriage is "a cultural universal," so is divorce. Fisher traces the history of marriage through the agrarian age and the Industrial Revolution. She writes that "all sorts of sociological, psychological, and demographic forces contribute to divorce rates." Some of these forces, according to Fisher, are individualism, self-fulfillment, financial freedom, and "nomadism" (the fact that most of us have moved away from home):[7]

> Sometimes we are so overwhelmed by thoughts and feelings that we don't really know what we want. Some of us are exhausted by our careers, children, or hobbies. We feel too busy to date or begin to cultivate a relationship. We find it difficult to express our feelings. We are still dealing with baggage from previous relationships. We are afraid of failure or rejection.

"Love and intimacy are at the root

of what makes us sick and

what makes us well,

what causes sadness and what brings happiness,

what makes us suffer and what leads to healing."

I've always been impressed by the way Dr. Dean Ornish, clinical professor of medicine at the University of California in San

Francisco, writes about love. In his book *Love and Survival*, he says "love and intimacy are at the root of what makes us sick and what makes us well, what causes sadness and what brings happiness, what makes us suffer and what leads to healing. If a new drug had the same impact, virtually every doctor in the country would be recommending it for their patients."[8]

Dr. Ornish says we are creatures of community:

Those individuals, societies, and cultures who learned to take care of each other, to love each other, and to nurture relationships with each other during the past several hundred years were more likely to survive than those who did not.... The real epidemic in our culture is not only physical heart disease, but also what I call emotional and spiritual heart disease—that is, the profound feelings of loneliness, isolation, alienation, and depression that are so prevalent in our culture with the breakdown of the social structures that used to provide us with a sense of connection and community.

As a society, we have secured our physical needs. Psychologist Abraham Maslow defines a "hierarchy of needs." In this hierarchy, once our physical needs for food, air, sleep, shelter, and sex are met, we pursue our higher-order needs, such as emotional needs for love and pleasure, belonging, and spiritual needs of meaning and purpose. As one need is satisfied, we move to fulfill another need. Our needs for belonging, meaning, and self-actualization also drive us to search for committed, monogamous relationships.

SEVEN BENEFITS OF A COMMITTED RELATIONSHIP

There are many benefits to a committed relationship beyond the obvious survival of the species. I was a marriage counselor for many years, yet I didn't know what the real benefits of a relationship were. Based on recent research, I believe these are what we really want in our lives:

1. Companionship

We are social beings who are comforted by closeness. Married people are healthier and happier and live longer than singles.

Most people have similar needs for companionship. At the end of the day, we all need appreciation, positive strokes, and quality time together. If you look behind these basics, all of us have an emotional need to love and be loved.

2. Intimacy

Intimacy means connection, not just feeling good. All of us want intimacy in our lives, but it can be challenging. We want to be close, but not too close. We can't handle too much closeness. There's this closeness-distance dance that most of us do: "Come here, come here, come here. Oh, that's too close!" And then, "Get away, get away, get away!" In a committed relationship, emotional closeness, love, trust, and mutual support improve over time. These qualities are much more difficult to achieve outside of a committed relationship.

Author Pat Love, Ed.D., in her book *The Truth About Love* explains that one of the physical benefits of intimacy is oxytocin. This "cuddle drug" is the hormone secreted by nursing mothers and after orgasm by both partners. Moreover, it is released in positive and healthy relationships in the presence of a long-term partner. Oxytocin is what makes us feel connected and blissful just being with him/her.

In an intimate relationship, we can truly grow emotionally. Satisfying intimacy requires skills that can only be learned in a committed relationship. You can't learn relationship skills alone! My colleague, Hedy Schleifer, once expressed this in a way that really struck me. She said, "Intimacy and love expand our essence and can deepen and grow infinitely." Over time, in a committed and intimate relationship, we can learn to:

 a. be fully present and receive our partner fully during good and hard times.
 b. communicate our issues and needs immediately with love and acceptance of our partner.
 c. stay connected when upset (instead of withdrawing or attacking)

d. express frustration positively, with an attitude of generosity and adventure for the opportunity to connect more deeply and grow even more.

e. receive our partner's issues and requests positively, welcoming them as opportunities to connect more deeply and grow even more.

Wouldn't it be wonderful to be in this kind of an intimate relationship? It is completely possible. Philosopher Martin Buber sums up intimacy beautifully: "When I meet thou, we are in eternal time."

Intimacy and love

expand our essence and can

deepen and grow infinitely.

---

3. Family

Both children and adults thrive in an environment of stable, long-term, multigenerational relationships. Indeed, we all have a survival of the species drive within us. The fact that we come together to have children is outside of our awareness; it's an inborn force. Still, in the end, it's certainly a benefit to stay together in a supportive environment.

In 2002, *Why Marriage Matters: Twenty-One Conclusions from the Social Sciences*, emphasized the fact that children do well when raised by loving, healthy, and committed parents. (My motive here is not to push unmarried people to get married as if that in itself could help them and their children. I'm talking about two parents who get along, i.e., are not an abusive relationship.) In this report, thirteen of the top scholars on family life shared their findings on decades of research. The report showed that parental divorce reduces the likelihood that children will graduate from college and achieve high-status jobs. Children who live with their own two married parents enjoy better physical health on average than children in other family forms. The health advantages of married homes remain even after taking into account socioeconomic status. Moreover, parental divorce approximately doubles the odds that adult children will end up divorced.[9]

4. Economics
Committed couples are usually financially more successful than singles and non-committed partners. Once again, it was Dr. Waite who concluded that married people have more money. From her own analysis of a National Institute of Aging survey of 12,000 people ages fifty-one to sixty-one, Dr. Waite found that married people have more than twice as much money on average than unmarried people. Married couples not only save more, but married men also earn up to 26 percent more than single men.[10]

Similarly, married women earn more than unmarried women, but only if they have no children. When they have children, "they trade some of their earning time for time with their children," Dr. Waite said. If the women continue to work, she added, they have difficulty getting child care, and experience stress trying to balance two sets of demands.

Moreover, committed couples appear to be less anxious when it comes to money. *Redbook* and *SmartMoney* magazines teamed up on a story called "The Truth About Women, Men and Money" in which couples across the country divulged information about their financial lives. They surveyed more than a thousand men and women between the ages of eighteen and fifty, all married or part of a committed relationship. The conclusion: "For years we've been hearing about how men and women clash over cash, but these days things are different. Whether both partners make the same salary, one of them earns more or there's a stay-at-home mom (or dad) in the house, most couples aren't wasting time arguing over finances, our survey revealed.... When asked, 'Is money a source of fights in your relationship?' only 7 percent of respondents said that it's the biggest cause, while the majority (62 percent) said 'rarely or never.'"[12]

Lastly, a 2003 Census Bureau report shows that married couples have higher median incomes ($62,405) than do single females ($29,307) or single males ($41,959).

5. Community

Extended family, neighbors, churches, and other forms of networks of supportive relationships thrive on the stability of committed relationships. Sometimes during a lecture, Dr. Dean Ornish asks his audience whether all four of the following statements are true for them:

- You live in the same neighborhood in which you were born and raised and most of your old neighbors are still there

- You've been going to the same church or synagogue for at least ten years

- You've been at the same job for at least ten years and most of your coworkers from ten years ago are still there

- You have an extended family living nearby whom you see regularly

---

Extended family, neighbors, churches, and other forms of networks of supportive relationships thrive on the stability of committed relationships.

Dr. Ornish reports that in an audience of three thousand people, maybe ten or twenty of them will raise their hands. And not just in San Francisco or New York or Los Angeles, but also in Ames, Iowa, or Omaha, Nebraska. So, the community that we have by being in a committed relationship keeps us from being isolated and provides a supportive connection for others.

6. Regular, safe, good sex

Committed, monogamous partners have more and better sex than singles and noncommitted partners. *Redbook* magazine ran a feature—"How to Make Love to a Married Man (Your Husband)"—based on the findings from a 2001 University of Chicago study on sexual satisfaction. In this study, Linda J. Waite and Kara Joyner revealed an important fact: married men, not their single counterparts, are the most physically and emotionally fulfilled when it comes to sex.

One forty-four-year-old married man interviewed for the story said, "Maybe some of the crazy lust has dissipated, but the love has expanded and become more profound. So the feelings of sharing have never been stronger than in the moments that follow sex. That's when I think to myself, 'This is what sex is all about.'"

But it's not just about better sex. In today's world, a monogamous relationship also equates to safer sex. As a single, you know that dating can mean putting yourself at risk. When you're in a committed, monogamous partnership, you don't have to live in fear of HIV or STDs.

7. Mental/emotional/physical health

Married adults live longer and have fewer mental and emotional problems than single adults. In fact, a ten-year study of ten thousand people in the United Kingdom found that living alone might shave several years off a single person's life. The findings, published in the Journal of Health Economics, show that long-term singles are at risk of mental illness and depression and of becoming sicker earlier. In The Case for Marriage, Gallagher and Waite sum up their research, "Being unmarried can actually be a greater risk to one's life than having heart disease or cancer" and "marital status was one of the most important predictors of happiness."

Dr. Waite also found that "marriage changes people's behavior in ways that make them better off." Married partners monitor each other's health, for example. They drink less alcohol and use less marijuana and cocaine. From detailed reports on fifty thousand men and women followed from their senior year in high school to the age of thirty-two by University of Michigan researchers, Dr. Waite discerned a steep increase in "bad behaviors" among those who stayed single, but a "precipitous drop" in bad behaviors like the use of alcohol or illegal drugs among those who married.

Drawing heavily on a study of thirteen thousand adults assessed in 1987 and 1988 and again in 1992 and 1993, Dr. Waite demonstrated the positive impact that marriage has on mental health. The study, conducted by two psychologists at the University of Wisconsin, Nadine F. Marks and James D. Lambert, and published in The Journal of Family Issues, states it is not just that people who remained married reported significantly higher levels of happiness than those who remained single.[11] The data showed that those who separated or divorced over the five-year period became, in Dr. Waite's word, miserable.

In 1998, the University of Chicago's Dr. Waite presented her findings at the second annual Smart Marriages Conference in Washington. Countering conventional wisdom that marriage is bad for women but good for men, Dr. Waite found that marriage brings considerable benefits to both women and men. It lengthens life and substantially boosts physical and emotional health. In a large national sample of adults followed for eighteen years beginning at the age of forty-eight, slightly more than 60 percent of divorced and never-married women made it to sixty-five, as opposed to nearly 90 percent of married women. Widowed women, for reasons not entirely clear, fared almost as well as married women. Among men, however, those unmarried for any reason—whether widowed, divorced, or never married—had only a 60 to 70 percent chance of living to sixty-five, versus 90 percent for married men.

Dr. Waite further proved her case in The Case for Marriage, written with Maggie Gallagher in 2000. Waite and Gallagher address what they term the five myths of marriage, including "Marriage is mostly about children" and "Divorce is usually the best answer for kids when a marriage becomes unhappy."

The book is based on eighteen years of research by Waite; Gallagher is director of the Marriage Program at the Institute for American Values. "Marriage is not just a label or a piece of paper, marriage is a creative act," Gallagher told the Washington Post in an interview. "When people invest in a marriage, it changes the way they look at the world and act—they're more willing to invest in their future together—and it also changes the way people look at you. You do get special status."

SEVEN BENEFITS OF A COMMITTED RELATIONSHIP
1. Companionship
2. Intimacy
3. Family
4. Economics
5. Community
6. Regular, safe, good sex
7. Mental/emotional/physical health

In the book, Waite and Gallagher state that:
- Nine out of ten married men will make it to age sixty-five, but only six out of ten single guys will do so.
- Only 5 percent of dating men who said they didn't expect their relationship to last reported they were extremely emotionally satisfied with sex, compared with 48 percent of married men. Meanwhile, 7 percent of single women in short-term relationships said they were extremely satisfied physically with sex, compared with 41 percent of married women.

- Married people—with or without children—were less depressed and more emotionally healthy than comparable singles.

"Marriage gives us a starring role in someone else's life," Gallagher wrote. "We talk about single people being free to do whatever they want. People who matter a lot to others aren't free to do whatever they want. It's a trade-off."

* * *

Indeed, Angela was feeling miserable. But she was grateful for her good friend Gretchen, who kept trying to pull Angela out of her funk. Gretchen was training as a relationship coach. Previously a social worker, Gretchen had switched careers and completed six months of classes so far. On Saturday, the two friends met at their favorite Italian restaurant for Caesar salad and pasta. As they sat together in a quiet corner booth, Angela told Gretchen about her list—the one in which she detailed the hundred things she wanted to do, be, and have in her life.

"I really want to hear it! Come on, tell me!" Gretchen said.

Having anticipated her friend's reaction, Angela had brought along her notebook.

She pulled out her list and started to read: "People who love and honor me. A big house with lots of light and vibrant plants. I want to be strong and fearless—" As she read her list out loud, her eyes filled with tears.

"You're incredible!" Gretchen said, putting her arm around Angela. "I'm so proud of you for doing this. Keep going!"

When Angela had finished reading, Gretchen said that she noticed certain themes in her list. It was obvious that Angela really valued family, and being in an open and communicative relationship.

"I'm sorry to point this out," Gretchen added, "but Matt didn't seem to value the same things you do."

"But I do have a lot about traveling here!" Angela said, defensively.

"That's true. But it seems that your list is mainly focused on having a life that is filled with love, honesty, and support."

"I guess you're right. Matt didn't really give me any notice about taking off. He was gone, just like that. He didn't even say goodbye to my son."

Gretchen nodded.

"He was so distant from his own family," Angela continued. "And he didn't have any close friends, unless you count me."

"I know you enjoyed all those weekend getaways," Gretchen said. "They sounded like fun."

"Fun," Angela repeated. "That's what the relationship was in a nutshell. But within a few months, we jumped from dating to mating. I was waiting for him to move in with me. I guess I was so desperate to be with a man that I was blind to the reality of who he really was."

"Well, if it makes you feel any better, I ran into our mutual friend Chris today at the grocery store, and he heard that Matt was just hanging out in Arizona by himself, playing bridge all day on the computer."

"Aaaaahhh!" moaned Angela. She put her head on Gretchen's shoulder and started to laugh uncontrollably.

* * *

While I've desired a successful life partnership as long as I can remember, I never really understood why it was so important until learning the facts shared in this chapter. We appear to be wired to thrive in a committed relationship, and the research shows that there are good, solid reasons to "find the love of your life and the life that you love."

Today, we are like relationship pioneers, following our dreams into uncharted territory without actually knowing exactly where we will end up or what our destination will look like. Some of us have vague fantasies or idealistic dreams. Some of us have rebelled against commitment by getting divorced to pursue mirages of greener pastures. Some of us have "hooked up" for fun and recreation, cohabited for sex and companionship, or gave up the dream of finding a life partner and reproduced using anonymous donors. We have learned in this chapter that the overwhelming majority of people do want a committed relationship with a soul mate. However, we all start this quest as singles. ✄

CONSCIOUS DATING PLAN EXERCISE NO. 2:

Please refer to Chapter 15 to write your answers.

What can you do when you're single to prepare to find your life partner?

1. Imagine that you have ten billion dollars and ten years to live. Sit down in a quiet place and imagine one hundred things you would want to do in your remaining years.

2. Don't forget the small things in your list, especially those things that make you feel loved.

3. If you get stuck, put the list down and pick it up again in a day or so.

Why "Dating" Doesn't Work: The 14 Dating Traps

Do you like the way the singles scene works? Truth be told, most of us don't. The old ways of dating and mating just aren't effective anymore. Why not? What exactly is going wrong? This chapter explains why current dating practices don't work.

When talking about these Dating Traps, I often share my tongue-in-cheek unwritten "Dr. Laura" title for singles: "Fourteen Stupid Things Singles Do to Mess Up Their Lives." We've all been there. A "dating trap" is an unsolvable problem that results in unhappiness in a relationship. Getting out of the trap often means leaving the relationship. When single, you can do a lot more than you realize to avoid these traps and better prepare for a successful and lasting relationship.

This list of dating traps is based on my personal experiences, my friends' and clients' experiences, and just plain observation. Most of the traps are obvious: they are inauthentic and fear-based and result in poor relationship choices. Perhaps you're afraid that you're not going to get what you really want, or that you'll be single for the rest of your life and always be unhappy. When you're afraid, you try to protect yourself. But the truth is that when you act out of fear, you end up creating the very things that you're afraid of.

One of my favorite introductory seminars that I lead for singles is the "Dating Traps Game," a takeoff of the Dating Game. First, we split into small groups, and each group is assigned a set of two to four dating traps. The groups share their "war stories" and then vote on the best war story for their assigned traps. Finally, the small groups come together and as a large group we share the winning war stories for each trap. It's amazing how easily participants can relate to each other's experiences, and how funny these follies seem after the fact!

A "dating trap" is an unsolvable

problem that results in unhappiness

in a relationship. Getting out of the trap often means

leaving the relationship. When

single, you can do a lot more than you realize to

avoid these traps and prepare for a successful and

lasting relationship.

At the end of the seminar, we also go over the "Ten Principles of Conscious Dating," which are discussed in Chapters 5-14. At the end of the Dating Traps Game participants complete a handout that you'll find at the end of this chapter. After reading this chapter, I urge you to answer the questions at the end as honestly as possible.

1. Marketing Trap
You believe that you need to make yourself more appealing to attract and "sell" yourself with attractive packaging and presentation. When you fall into the Marketing Trap, you fear that nobody will want you as you really are.

If you browse through your local personal ads, you'll see that most of them are just marketing hype. They tell you very little about the real person behind them. When dating, many single people assume they will not be attractive or acceptable as they are. In fear of rejection, they use a "marketing" approach to attract potential partners.

I know a single forty-year-old man whom his friends refer to as "Mr. Casual." His favorite place to shop for clothes is the local surplus store. He wears hiking boots every day. However, when one of his friends sets him up with an attractive young woman who loves the opera, he wants to impress her. A week after their first coffee date, he invites her to the opera (although personally, he abhors opera music). Not only does he buy box seats, but also he dresses up in a tuxedo. When he shows up at his date's door awkward and uncomfortable, it's painfully obvious that he is trying to impress her. Presenting a version of someone else does not work.

Be your best when you show up for a date, but don't present yourself as someone you're not. By "marketing" yourself, you risk disappointment and relationship failure.

I've also seen women fall into the marketing trap. I recently spoke with one rather conservative woman who wears a dress suit to work and slacks and sweaters on weekends. Yet, on a recent date with a man who was four years younger, she splurged on a new outfit: a slinky skirt with a long slit up one side and a V-neck silk blouse that showed some cleavage. She showed up as a woman who was not her.

It's normal and fine to dress up for a date. But there's a difference between primping and getting an extreme makeover. While it's important to look your best when you show up for a date, don't present yourself as someone you're not. By "marketing" yourself, you risk disappointment and relationship failure. When the excitement and promise of the "sizzle" conflicts with the reality of the "steak," one or both of you are left feeling disappointed and angry.

2. Packaging Trap

The Packaging Trap is the opposite of the Marketing Trap. Instead of seeking to sell yourself with attractive packaging, you focus on the packaging of others.

Women commonly dislike being evaluated or pursued by men solely for their physical attractiveness, and are offended by comments such as "She's so hot!" Similarly, men commonly dislike being evaluated or pursued by women for their job or money, and wonder sometimes why women can't see past their bank account.

When we don't know someone, it is natural to focus on the outside packaging. It is also understandable to be attracted to something that is very important to us, such as looks or money. Deep down we know that potential partners are just like us. We all want to be viewed as multidimensional beings—not just a body or a wallet. Yet, in dating—whether we are straight or gay, young or old—unconscious singles commonly focus on a packaging quality that attracts them, and then wonder why their relationships don't work.

Deep down we know

that potential partners are just like us.

We all want to be viewed as multidimensional

beings—not just a body or a wallet.

In our culture, we commonly objectify people by focusing on their age, gender, race, clothes, hair, weight, job, finances, and other external characteristics. Then we often make generalizations about who they are. When scouting for potential partners, it is common for some singles to focus on the packaging first, then not see much else beyond that. This works both ways—rejecting some people because of their packaging, and pursuing others because of their packaging.

Focusing on packaging can interfere even when unintentional. For example, in my story, which you read in the Introduction, when Maggie and I first posted our profiles on Match.com, our searches missed each other. We missed because I selected five foot two as my minimum height requirement for a partner (Maggie is five foot one and a half inches) and she selected her age and older (I'm eighteen months younger). Neither of us intended to discriminate based upon such external packaging characteristics, or to reject potential partners who were younger or shorter. Fortunately, Maggie had the intelligence to modify her search criterion to include men a few years younger, and found me! And I'm very glad she did.

It is understandable to have preferences and reactions to external packaging; however, if our goal is an internal experience—such as to be happy, loved, and fulfilled in a relationship—we must balance external preferences with internal ones. We all have some requirements related to packaging—such as race, height, age, and even body type or weight—but I recommend de-emphasizing external characteristics that don't have much to do with a quality relationship, and instead emphasizing what you require to have the life and relationship you want.

The 2001 movie *Shallow Hal* is a great example of the packaging trap. Hal (played by Jack Black), a single guy obsessed with external packaging, was hypnotized by Anthony Robbins to see only the person inside and pursued Gwyneth Paltrow's illusionary slim character. Then, when the hypnotic spell broke and he saw her actual obesity, he decided that her weight didn't inter-fere with his love and desire for her.

3. Scarcity Trap

You believe there is a limited supply of possible partners, and therefore think that you have to take what you can get or be alone. The Scarcity Trap results in relationship failure because there is a temptation to settle for less: you believe you can't get what you really want because there is not enough to go around. Unfortunately, it's a self-fulfilling prophecy because when you expect less, you get less.

When you expect less, you get less.

Forbes magazine runs an annual feature called "Best Cities for Singles." The article ranks the forty largest U.S. metropolitan centers as the best and worst places to live if you're single. Each metro area is ranked based on supposed "quantitative data" including nightlife, culture, job growth, number of singles, cost of living alone, and "coolness."[1]

The piece leaves readers with the impression that if they don't live in one of the top ten cities—such as Austin, Denver, or Boston—their chances of finding a mate are very slim. Not only does this article instill fear in singles—such as, "How sorry is the singles scene in Cleveland?... most Clevelanders flee the city for the burbs as soon as they can"—but the artwork further feeds into the scarcity trap. The photos shown alongside the "Top Ten Cities for Singles" article show couples touching each other and laughing; while the "Top Worst Cities for Singles" illustrate singles standing far apart from each other at a bar, and a single checking his cell phone.

Readers living in one of the worst-ranked cities are left feeling, "Well, does that mean I'm screwed?" It's scary for many who read such articles. Readers can feel desperate, thinking, "Man,

I'm going to have to take what I can get here. I can't afford to be choosy." Or, "It's not in the cards for me." Or, "There aren't enough potential partners to go around." Or even, "I'll have to move if I ever want to have a meaningful relationship." If readers don't know any better, they might settle for less. Many do.

The idea that dating is a numbers game is nonsense. The truth is: it just takes one! Finding your life partner has no relation at all to how many singles are living in your area. It's about quality, not quantity, as well as applying the strategies for conscious dating that we will cover later in this book.

4. Compatibility Trap
Singles who fall into the Compatibility Trap believe that if they're having fun with someone and getting along well, then they are compatible and a committed relationship will work. The Compatibility Trap is a very common one because when you first meet someone, it is so easy and seductive to assume that if you're having a good time together, then you're well-matched. Unfortunately, short-term fun and long-term compatibility are not the same.

There is a vast difference between a

dating relationship—in which the focus

is on fun and recreation—and a serious, long-term,

committed relationship.

First and foremost, there is a vast difference between a dating relationship—in which the focus is on fun and recreation—and a serious, long-term, committed relationship. The criteria and process for choosing somebody whom you date casually are very different from choosing a life partner. Many couples end up making a commitment because they have fun dating. But when the dating ends—and you both decide to become an exclusive couple—the fun ends, too. Just because you are having fun together doesn't mean a successful life partnership will result.

Certainly, singles need to be out there and have fun! But for a lot of people, fun is the primary criteria they use for dating. The pattern in our culture is one in which we pursue people who are fun and attractive to us. But time and time again, "recreational dating"—socializing and spending time with people in order to have a good time—quickly turns into a "mini-marriage."

I recall one woman in her mid-fifties, Sharon, who came regularly to our Friday Night Socials for singles. One evening, she told me how frustrated she was with dating. Sharon had been planning and saving for retirement, an important focus in her life. She had no problem finding men to date. Most had lucrative jobs, but they were not security-minded like her. One man was a ski bum. Another man was putting all his money into his boat. She would get involved with these men, and then break up because they didn't meet her requirements for financial security. When I asked Sharon why she continued to date them, she said, "But they're so much fun!"

I pointed out to her that just having fun didn't mean these men would meet her requirements, or "nonnegotiables." (I discuss requirements in more detail in Chapter 5. In short, requirements are what you must have for your relationship to work for you; if one requirement is missing, the relationship will fail.)
Sharon slapped her forehead: "Yeah, you're right!"

It is possible to convert a recreational relationship into a serious, long-term, committed one—but only if 100 percent of your requirements are met. If one requirement is not met, it will become an "unsolvable problem." Unsolvable problems are the ones that usually cause relationships to break up. Imagine the clarity you would have if all your requirements were spelled out before you entered a relationship. And before making a commitment, you would be certain that all your requirements were being met. Then, any problems that arise are going to be solvable ones. Wouldn't that be great? Well, it's completely possible, but it takes some preparation and self-awareness.

5. Fairy-tale Trap

In the Fairy-tale Trap, you believe that finding your soul mate will just happen. You expect your ideal partner to magically appear and whisk you off to live happily ever after—with no effort at all on your part!

As children, we all fantasize. When you were a kid, you might have thought "I'm going to live in a castle one day!" or "I'm going to be a football hero." As adults, how many of us dream about winning the lottery? Growing up can feel scary, and some people have a hard time letting go of childhood fantasies. Many of us unconsciously expect that what we want in our lives will somehow just happen, and we can't, or we don't need to, do anything but wait passively for it to happen.

Every week, we watch fantasy relationships play out on TV with reality shows like The Bachelor, The Bachelorette, Joe Millionaire, Hooking Up, Blind Date, elimiDate, Date My Mom. We see a handsome Texas lawyer eliminate nineteen princesses—their hair shining and eyes sparkling—one by one until he chooses the winner. A few nights later, the inheritor of his family's estate is deciding which young lovely beauty will dine with him at the countryside villa. These women—who often appear desperate and scared—simply hope to be "the one."

Maintaining this fantasy mind-set in real life does not work. Finding the love of your life is not about hoping to be picked. Nor is it about sitting down and making a list of your future partner's ideal traits—what your prince or princess is like—and waiting for the magic to happen. It's about knowing yourself first so that you can be the chooser, rather than waiting to be chosen. (In Chapters 6 and 7, we will discuss the strategies you can use to take personal responsibility for your relationship choices and outcomes.)

Finding the love of your life is not about hoping to be picked... It's about knowing yourself first so that you can be the chooser, rather than waiting to be chosen.

---

6. Date to Mate Trap

In this trap, you become an "instant couple" with someone you are dating. Many couples will say, after just a couple of weeks or a month of dating— "We really want this to work," or "We're very committed to each other." In the Date to Mate Trap, you believe that if you develop an exclusive relationship with someone when you are dating, a successful committed relationship will eventually happen. This dynamic is also known as the "mini-marriage" or "serial monogamy."

I compare this trap to taking an extended test drive with a car. When you are car shopping, you visit the dealer and try out a variety of cars for short rides around the block. You ask questions, keep your options open, and have fun. Those who fall into the Date to Mate Trap sign the lease for the first car they test drive without investigating possible unsolvable problems that might arise along the way.

This approach is a costly use of time and emotional energy. The Date to Mate Trap results in relationship failure because there is a big difference between a dating relationship and the complexity and challenges of a long-term relationship. Can you imagine entering a relationship with everybody you date? There's a certain amount of inertia created because you're going out with this person and are exclusive with him/her. There is a pressure for this person to be "the one," and for this relationship to work.

The Date to Mate Trap is like trying to fit the round peg into the square hole: "OK, it doesn't quite fit, but it is close enough." And people attempt to solve unsolvable problems. Unsolvable problems are heart-wrenching and you shouldn't need to deal with them unless you're in a committed relationship. If you choose carefully, you may not need to deal with unsolvable problems at all.

There is a very big difference between a dating relationship and the complexity and challenges of a long-term relationship.

When I explain the Date to Mate Trap to singles, they often respond, "But if you don't date to mate, then what do you do?" Unfortunately, this trap is the cultural norm in dating. Fortunately, singles can learn how to date consciously, as you will discover in the next few chapters.

7. Attraction Trap

You fall into the Attraction Trap when you make your choices based solely on feelings of attraction. You interpret a strong attraction to someone as a sign that this relationship is a good choice and is meant to be. In the midst of infatuation, you ignore red flags and the relationship eventually fails.

The Attraction Trap is a kind of paradox because we do need to feel attracted. The chemistry has to be there. You can't just get together with someone you're not attracted to! But this trap is about following your feelings of attraction as if that's all you need to make a relationship work. When you were twelve or thirteen, you probably had a crush on someone in class. Everything looked good and felt good. You didn't stop to think about the consequences and just went for it. I'm NOT saying that we should ignore all this junior high school excitement. I'm saying that attraction should be a given, but by itself is not enough to keep us together.

Attraction is like the radar that helps you find your target. But the Attraction Trap is blindly following this radar. In conscious dating, we use our feelings of attraction as information. We need to stop and ask ourselves why we are attracted to this person and whether he/she meets our requirements. Author Harville Hendrix, Ph.D., calls the unconscious partner choice the "imago," meaning that you're attracted to someone because of your childhood, your caretakers, and your past experiences. These unconscious choices often result in repeating unproductive past patterns and results in failed relationships.

Attraction is like the radar

that helps you find your target.

---

8. Love Trap

The Love Trap is powerful and alluring because we all deeply want to love and be loved. You fall into the Love Trap when you interpret infatuation, attraction, need, good sex, and/or emotional attachment as "love." Subsequently, after you discover that love is not enough to meet your requirements, your relationship fails.

Romantics are especially vulnerable to getting caught in this trap. Romantics believe that "if it feels good, it must be love" and think that "love is all you need" and "love conquers all." Romantics use these beliefs as their primary motivators when seeking a relationship. Then, when the relationship isn't working out, they spend their time trying to recreate their initial experience of infatuation. Time and time again, I've heard people say—after the first two weeks of a relationship—"This has been the best time of my life!" They feel so in love, so they believe it must be a good relationship. In a short time, the initial infatuation is gone; then they spend the rest of their time together struggling to get it back.

9. Sex Trap

The Sex Trap is similar to the Love Trap, where singles interpret good sex as love. But those who fall into the Sex Trap go even further, because for these singles, having sex carries immense meaning and consequences. A great summation of the Sex Trap is that often-heard stereotype, "Women use sex to get love, and men use love to get sex."

Falling into the Sex Trap usually means one of two things: singles believe that sex is a necessary test of compatibility; that is, if the sex is good, then the relationship will be good as well. Or, more commonly, all consciousness goes out the window, and one or both formerly level-headed singles consider themselves a committed couple as soon as they have sex.

Rather than looking at whether this other person might be a match on levels other than physical attraction—such as long-term requirements, needs, and wants—you are blindsided by the chemistry under the covers. It can be challenging to keep in touch with reality and stay conscious when all those hormones are running wild.

Our body reacts to someone we are attracted to by producing hormones such as PEA or phenylethylamine (natural amphetamine), dopamine and norepinephrine (natural mood enhancers), and testosterone (increased sexual desire), which makes the opportunity to have sex with someone we are attracted to extremely hard to resist. Then, after orgasm, we produce oxytocin (which acts on the hypothalamus to produce emotions), which makes us feel very close to and bonded with our sex partner. These chemical reactions are involuntary and strong, leading to powerful feelings of attraction, excitement, love, closeness, and well-being. But when problems arise, you often rationalize by thinking, "Well, we've got problems, but the sex is great." By falling into the Sex Trap, you (although it's hard to admit it) prioritize physical intimacy and regard the rest as optional. Whether you are aware of it or not, your main criterion for a relationship is sexual attraction and physical compatibility.

It can be challenging to keep

in touch with reality when all those

hormones are running wild.

I do want to point out that chemistry is very important. Yet, chemistry is a given that we can't control in a relationship; it is either there or not there, and it must be there for the partnership to work. If it is not there, we can't "make" it happen, though sometimes it can grow over time. Those who pursue a relationship based upon sexual chemistry risk relationship failure when the hormone-induced intoxication wears off and reality hits.

10. Rescue Trap

The Rescue Trap is enticing as you hope that a relationship will solve your emotional and financial difficulties and bring you happiness and fulfillment. It's like winning the lottery. You then avoid taking responsibility for your life challenges and expect to be rescued from them. When problems multiply instead of disappear, the Rescue Trap results in desperation, neediness, and relationship failure.

I've seen women especially jump into this trap over and over: "When I meet the right partner, my life will be wonderful. Oh please hurry and rescue me!" They feel like they can't make it on their own, whether it's about paying the bills or raising their children. This attitude typically results in neediness and desperation.

In the Rescue Trap, you're not taking responsibility for your life because you're expecting some outside magical solution. You tend to live with your problems rather than solve them. And then, in a relationship, your problems multiply instead of disappear. In the end, your debt increases, your children get rowdier, and your relationship eventually fails.

Although it feels good to be needed,

someone who needs you is not necessarily able to

give you what you need.

---

11. Codependent Trap

The Codependent Trap and the Rescue Trap both capture those of us who don't like to be alone and need to focus our life on someone else. You expect someone will love you and give you what you want by giving the other person what he/she wants. You attempt to earn love and happiness by acquiescing, nurturing, giving, and helping. Needing to be needed often results in unconsciously attracting and choosing a relationship with a person who needs you but—as you later discover—is unable to give you what you want.

Codependents are convinced that no one would want them for who they are, and thus feel good when they are needed. This is my own most common and riskiest trap. My first two marriages were to women who attracted me because they needed me—first to leave home and escape controlling parents, then to leave a dead first marriage. It felt so good to help them make their transition toward the life they wanted, but neither was a good foundation for a committed relationship.

Codependents really want to be in a relationship. You feel unworthy as you are and that you need to earn love. You pursue relationships because you feel incomplete when you're not in one. You want to be the hero and therefore seek someone who wants to be helped. But you learn the hard way that although it feels good to be needed, someone who needs you is not necessarily able to give you what you need in return.

12. Entitlement Trap

Those who fall into the Entitlement Trap seem to believe (often unconsciously) that you deserve to get what you want in your life and relationships without effort or change on your part. As you rely on your partner to bring happiness and fulfillment, you inevitably experience disappointment.

We're bombarded daily by messages that reinforce the Entitlement Trap. The media's message is: you deserve to drive that new SUV and to live in that two-story house with the manicured yard and view of the water. In a relationship, this translates into feeling that you're entitled and deserving. Your attitude toward your partner is "What can you do for me?"

Very attractive and/or wealthy people seem to fall into the Entitlement Trap most often. For example, I have met many beautiful women who feel that they deserve to be catered to. From early on, they have been given the message that the whole world will wait on them. All they have to do is sit back and look pretty. And I have spoken to wealthy men who think that they don't have to work on relationships. Just as they buy things in everyday life that make them feel good—whether it's a new DVD player or a hot tub with jets—they can buy love. Unfortunately, a relationship doesn't work out when you believe that you're entitled.

13. Virtual Reality Trap
In this trap, you believe that "what you see is what you get." Instead of using actual experience and knowledge to make long-term relationship choices, you make your decisions based on short-term impressions and inferences. By seeing only what you want to see, you are blinded to the reality and the relationship fails.

Instead of dealing with the reality

before me—that my wife was

addicted to these medications—I saw what

I wanted to see and clung to our marriage.

I lived in "virtual reality."

With my second marriage, I fell into the Virtual Reality Trap. After numerous failures to get pregnant, my wife and I decided to give in vitro fertilization (IVF) a try. It was a long and costly process and, in 1998, our twin boys were born. After their birth, I didn't think much about the medicine bottles floating around our house; I'd gotten used to seeing various kinds of prescription medication during IVF. When I did bring up the issue, my wife denied there was a problem. I believed her. Nonetheless, within a short time, I discovered that indeed she was addicted to the prescriptions. She went into rehab with many promises to change, which I also believed. When she got out, she relapsed and made more promises. Instead of dealing with the reality before me—that my wife was addicted to these medications—I saw what I wanted to see and clung to our marriage. I lived in "virtual reality." But when the pattern continued to repeat— rehab and relapse, rehab and relapse—I finally gained the insight to look behind her promises and see that from the beginning, I had overlooked what was truly real.

The Virtual Reality Trap is the opposite side of the Marketing Trap. In this case, you're reacting to the external presentation and packaging as if they are real. How many of us have gotten involved in relationships focusing on "potential" (another word for the Virtual Reality Trap), hoping that some things that we really need to happen will get better or change over time?

14. Lone Ranger Trap

The Lone Ranger Trap is one of the most pervasive and common. You live your single life focused on your goal of finding your life partner and believe that the other relationships in your life are less important and that you don't need anyone's help. You evaluate the people you meet for their relationship potential and don't take the opportunity to cultivate new friends. In turn, you feel isolated and think there's a scarcity of potential partners. Therefore, you risk settling for less than what you really want because you are alone yet so focused on finding a partner.

Lone Rangers focus so much on the goal

of finding a mate, they isolate themselves, feeling

even more alone and desperate.

Those of us who fall into the Lone Ranger Trap go about dating by shoving friends and family out of the way while asking, "Is this the one? No. Is this the one? No." By focusing so much on the goal of finding a mate, you isolate yourself. You have not developed a support system or network, and you do not have experiences with a variety of people. So, in the end, you truly feel alone.

The Lone Rangers share a few basic characteristics. First, you want to feel grown up and live your life thinking, "I can do it myself!" Second, you are ashamed about being single and want to have a partner at your side as soon as possible so you can look and feel better. Third, as an isolated single, you then become an isolated couple. Sadly, Lone Rangers exclude others and focus their needs on their partner. Lastly, Lone Rangers also often fall into the Scarcity Trap. When you can't see beyond your own resources, it feels like no one is out there for you.

I believe that to be successful in any area of life, you need to have supportive people involved. We are social beings; no one is successful alone. The complexities and conflicts of any relation-ship—whether it's a partner, friend, or family member—can prove to be challenging. But how you relate with friends and family will play out in your life partnership, so you might as well set yourself up for success and learn how to handle relationship challenges when you're single. ✣

CONSCIOUS DATING PLAN EXERCISE NO. 3:

Please refer to Chapter 15 to write your answers.

Let's play the Dating Traps Game!

1. Which dating traps have you fallen into?

2. Which trap is your riskiest?

3. If you could give yourself some expert advice, what would you say?

4. What will you do to follow your own advice?

Being Single Is an Opportunity!

Being single is like being on a sabbatical from a committed relationship. When you take a sabbatical from your job, you focus on professional goals, personal goals, and activities that you couldn't pursue while working full time. While you are on this sabbatical, what goals and activities will help you have the life and relationship you really want? What personal, lifestyle or professional goals can you accomplish while you're single that will enhance your life and future relationship? Being single is an opportunity to ready yourself to attract the love of your life.

BEING SINGLE IS NOT A DISEASE

If you were to take an informal survey of single relatives and friends, you might hear an overwhelming "I just want to be in a relationship!" Many singles view their status as an undesirable state that they want to change as soon as humanly possible. Many singles unknowingly subscribe to a myth that if only they were in a relationship they would be happy.

As a single, if you are not happy with your life or yourself, a relationship will not fix that. Many singles sign up for my Conscious Dating Relationship Success Training for Singles (RESTS) classes because they don't want to be single anymore. Often, they send in their applications out of desperation and fear. They are hoping that by the end of the course, they will have met the love of their lives. However, many realize by the end of the class that their job right now is to pursue their dreams while they're single, that being single is an opportunity to enjoy their current life while preparing themselves for future success in having the life and relationship they really want.

If you are not happy with your life or yourself, a relationship will not fix it.

Cathy taped up her last cardboard box and sighed. She would be leaving Denver in two weeks. While she was devastated that her marriage was over, she was slowly realizing that her divorce was turning into an opportunity. Cathy's life would no longer revolve around Brad, her alcoholic husband. For a decade, she had suppressed her dream of having a family while she took care of Brad's hangovers.

Now, instead of waiting for her hung-over husband to wake up every Sunday, Cathy walked to the downtown bookstore and zoomed straight for the self-help section. She picked up one book on alcoholism that said that adult children of alcoholics often enter relationships in which they take on a codependent savior role. They feel a need to save and look after their substance-abusing mates as they did for their parents. Cathy clearly remembered nursing her father's hangovers. And her mother's role-modeling had taught her from an early age to cover up the alcoholism by throwing out empty bottles before friends came over or by explaining that her father needed to take a nap when he was really sleeping off the previous night's binge.

Cathy was going to move back to her hometown of Cincinnati. The move would be scary and daunting, but she was ready to deal with her pain. When the big day arrived, Cathy dropped her last box in the back of the moving truck with a thump and a sigh of relief.

Everything she'd accumulated over the past two decades was there: the pottery she had made in college, the dolls she had collected from rummage sales, kitchen supplies, bedding, stereo system, and sofa. However, she intentionally left behind the bed she and Brad had shared. It felt very symbolic not to take it with her.

Cathy's friend, Melissa, was driving with her from Denver to Cincinnati. Melissa was the only friend whom Cathy had hung onto during her isolated marriage. They had packed a special picnic basket for the long drive and brought along a stack of their favorite CDs. As Melissa took the wheel, Cathy stared out the window. She was thinking about her past. When she had married Brad at age twenty-eight, she knew he had a drinking problem. During the fast and furious six months they dated before getting engaged, he was often hung over on weekends. He worked long hours as a carpenter, and she had chalked off the extra beers as something he did to ease the heavy day's work load. Still, she had figured that after they were married, he would stop going out with his buddies. Not so. At least one Friday a month, Brad would stumble home at 3 a.m. and fall asleep on their sofa. Cathy tried to remember what exactly attracted her to Brad. When they met, most of her friends were already married and had children. She had been feeling like an old maid. Dating had been easy—men were drawn to her fire-red hair and blue eyes—but she had been feeling desperate to settle down. Brad, who was then thirty-two, had been under a lot of pressure from his family to tie the knot. He and Cathy had met through mutual friends at a party and quickly jumped into seeing each other a few times a week, leaving little space for introspection.

You have a full and rich life ahead of you.

A few years into the marriage, after Cathy had difficulty getting pregnant, the relationship turned rocky. They had intense discussions about fertility treatments—would IVF work? could they afford it?—after which Brad often went out drinking. At that point, Cathy went to see a therapist and starting taking antidepressants. She questioned the future of her marriage, but the last thing she wanted to do was break up as her own parents had. Eventually, she gave up trying to have children.

As they drove on, Melissa told her that she'd felt so worried when Cathy hadn't returned her phone calls.

"I'm sorry," Cathy said. "I was so ashamed. It got so crazy at one point that if he didn't come home by 10 o'clock on Fridays, I actually went down to the bar to find him. I thought I could drag him home, but we would end up screaming at each other on the street corner."

Melissa turned her eyes away from the road and looked at Cathy. "You have a full and rich life ahead of you."

* * *

THE SINGLES BLUES

David Bentley, one of my colleagues who coaches singles, has identified a "syndrome" which he calls "The Singles Blues."[1] It's when you feel inferior because you don't have a partner, or when being single overwhelms you so much that you just want to crawl under the covers and hide. David identifies four "symptoms" of the Singles Blues. Do you recognize any of them in yourself?

1. **Holding onto the Past:** When it comes to dating, do you hesitate to make the first move because in the past you got snubbed by someone or turned down for a date? Are you waiting for others to approach you? Do you become depressed and/or angry when they don't? Holding on to the past can cause us to take the same unsuccessful actions we've always taken, expecting them to work this time if we just try harder. Sometimes we even hold onto physical objects from the past. Do you still have love let-

ters from a former sweetheart who is now married and has six children? Is that faded rose from your first date still pressed between pages of Rumi poems? Isn't it time to get rid of the physical and emotional remnants of the past and embrace your present and future?

DO YOU HAVE
THE SINGLES BLUES?

- **Holding onto the Past**
- **Negativity**
- **Excessive Guilt**
- **The Paralysis of Analysis**

---

2. **Negativity**: Do you make derogatory remarks about previous partners? Are you cynical about your friends' relationships? Do you obsess over the negative aspects of being single or about being successfully partnered? When you're positive and feel good about yourself, you find positive qualities in the world around you.

3. **Excessive Guilt**: Many of us assume too much responsibility for what happens to us in our world. For example, if you're over twenty-five and not in a long-term relationship, you might think that something is wrong with you. If you've broken up with a lover or divorced your spouse, you might feel no one else will want you. We all make mistakes, but the only failures are the mistakes from which we fail to learn. Guilt is a useless emotion that prevents us from dusting ourselves off and getting back into the saddle. It is important to accept responsibility for our part in any situation, but only our part.

4. **The Paralysis of Analysis**: Do you ever find yourself unable to move in any direction? Have you looked at every possible angle of past, present, and future relationships until you are

totally confused? Are you filled with fear about the misfortunes awaiting you on the relationship scene? If so, stop analyzing and take some action. Any action, even the wrong one, is going to get you moving. Action absorbs anxiety. Decide what first baby steps would be appropriate and take them. After you've moved a bit, decide what steps to take next. If the first action produced positive results, keep moving in the same direction. If not, then choose a new direction. Standing still and analyzing only prevents you from moving down the path of your life.

LEARNING BY FALLING DOWN

A new relationship is not the "cure" for the loneliness of your last breakup. Instead, the cure can lie in the breakup itself. When a significant relationship ends, we can feel like a failure. But what if we turn this around and see the breakup as an opportunity to evolve? Significant life challenges—such as relationship breakups—present us with the opportunity to grow, learn, become better people, and accomplish more in our lives. Notice that I use the word "challenge," and not "failure." That's because if we are challenged, there must be something that we need to learn.

I recall teaching my children to ride two-wheeled bikes. At times it was scary for them, but I helped them overcome their fear to learn this important skill. I've always enjoyed bike riding, and have taken my children in bike trailers and seat carriers when they were little, followed by giving them bikes with training wheels as they got older. It's been my tradition to get each of my children a new two-wheeled bike on his/her fifth birthday and teach him/her how to ride. My oldest daughter caught on fast and learned to ride on her own after just an hour of assistance. My twins and former step-daughter needed multiple lessons spaced out over a few weeks, but they caught on pretty fast. My former stepson, however, had a fear of getting hurt and cried a lot when he fell down, even though he wasn't really hurt. I encouraged him, telling him how important it was to get back up after you fall. Falling down is not a failure! This story applies to the challenges we have in relationships: You don't learn by avoiding risk or giving up and being hard on yourself for making mistakes or failing. Falling down is how we learn.

THE NEW SINGLE VERSUS THE OLD SINGLE
Fortunately, the stigma of being single is changing.

Just a couple of decades ago, many singles felt there was something wrong with them if they were not in a relationship. I refer to this mind-set as the "Old Single," meaning one who lives in fear that something is wrong with them because they're single. In the 1980s, books such as *Singles: The New Americans* were published, in which the experts psychoanalyzed singles who placed personal ads. (One professor of psychology said this "reminds me of the casting couch–impersonal, for sex only, exploitative.") These books highlighted singles who talked about their boring nights, all the money they spent on going out, and their loneliness.

Today, however, you'll find very positive books about what I call the "New Single," who is conscious and embraces being single. Books such as *Urban Tribes: A Generation Redefines Friendship, Family, and Commitment* and *Quirkyalone: A Manifesto for Uncompromising Romantics* are geared toward singles who see the value of being single, and know there are learning opportunities in relationships that don't work out for the long term. The New Single has a goal of finding a life partner, but is truly satisfied by being single for now. The New Single has goals, but there is no panic or desperation because he/she has not yet achieved these goals. The New Single is content being where he/she is right now. In our culture we always want to be ahead of where we are. But the conscious single is not in a hurry.

Ethan Watters, who wrote *Urban Tribes*, defines an urban tribe as a group of city dwellers who have formed a bond through a common interest, such as work or a social or recreational activity. Watters is referring to the rise of support networks for the growing class of creative single people inhabiting leading urban centers in the United States and around the world. [2]

Similarly, Sasha Cagen coined the word "quirkyalone" in her book, which "stands in opposition to saccharine, archaic notions of romantic love. It stands for self-respect, independent spirit, creativity, true love, and confidence." *Quirkyalone* begins with a timeline of Quirkyalones Throughout History, in which she quotes Socrates ("The unexamined life is not worth living"); Virginia Woolf (whose book *A Room of One's Own* articulates the need for space to be creative and develop as an individual); and the notorious 1986 Newsweek article, "Single Women Over 40 Have Less Chance to Marry than to Be Killed By a Terrorist," after which shock waves of anger, despair, and disillusionment swept the country. Cagen dispels the myth that wanting to be alone is negative or strange: "Putting *quirky* together with alone implies the ability to enjoy one's aloneness, whether one is single or not."[3]

Cagen's first-person essay—"The Quirkyalone: Loners Are the Last True Romantics"—was published in 2000 by *Utne* Reader. In it, Cagen wrote: "For the quirklyalone, there is no patience for dating just for the sake of not being alone." That's because quirkyalones have "unique traits and an optimistic spirit; a sensibility that transcends relationship status." Her book includes a chapter called "Marry Yourself First: The Mini-Trend of Self-matrimony," in which she details what some single people are doing today instead of getting married: throwing a bigger thirtieth or fortieth birthday party; buying their own homes; or even signing up for their own registries (formerly known as bridal registries) to get their share of flatware, crystal, and slow cookers.

The New Single is also very aware of the high failure rate of committed relationships. In her chapter "Quirkytogether," Cagen writes: "At the core, quirkytogether values the idea of two fully formed human beings coming together for a partnership rather than a merging of souls—it's not the soul mate idea of finding the other half to complete you, but about finding a lively and dynamic partnership that still allows you to be fully yourself."

In today's world, when you're more cautious and conscious about relationship choices, you might find yourself more cynical and staying away from romantic illusions. However, the current trend of increased cohabitation and a decreasing marriage rate implies that many are attempting to avoid failure by avoiding commitment, which doesn't work either. While being single is not a disease, it need not be a chronic condition.

MAKING THE MOST OF BEING SINGLE

One of the reasons that I enjoy working with singles is that they are usually very motivated. Often, they come to me very excited to share their goals. Together, we talk about the many advantages of being single. You have the freedom and flexibility to live the life you want, how you want, and where you want. It is a bit like being in college: You can have fun, learn a lot, and prepare for the rest of your life. But just as you can party and skate through college, you can party through your single life until the fun ends and the reality of life catches up with you. You might be unprepared for what comes next. However, with effort, awareness, and intention, you can have fun while preparing yourself for the life and relationship you really want.

You have the freedom and flexibility

to live the life you want,

how you want, and where you want.

When Cathy returned to Cincinnati with all her belongings in the back of the moving van, her father met her and wrapped his arms around her. He helped her move her belongings into the in-law unit behind his house, a small, sunny studio with a fuchsia blooming outside her door. She promptly hung her collage of her life vision over her bed.

Within a week, thanks to the contacts she'd made in Denver, Cathy had a new job and a new therapist. The antidepressants kept her energy up, and the adrenaline from the excitement of her big move energized her. She even called a couple of girl-friends from high school, also recently divorced, and they start-ed to meet regularly for dinner.

Still, at night, when Cathy climbed under the covers alone, she thought about all the things she had given up for her marriage. Rather than pursuing her dreams—for example, having a fami-ly—she had adapted to her alcoholic husband. Ever since she could remember, she had been passionate about children. After trying unsuccessfully to have children for years, Cathy came up with the idea of opening a daycare facility in their home. But Brad had said: "If we can't have children, I don't want to take care of other people's children!"

Cathy knew that it was time to figure out what she really want-ed in her life. She decided that for the next few months she was going to focus on three things: her new job, her search for her own apartment, and her life vision. She had the perfect oppor-tunity to recreate her life, but she wasn't sure how to go about it. For now, she was not interested in dating anybody. She want-ed to focus on what she was really passionate about: children!

In therapy, Cathy often said that she felt like a failure because she'd married an alcoholic, enabled his alcoholism, and stayed in an unhappy marriage for so many years. But her therapist told her over and over, "Cathy, you have not failed. Your marriage was an opportunity to learn about yourself, and you are certainly doing that." Cathy's therapist recommended a variety of support groups. The first one, about recovering from divorce, was a group of six women who focused on a number of topics: stages of recovery, anger and grief, self-identity, loneliness, forgiveness, and begin-ning again. Occasionally speakers came and Cathy took mental notes. She also made some new friends. Cathy felt like she'd final-ly faced the reality that her marriage had been an unhealthy one. While Cathy felt far from ever being in a committed relationship again, she wanted to take the next step to discover more about herself, with the possibility of loving again. One night she turned on her laptop. She searched for "relationships" and "conscious" and found herself on my site called, "Conscious Dating: Finding the Love of Your Life in Today's World."

Cathy was familiar with the profession of relationship coaching, having been part of the therapy world for years. Right then, she decided to sign up for my Conscious Dating Relationship Success Training for Singles (RESTS) course online.

* * *

Unfortunately, many singles are uncomfortable being single and want to be in a relationship, even if it means repeating past patterns. Rather than looking at their lives and relationships as intertwined dynamic processes, they view relationships as a commodity to possess or "have." The truth is that a relationship is a long-term project, not a short-term venture. Finding the right relationship is not like buying clothes; you cannot just choose one off the rack and take it home—mission accomplished!

Relationships are a long-term project,

not a short-term venture.

Finding the right relationship is not like

buying clothes; you cannot

just choose one off the rack and take it home.

It can be challenging to step back and examine whether you are ready for a relationship, and to know what you really want. Getting divorced can be quite a wake-up call for someone who strongly desires and intends to be married for life. Being single can be a time for carefully planning how to get what you really want in your life and in a relationship. Life lessons, such as divorce, force us to confront our shortcomings and teach us that our expectations and goals are not a guaranteed reality.

Because we are all single for a significant part of our lives, we should embrace and make the most of being single. In Chapter 3, we discussed the "dating traps," those unsolvable problems that result in unhappiness in a relationship. Getting out of the trap often means leaving the relationship. What's important to remember is that when you are single, you can use this time and space to avoid these traps and prepare for a successful and lasting relationship. The next ten chapters of this book will cover the Ten Principles of Conscious Dating, which detail how to avoid the dating traps and find your life partner. Right now is your chance to use being single to:

- let go of the past
- take responsibility for your life
- discover who you are
- re-create your life
- have the fun and freedom you had (or wish you had had) as a child

---

Being single can be a time

for carefully planning how to get what you really

want in your life and in a relationship.

You may recall Angela in Chapter 2, whose boyfriend Matt split town because God supposedly commanded him to go. Now that Angela was single again, she had time to reflect on her life. For the first time in years, she was writing in her journal. Every morning, Angela woke up at sunrise and wrote. Sometimes she felt whiny, writing about her frozen dinners and being alone on the weekends. But other days, she let her mind wander to an imaginary future in which she woke up next to an incredibly warm and supportive partner, a man who served her coffee in bed and left love notes under her pillow.

Exactly one month after Matt took off, Angela was back on the treadmill at the gym. "Hi there! Long time no see," said a voice behind her. Angela turned her head to see Jerry, the good-looking middle-aged man who often chatted with her in the sauna. His brow glowed with sweat as he got on the treadmill next to her. He looked taller than she'd remembered, and his eyes were a very clear hazel.

"Oh, hi," Angela said, feeling shy, but glad to see him. Jerry told her that he'd just come back from a one-week meditation retreat in the mountains. She commented that it must have been a great way to spend a vacation and recharge oneself from work. But Jerry corrected her: "Actually, I'm not working right now."

Angela turned her eyes back toward the treadmill screen, suddenly guarded. Jerry tried to explain: "Ten years ago, I started my own computer programming business and worked hard, long hours. I sold it six months ago and decided to take some time off to enjoy life as I figure out my next move."

A man who didn't work turned Angela off. Lazy, she thought. Just like Matt. The last thing she needed to was to get involved with another unemployed man. She stepped off the treadmill to work out with weights in the next room. She gave Jerry a wave.

Twenty minutes later, who should walk into the sauna behind her but Jerry. Angela breathed in deeply, all that hot, dry air getting stuck in her chest. They chatted about his retreat in the Virginia mountains, and her plans to take her son ice skating on Christmas Day. Then Jerry cleared his throat, and asked Angela if she'd like to go out for dinner some time. Angela wasn't sure. She felt flattered, but was turned off by the fact that Jerry didn't have a job. He told her that he was going to leave his card at the front desk.

When Angela got home, she called her best friend, Gretchen, who was training as a relationship coach.

"It sounds wonderful!" Gretchen said.

"Wonderful?" Angela said. "But he doesn't have a job. How come I get all these guys without jobs?"

"It sounds like he's a hard worker, though, and he's just taking some time off."

"Yeah, that was Matt's story, too," Angela said.

Now that she was single, Angela could

step back and examine

what she really wanted in a relationship.

"No," Gretchen corrected her. "Matt inherited his money from his family. He hadn't held a real job for years."

"Well, I don't want to go out with another guy who might suddenly decide to take off—"

"Angela, just because someone has a job doesn't mean he's going to stick around. What if his company suddenly offers to transfer him to another state?"

Angela was silent, taking in her friend's wisdom.

"Look," Gretchen continued. "Is it really about having a job? Isn't it actually about stability?"

"I guess you're right," Angela said. Now that she was single, Angela

could step back and examine what she really wanted in a relation-ship. She was taking the time to get clear about her expectations. She could proceed cautiously, without rushing into anything.

* * *

USING OUR RELATIONSHIPS AS MIRRORS

Single again, Angela was using her time wisely to reflect on her past. Shakti Gawain, a pioneer in the field of personal growth, has written and spoken much about relationships as mirrors, which is the process of letting our relationships reveal what we need to learn. (This will also be covered more in depth in Chapters 10 and 11.) Gawain believes that our primary relationship is with ourselves:

> Our relationships with other people continually reflect exactly where we are in that process. For example, for many years I yearned to find the right man to be my life partner. I created many relationships with men who were unavailable or inappropriate in certain ways. Eventually, I realized they were reflecting my own inner ambivalence about committed relationship and the ways that I didn't truly love myself. It was only after I did some deep emotional healing work, learning to truly love and be committed to myself, that I met a wonderful man who is now my husband.[4]

* * *

Curled up on her sofa with her notebook and pen, Angela jotted down what she remembered about her relationship with Matt. She and her husband of ten years had divorced when she was thirty-eight. They had grown apart, but remained good friends. She had gone out with a couple of men, but the attraction died out after a couple of months. Her son was entering adolescence and although he spent every other weekend with his father, she felt an inner pressure to find a good male role model for him. She had been set on the idea of having a traditional nuclear fam-ily. Time had seemed to be running out—when she met Matt.

Matt had approached her at a reading by one of her favorite authors—Margaret Atwood—and they'd gone out for coffee. He was fun and made her laugh. Like her, he enjoyed reading and seeing out-of-the-mainstream movies. While walking Angela back to her car, Matt stopped and bought her a red rose. His romancing was hard to resist after the dry spell she'd been through. Within a month, they were spending all their time together and going on weekend trips to the mountains and ocean.

Angela initially saw Matt as future partner material, but she soon discovered that he was distant from his family and only saw them once a year. He had few friends, and he was not very enthusiastic about hanging out with her son. Still, he had swept Angela off her feet with weekend getaways and expensive gifts. Also, the sparks had been flying. Angela had not slept with any-one for a year and Matt had been eager to please her in bed.

As time passed, she chose to ignore her important criteria for a life partner, such as a man with a clear and purposeful vision and close relationships with his family and friends. Angela also realized that, initially, she had kept Matt from her friends. She had feared they would be put off by his sometimes sarcastic sense of humor. And most of the time, they had been skipping town for the weekend. By the time three months had passed, Matt and Angela had become a couple and were in what seemed like a committed relationship. So, when Gretchen finally met Matt—and openly disapproved—Angela got defensive.

***

Gawain compares this process of reflection to being an artist. When you are painting, you typically have a sense of what colors you want to use, or what brush stroke you're going to try. As you paint, you get feedback from the painting itself. You are looking at your creation and it's telling you about yourself. Gawain says that this is how she looks at her own life.

She adds:

It's very difficult to look inside ourselves and see what's going on in there—particularly to see what we're unaware of. That's why it's important to look at our relationships as mirrors of our inner processes. Used in this way, relationships become one of the most valuable sources of healing and teaching in our lives. To understand how this works, we need to remind ourselves that we each, through our individual consciousness, create and shape how we experience external reality. This is as true in our relationships as in every other area of our lives—the relationships we create and shape reflect back to us what we are holding within our consciousness. We draw to us and are drawn to people who match and reflect some aspect of ourselves.[5]

* * *

After staying up late reflecting, Angela went to bed and fell into a deep sleep. The next morning, she called Jerry. His machine picked up. She said: "Hi, Jerry. It's Angela. I would be pleased to join you for dinner one night." She was curious to see which parts this new man would reflect of herself. She was ready to be conscious.

Being conscious means taking ownership for your part in what happens in your life.

Being conscious means taking ownership for your part in what happens in your life. If you see your relationships as mirrors, you can see yourself more clearly in every interaction you have with others. Being unconscious often means that you attribute your outcomes to external forces, events, and people. Being conscious gives you the opportunity to choose to learn and grow. Conscious Dating is about using this time in your life to learn more about yourself and relationships so you can truly find the love of your life and the life that you love.

CREATING A SUPPORT COMMUNITY

The most common lament I hear from today's singles is the difficulty they have meeting potential partners. This problem did not occur in past generations when we lived and worked in a community of family, friends, neighbors, and coworkers, all of whom would typically help introduce singles to each other. Without this support system, today's singles increasingly rely upon dating services and personal ads, and then wonder why they have so little in common with the people they meet through these services. Remember that relationships are about connection, and start by asking yourself how you can improve the quality and quantity of ALL your relationships. Without a built-in community, today's singles must create their own support system, like Ethan Watters' urban tribes.

Without a built-in community,

today's singles must intentionally create

their own support system.

When you take a sabbatical from your job, you focus on goals and activities that you typically couldn't do while working full time. While you are on this sabbatical from romantic relationships, it's an opportunity to build your support community. You can make new friends and allow new people into your life when you're not looking at everyone as a potential partner. You can take more risks to enrich your life when you're free to make choices and aren't worried about how your partner will react. You can focus on yourself instead of your partner when you try new things.

* * *

Cathy was finding a supportive community in her Conscious Dating Relationship Success Training for Singles (RESTS) class. Every Thursday night, Cathy got home from work at 5 p.m. and "met" on the phone with her class, a group of eight men and women. The first couple of weeks, Cathy had a blast envisioning her perfect life by writing out all the things she wanted to do, be, and have in her life. It became clear that she really wanted to get the proper credentials to open a daycare center. She also met separately one night a week with her coach, Patty, to further clarify her thoughts and feelings.

One of the most challenging classes for Cathy focused on her values and life purpose. In one exercise, she needed to envision her family and friends toasting her on her eightieth birthday. She was asked to write what significant people in her life would say about her: how they appreciated her, what she meant to them, how she was important to them, and why they loved and respected her.

Cathy felt so silly, as if she were bragging about herself.

But Patty encouraged her: "Go for it, Cathy! This is a celebration of your life! This is your opportunity to talk about how you shine!"

Cathy took a deep breath and read her toast on the phone:
My eightieth birthday party takes place on top of a mountain as the sun is shining. My father is there, along with my brother and his family. All my close friends from the past and present are with me too.

First, my friends take turns talking about me. They say, "Cathy is an incredibly generous, warm, and loving woman. She is one of those unique people to whom children are drawn. She has the most contagious laughter, and you can't help but smile in her presence. She's very intuitive, especially when it comes to young children. We have witnessed her growth over the years and felt intense pride."

When Cathy got off the phone, she was giddy and excited. She knew that now she could finally do what she'd always wanted...

Then, it's my father's turn. He says, "Cathy has always been a giver, and I've witnessed with pride as she learned to give more and more to herself as she got older. I watched her grow in many ways, whether it was in her career or in her love life. It has made me so proud to be the father of such a beautiful woman, both on the inside and outside."

Lastly, a group of my nieces, nephews, and grandchildren speak. They say, "We want to acknowledge Cathy for being one of the most generous human beings in the world. We also thank her for always opening both her heart and her home to us."

By the time Cathy stopped reading, tears were falling down her cheeks. "I love it!" Patty cheered. "Bravo!"

When Cathy got off the phone, she was giddy and excited. She knew that now she could finally do what she'd always wanted: open a daycare center! Now that she was single, she would embrace life as an adventure and finally live the life she wanted.

Both Angela and Cathy were grieving the ends of their relationships. But they were also using the time to turn their situations into opportunities. That's why Angela decided to write in her journal again. And why Cathy decided to sign up for my Conscious Dating

Relationship Success Training for Singles (RESTS) class. When you're single, you can take the personal growth workshop that you always wanted to take. You can go back to school. You can travel to a faraway country. You're free to expand your world and yourself. A relationship can narrow these opportunities tremendously as you make plans and decisions with your relationship in mind.

Relationships happen anyway. They do! If you look back on your life, you will find that you met people and formed relationships without any plan or intention. As social beings, this is what we humans do. When you are single, you may feel alone and desperate, but even if you did nothing to meet a partner, eventually you would have opportunities to do so and form a relationship. Since relationships happen anyway, you can relax and not push the outcome. Instead, you can focus on the process of living your life consciously, building a community of emotionally satisfying relationships all around you and allowing your support community to help you attract the kind of partner you really want.

* * *

The remainder of this book covers my Ten Principles of Conscious Dating and will give you the information and tools you need to make good relationship choices while single. These choices can result in the life and relationship you really want. While there is no quick fix, I think you will find that *Conscious Dating* is very doable and can set you on a path that will help you find your life partner sooner than you might expect as you are living the life that you love. ✄

CONSCIOUS DATING PLAN EXERCISE NO. 4:

Please refer to Chapter 15 to write your answers.

How can you turn being single into an opportunity?

1. At this point in the book, can you come up with at least three things that you've always wanted to do but have not done, due to finances, time constraints, or the fact that you were in a relationship?

2. On a scale of 0 to 10, does being single feel like an opportunity to you? (With 10 being very excited and positive)

3. If you did not write down a 10, how can you close the gap to be closer to being a 10? For example, is there something that you let go of or suppressed in your last relationship that you can do now? What have you always wanted to do in your life that you held back from doing until now?

4. Finally, pick one of the three things from Question 1 that you will act on today!

FIRST PRINCIPLE OF CONSCIOUS DATING:
Know Who You Are &
What You Want

Learn what differentiates Conscious Dating from other advice for singles. Discover the First Principle of Conscious Dating: know who you are and what you want. You will learn how to be clear about your life purpose, requirements, needs, and wants. Try as you might, relationships that are not aligned with these key concepts are doomed.

THE TIP OF THE ICEBERG

Two weeks after Cathy reached Cincinnati, her divorce papers arrived in the mail. As she was reading them over, the phone rang. It was one of her old girlfriends from high school, calling to see if she wanted to go out for dinner with a group that night.

Over dinner, Cathy's girlfriends teased her about being a free woman. "What are you going to do first?" one of her divorced friends asked her. "How about Match.com? Even better, let me set you up with this cute guy I know at work!"

Cathy blushed. Dating again? The possibility was terrifying—and maybe just a bit thrilling.

The day before, Cathy had received a new homework assignment in my Conscious Dating Relationship Success Training for Singles (RESTS) teleclass. She knew this was going to be an intense task. For the past few weeks, homework had focused on various vision exercises. Cathy now had a lot of information about how she wanted her life to look. It was time to sum up everything. What were her values? How did she envision work, family, and fun? What was her life purpose?

WHAT IS YOUR VISION?

Making good long-term relationship choices requires clarity about who you are and what you want. Many of us think we know exactly what this looks like. All singles have their "list." But really, most singles see just 10 percent of their life Vision. It's like an iceberg, with the tip above the water representing your clarity about who you are and what you want. Your success and happiness depends upon the 90 percent that lies hidden below the surface.

Cathy's coach had sent out an incredible picture of an iceberg. Cathy clicked on the photo to open it. She had no idea that an iceberg went so deep. (No wonder the Titanic *went down!) Cathy printed out the photo and tacked it to the wall above her computer. Then she made a cup of tea and sat with her spiral workbook. She looked at a line she had written in her workbook and read it over and over:*

"If my life were absolutely perfect and I were guaranteed success, I would—"

Making good long-term relationship choices requires clarity about who you are and what you want.

All of us have core truths that, believe it or not, are often stronger than our commitment to a relationship. John Gottman, Ph.D., professor of psychology at the University of Washington, is world renowned for his work on marital stability and divorce prediction. Gottman says that 69 percent of conflict between couples results from perpetual problems related to unrealized dreams or expectations.[1]

All of us have core truths

that, believe it or not, are often stronger than

our commitment to a relationship.

As I interpret Gottman's research, most of the conflict between couples is actually about our life Vision. Sometimes our Vision is unconscious, and we don't realize why the relationship is not working. Gottman says that couples in happy marriages tend to have less conflict because they do a better job of repairing the damage from a fight or disagreement. Some people are effective in making repairs and others are clumsy or ineffective. But that's not important, says Gottman. "It's really a matter of whether they had enough emotional savings in the bank that makes repair attempts work, and that comes from the quality of the friendship between the couple." One of the best ways of nurturing friendship is to keep what Gottman calls a richly detailed "love map."

"That's my term for the imaginary place in your head where you store all of the relevant information about your partner's life—their dreams, aspirations, worries, and fears," Gottman explains. "Couples with love maps remember the major events in each other's history, and they keep updating their information as the facts and feelings of their spouse's world changes.

"Love maps are about knowing your partner and being known. One of the most important things in marriage is being and staying interested in your partner and keeping your partner interested in you. No gimmick—flowers, candy, or a candlelight dinner—works unless your partner is genuinely interested in you and their face lights up when you enter the room."

WHAT ARE YOUR REQUIREMENTS?

Requirements are the basic foundation of your Vision for your relationship. Each of us has nonnegotiable Requirements that must be met if a relationship is to work. You can figure out your Requirements by asking, for example, "Could the relationship possibly work if this didn't happen?" Or "If I had everything but this, could I still make it work?"

By "nonnegotiable," I mean that the Requirements must be met for the relationship to work—no ifs, ands, or buts. If one requirement isn't met, the relationship most likely won't work, even if you try to compromise or let go of it. The best evidence for the existence of Requirements is the high divorce rate.

Could the relationship possibly work if this didn't happen?

Every marriage starts out with two people making a commitment to be together forever, and they usually mean it. I don't assume they take the idea of divorce lightly. (I certainly didn't.) Then, at some point later they are in the painful position of really wanting a relationship to work and usually trying very hard to make it work, and then letting go of the relationship, even though they would rather have stayed together. This force causing so many couples to break their vows despite their best efforts and intentions must be very, very powerful. I call this force Requirements, which are the basic ingredients of our Vision.

Even when a relationship meets those Requirements, it does not guarantee a happy or fulfilling relationship. All relationships have problems or challenges. But unmet Requirements tend to be relationship-breakers. For example, an affair typically results in a severe problem that must be solved if the relationship is to continue. Think of a relationship as a cake. Requirements are the basic ingredients—the flour, sugar, and eggs. If one ingredient is missing, you will not have a cake. You will have something else!

All relationships have problems or challenges. But unmet Requirements tend to be relationship-breakers.

In her journal, Angela wrote on the top of the page: "My Perfect Partner." She wanted him to have a full-time job and a habit of paying all his bills on time. If he had young children, she was not interested. She wrote on and on, making a list of a hundred traits for her ideal partner.

She was excited to share the list with Gretchen, who had recently become certified as a relationship coach. After skimming over the pages, Gretchen pushed Angela's journal aside and said, "I'm so proud of you for doing this!"

"Me, too," said Angela.

"But I think we need to talk about Requirements for a relationship. You have written up a list here that describes your ideal partner. It's a start, but the reality is, even if you make a list of one hundred traits for your ideal partner, and you find a guy who meets all hundred, you could still be miserable."

"I don't believe that!" Angela said. "Try me!"

"Let's take a look at your list. Your first item is, 'A good listener.' Now, a good listener might mean a man who makes eye contact with you when you're talking. Is that what you mean? What's really important to you here?"

"Not just eye contact," Angela said. "I want to be with a man

who's interested in knowing where I'm coming from. I want him to be able to let go of his ego sometimes in order to pay attention to me."

"What I'm hearing is that you want to be deeply heard and understood," Gretchen said.

"Yes. I want someone to stop talking about himself long enough to listen to me. I guess what I mean is that I want to be validated."

"So, you want to be present for each other in a relationship."

"Yes!" Angela said. "That's it."

"Good. To clarify this requirement, we can change 'a good listener' to say, 'deeply listen to each other' or 'be present for each other.' Let's keep going. 'No young children.' Can you tell me what you mean?"

"Well, now that my son is a teenager, he'll be leaving home soon. I don't think I could do the parenting thing all over again, say, as the stepmother of a toddler or a little one."

"How about a man with young children who are not living with him?"

Angela thought for a moment. "No. Young children need and deserve to be the priority, and I want our relationship and life together to be the priority."

Gretchen skimmed down the list, pointing out another trait that might be refined and clarified as a Requirement: "Honest."

"Honest," Angela repeated. "Yeah, I see how that's just a word. In part, I'm reacting to the fact that Matt was not honest with me."

"So, what do you really mean by honest?" Gretchen said. "What is the experience of honesty that you are looking for in a relationship?"

"I want to be with a man who tells me the whole truth, and doesn't hold anything back."

"That's much clearer," Gretchen said. "So, write down, 'To tell the whole truth to each other, without holding anything back.'" Then, Gretchen asked, "I wonder, if you were totally in love with someone and he was in love with you, and he met all your Requirements, except that sometimes he held things back— because, perhaps, he feared conflict or didn't want to hurt your feelings—would you break up with him?"

"Of course not. We could probably work something out, especially if he was aware of it, valued honesty, and wanted to tell his truth."

What is your bottom line on this issue? What do you have to have for this relationship to be sustainable?

"Okay," said Gretchen. "So, telling the whole truth and not holding anything back might not be the actual Requirement. What is your bottom line on this issue? What do you have to have for this relationship to be sustainable?"

Angela thought hard for a moment. "That we value telling the truth to each other and do our best to do so."

The two friends leaned over the kitchen table, taking notes and making clarifications about Angela's Requirements. After an hour, she had rather clear definitions of her nonnegotiables for a relationship. Owning and naming exactly what she required challenged Angela, but now she felt less scared and confused.

WHAT ABOUT LOVE?

Requirements are probably the most important, controversial, and confusing concept in *Conscious Dating*. They are your core truth. They are the experience of your relationship in your Vision. As you become clearer about your Requirements, you also need to stay open to continuing to learn about yourself, because you might discover new Requirements as you are dating. Some examples of Requirements are: "addiction-free," "family oriented," "good listening," "financial responsibility," "open communication," "physically compatible," and "support each other's goals."

REQUIREMENTS:

- are nonnegotiable

- are black or white; there is not much room for gray

- are subjective; is the requirement met from your standards?

- have a lot of power. If you have to think about it, chances are it's not a requirement

- are behavioral events in the relationship, not traits of your partner

---

Requirements usually have the following characteristics:

- They are nonnegotiable; the relationship would not work if one were missing.
- They are black or white, met or not met. There is not much room for gray.
- While black or white, they also subjective; what matters is if the requirement is or is not met from YOUR standards.
- They have a lot of power. If you have to think about it, chances are it's not a Requirement.
- They are behavioral events, NOT traits of your partner.

One of my colleagues, coach Deki Fox, has this perspective on Requirements:

Requirements say *I like being touched by life THIS way.* Unfortunately, we all have some life experience that has touched us in ways we did not like, and this experience defines us to some extent. As we can OWN this definition or boundary and protect our vulnerability by clearly stating our Requirements, we are more alive and secure and capable of touching and being touched by others.[2]

Requirements say I like being touched

by life THIS way

Cathy was struggling with writing down her Requirements. Her list seemed to have mostly traits. She wrote down "spiritual." Her coach, Patty, asked her, "What is the experience of spirituality you are looking for in your relationship?" Cathy realized that her part- ner did not need to have a certain faith; she just needed to be able to share with him a belief in a higher power and the journey of finding meaning and purpose in life.

Cathy also wrote down "romantic." Her coach asked: "What is the experience of romance in the relationship you are seeking?" Cathy's partner did not necessarily have to be "Mr. Romantic" for her to have the relationship that she wanted. Cathy realized that if she focused on a certain trait coming from her partner, she would prob- ably be disappointed. For Cathy, it felt technical—almost nonemo- tional—to take notes about what would or wouldn't work in a rela- tionship. What about love? What about attraction? What about chemistry?

* * *

By focusing so much importance on Requirements, I am not discounting the importance and role of chemistry. As I see it, the problem is that our feelings and unconscious forces that attract us to a partner interfere with our objectivity. Then, singles fall into one of the "dating traps" (Chapter 3). I suggest that singles use their Requirements to balance their heart with their head and make sure their Requirements are met—no matter how attracted or in love they are.

Still, Cathy wanted to know: didn't she need to rely on herself to meet her own needs? Was she just looking for the right partner to meet her needs? Of course, I believe in taking personal responsibility for getting what you need in your life and relationship. I also advocate the need to make a good partner choice, because having your needs met is a combination of who your partner is and your efforts with your partner. Once you make a partner choice, you can't change who your partner is.

Choose your life's mate carefully;

from this one decision

will come 90 percent of

your happiness or misery.

—H. Jackson Brown Jr., Life's Little Instruction Book[3]

You need to find someone who lines up with all your Requirements—meaning that they will be met in the relationship, not that your partner delivers them all on a silver platter. Fulfillment in a relationship comes from working with your partner to get your needs met, not expecting it will just happen. The key is that your partner is capable of meeting your needs. You can't just choose anyone and then figure that you can make your Requirements and needs happen from your end. If you do that, you will be disappointed.

Fulfillment in a relationship

comes from working with your partner

to get your needs met,

not expecting it will just happen.

Coach Deki Fox has clarified for many singles what Requirements mean. She says:

> Requirements are the conditions we bring to life because of who we uniquely are. They also define how we have grown and developed up until this present moment. Requirements protect our vulnerable selves from harm. Requirements clarify the way my experience of life has shaped me. They say, "Here I am" with profound implications.

Requirements are the conditions

we bring to life because of who we

uniquely are. They clarify the way my experience of

life has shaped me. They say,

"Here I am" with profound implications.

Fox also points out that life experience generates Requirements:

> Owning and naming what we require optimizes awareness and puts us fully into life's flow. Each requirement is like having another paddle in the water as we move our relation-ship along the river of this lifetime. If you wonder if you have "too many"

paddles in the water, try sorting your Requirements according to "protect my vulnerability" (prevent being hurt) versus "fulfill my life purpose" (achieve important life goals) and see what happens.

Lastly, I want to point out one very important rule about Requirements. When you are starting to date, don't spell out all your Requirements! They are not a list that you carry around in your pocket. Just as you wouldn't share your financial statement on a first date, you would not reveal everything you're looking for in a partner. Consciously or not, if they like you and want to please you, prospective partners might be tempted to tell you what you want to hear.

Here's what I mean: Let's say one of your Requirements is to be with a partner with whom you can start a family. It would be a no-no to say, "Look, one of my Requirements for a partner is that he has to want to have children one day."

That's because, if your date is into you, he might be tempted to agree with you—even if he was unsure—just to make the relationship work. He might jump out of his seat—"Yes, I love children!"—even if he felt uncertain about kids.

Rather, you might casually mention in conversation, "One day, I'd like to have children," or, "Do you like kids?"

Then, watch his nonverbal responses. They will tell you everything you need to know. What are his facial expressions like? What is his attitude like? (Is he positive? Negative? Neutral?) After you mention children, does the energy level around both of you go up or down?

CREATING A CRYSTAL CLEAR VISION

Remember that your relationship is like a cake. Requirements are the basic ingredients: the flour, sugar, and eggs. But you also need to know why you are making the cake. This is your purpose, your reason for living. This is the higher meaning and legacy of your life, such as raising children or making a difference in your community.

When your relationship does not align with your purpose—even if you are unclear about your purpose—you feel empty and incomplete. No relationship will fix this.

When your relationship does not

align with your purpose—even if you are unclear

about your purpose—

you feel empty and incomplete.

But a cake requires more than just the ingredients. Before you start, it's important to know what you want the cake to look like. In a relationship, that corresponds to your Vision. Your Vision is your internal image of your desired outcome that acts as your inner guidance system, leading you toward certain choices and away from other choices. You feel content when you are on track with your Vision. You feel stressed when you are off-track, even if you are not conscious about why.

Your Vision is your internal image

of your desired outcome that acts as your inner

guidance system, leading you toward

certain choices and away from other choices.

Another colleague of mine, Dr. Philip Humbert, a psychologist and coach, says: "The single most critical factor in determining your future is a crystal clear Vision. Or, if you prefer, a dream that is big enough to be worthy of you." Humbert agrees that other things play a part in your future—such as skills, goals, a written plan, an attractive personality, ambition, and lots of energy—but the one that makes all the difference is your "big enough" Vision.

"A small Vision won't do it," Humbert explains. "Successful people find something huge, and devote their lives to it. It's something that seems to possess them, to drive them, to challenge them to overcome and to persist until they find a way. There's a wonderful quote from the ancient general, Hannibal: *'We will find a way, or make one.'*"

While talent, skill, money, and resources are all helpful, Humbert says that "in the end, a determined, focused sense of who you are and what you are going to accomplish is the most important ingredient for unusual success." He loves to share examples with his clients: Lee Iacocca said he'd turn Chrysler around, and he did. Oprah Winfrey dreamed of escaping poverty and making a difference, and she has. As a child, Hillary Clinton imagined herself as a person of power and influence, and she is.

* * *

Cathy wondered what her Vision was. She flipped back through her homework. She knew that being loving and joyful were very important parts of her life. But how did she go about being loving and joyful?

She recalled that at dinner with her girlfriends earlier that week, she had hugged each friend and given each woman a yellow rose in thanks for her support. And over dinner, she had recounted a story about their prom that had made them laugh so hard.

At last, Cathy jotted down her life purpose statement: "I am loving and joyful by encouraging openness and compassion from both myself and those around me." She read it out loud. Yes, her voice was alive and energetic! It felt right.

Next, Cathy envisioned being with a partner who also loved children. Maybe she could fill her life with children in another way, such as opening a daycare center. Cathy imagined living in a beau-

tiful and simple house with a yard where children could play. She also saw herself laughing a lot and making love passionately.
Cathy was satisfied as a manager in the health-care field, but something was missing. Yes, she was earning enough money to save for her retirement. But she wanted to be surrounded by children—young children. Maybe she would meet a partner who had children already. In the meantime, thoughts of starting a daycare center flooded her mind.

Our ability to identify our Needs and

get them met determines

our level of happiness and success.

WHAT ARE YOUR NEEDS?

We all have Needs. We need to sleep and eat. We need light to see and air to breathe. We need love and relationships. Needs are not a problem or a sign of weakness. Our ability to identify our Needs and get them met determines our level of happiness and success. If your relationship is like a cake, then your needs beyond the ingredients are the baking pan, bowls, utensils, oven, baking time, and temperature. The difference between Needs and Requirements is that you *can modify, negotiate, or substitute your Needs.* With Requirements, you can't. If you bake a cake in a square pan at 350 degrees for thirty minutes, or bake it in a round pan at 375 degrees for twenty-five minutes, it will still work. If you leave out the flour, it will not work. In a successful relationship, your Needs are the events that must happen for you to be OK or happy. If a Need is unmet, we experience stress or an "issue."

FUNCTIONAL NEEDS

Your relationship can be divided into functional and emotional Needs. *Functional Needs are the events you need to happen for your life and relationship to function optimally.* Most of us want to be with a partner who earns money to pay bills and helps with household chores and child rearing. If you need to pay your bills on time, it will create an issue in your relationship if your lights go out because your partner forgot to pay the utility bill.

Functional Needs revolve around those classic arguments about keeping the toilet seat down or putting the toothpaste cap back on the tube. If something continually bugs you, it's going to be challenging to let go of it. I'm the typical dad who walks through any room and shuts the light off if no one is in there. I'm also the one who gets annoyed when my kids leave all the kitchen cabinets open. Am I going to file for divorce because of this? Of course not! This is about a need for order. In my own life, I have a certain threshold for order. Some partners have called me a perfectionist. But it's not that I'm picky or a control freak. Rather, I just have a functional need for some order.

- **Functional needs are the events you need to happen for your life and relationship to function optimally, such as paying the bills on time.**

- **Emotional needs are what you need to feel loved, such as being called if your partner is going to be late.**

EMOTIONAL NEEDS
Emotional Needs are what you need to feel loved. Perhaps you would like your partner to call if he/she will be late. Or, you enjoy being greeted with a hug. Or, you want to be taken care of when you are sick. For most of us, the top desire in a relationship is to love and be loved. Yet few of us fully know or understand our emotional needs. Most of us do not become aware of a need until it is unmet.

For example, if you feel unloved when your partner is late and doesn't call, your emotional need is for him/her to be on time and to call if he/she is going to be late. If that need is not met, you will have more difficulty feeling loved by your partner. Another example might be the fact that your partner stays up late every night watching TV in the living room as you lie awake in bed. You want him to go to sleep with you. You might get very irritated at him for watching TV every night. But turning off the TV is not really the need. The need is the fact that you would like some affection, or maybe sex.

* * *

Cathy kept getting stuck: could she really rely on a partner to meet her needs? Shouldn't she take responsibility for her own needs?

One night, her divorced girlfriend Frances called. "So, can I set you up with this guy from my job?"

Cathy giggled. "Not so fast! Tell me a bit about him first. How old is he? Has he been married before?"

"Let's see, he's forty-five years old and he was recently divorced."

"How recent?" Cathy asked.

"He and his ex got separated last year, but to tell you the truth, I'm not sure if all the papers have been signed yet. They have three kids and there seems to be some complications about custody."

"Sounds messy," said Cathy.

"But he's a really nice guy!"

"I'm sure he is, but I feel strongly about not getting involved with a guy who has unfinished business. Let's make a deal: keep in

touch about him over the next few months, and if things get finalized, I'll consider a coffee date."

"It's a deal," said Frances.

This conversation was a good transition into Cathy's work on her Needs and Requirements. What were the nonnegotiables that would make or break a future partnership? The next morning, Cathy woke up and reread her coach's notes on Requirements:

"Requirements are those must-have, bottom-line, black-and-white, nonnegotiables!"

Cathy realized that she couldn't just go out and find some guy who matched all her traits, mark off her checklist, and get married. It took Cathy another few days to rework her Requirements. She did want a life with children. This could mean opening a daycare center, adopting, or having stepchildren.

At last, on Tuesday night, Cathy read her Requirements out loud on the phone:

"Our relationship is addiction-free."

"My partner and I are present for each other on every level: emotionally, physically, spiritually, and mentally. This also encompasses our belief in a higher power, and sharing our faith with the world."

"Our lives are filled with love for each other, children, friends, and family. This means we are committed to each other and our loved ones."

"We have a passionate relationship."

"We share dreams for the future: to have children in our lives, to live together in a warm and sunny house with a yard, to make

lots of home-cooked meals together, to laugh heartily, to grow individually and as a couple."

Cathy glanced up at the picture of the iceberg on her wall, letting out a deep breath. Then Patty coached Cathy a bit more on her Requirements.

"Sounds like you're ready for recreational dating," Patty said.

"Oh, I hate how that sounds! I don't want a bunch of random one-night stands."

Patty laughed. "Let's rephrase it then. You're not ready to meet your life partner, but you would like to get out there and practice your new skills. You might date more than one man at a time, but you're going to be clear about your level of commitment and keep your boundaries around sex."

"That's right on!" Cathy said.

* * *

Recently, one of my single clients asked me, "But what's the difference between needs and neediness?" Good question! I've juxtaposed these two concepts to give you some clues about creating successful relationships. Everyone has needs, even the most healthy and successful among us. Needs are present in all of us and are not a problem or a sign of weakness. Our ability to identify our needs and get them met determines our level of happiness and success. Neediness is a contrast to having needs. Neediness tends to be a sieve that will be empty regardless of how much you put into it.

NEEDS

1. are normal, valid, important
2. are present in everyone, including healthy and successful people

3. are necessary to survive and thrive
4. are best met by taking responsibility and initiative
5. stimulate action when they are unmet
6. are most effectively met by being assertive
7. result in contentment when met

NEEDINESS

1. comes from desperation and helplessness
2. is driven by emotional deficits
3. is an externalized problem and solution
4. results in a helpless/victim position
5. is insatiable
6. results in repelling others

Wants are the objects and activities that provide stimulation, fun, and pleasure. In a relationship, most of us want to go out once in a while for some fine dining. We want to take long walks on the beach with our loved one.

WHAT ARE YOUR WANTS?

As you know, the best part of the cake is the icing. Without the icing, your cake is still edible—perhaps even nutritious—but it is dry. In a relationship, the icing is your Wants. *Wants are the objects and activities that provide stimulation, fun, and pleasure.* In a relationship, most of us want to go out once in a while for some fine dining. We want to take long walks on the beach with our loved one.

When you imagine your dream-come-true relationship, it's not about being with a partner who keeps the toilet seat down. Rather, you're fantasizing about vacationing in the Bahamas together. Without fun, a relationship would be fairly boring, whether it's playing tennis, going camping, listening to music, skydiving, or just reading silently next to each other. Having your Wants met creates positive energy, which creates passion. However, if you make a partner choice based upon going on long walks on the beach, it is not enough for the relationship to be successful. Yes, it is important to have fun together. But Wants are not Requirements. Singles who make relationship choices based only on their Wants often have short-lasting relationships.

Wants also tend to be transient, changeable, and easily substituted. If they are out of chocolate, mocha will be fine. While I might want to go to the Bahamas, Hawaii would be great too. Wants often change. I might eat steak tonight, and then be in the mood for fish tomorrow. Maybe I had chocolate ice cream for dessert tonight, but tomorrow I will want apple pie. Remember what I said about eating cake without icing? It might be dry, but it is still nutritious. Often, under stress, the icing is the first to go. When couples are feeling stressed—because, for example, they are new parents or dealing with a chronic illness—Wants are the first to disappear, but in itself that doesn't threaten the relationship.

We have a Vision for our life and relationship, Life Purpose, Values, Requirements, Needs, and Wants—whether we are aware of exactly what they are or not. Requirements are part of who you are, just as you are left-handed or right-handed. You might require children and a family, or you might desire a child-free partnership. You might require monogamy, or you might be fine with an open relationship.

When we live our life aligned with our values, we fulfill one of our highest needs: for our life to have meaning. When we are not living in alignment with our values, we become bored, numb, or depressed. To feel fulfilled in a relationship and choose a life partner wisely, we must choose in alignment with our Vision, Requirements, Values, and Life Purpose. After working with singles for many years on their Requirements, I find that the typical number seems to be between eight and fifteen. So, if you have twenty or thirty Requirements, you might want to go back and revise. ✗

CONSCIOUS DATING PLAN EXERCISE NO. 5:

Please refer to Chapter 15 to write your answers.

Who are you? What do you want?

1. Make a list of your last three relationships that did not work out.

2. For each relationship, identify the top three reasons it ended.

3. Now look back over your list and ask yourself whether each reason was a Requirement or a Need. These test questions will help you determine the answers:

    A. Test Question for a Requirement:
    If you fell in love with someone who was very attractive and also independently wealthy and you really wanted this relationship to work, but _____ was missing, would you stay or break it off?

    If it would be possible for you to stay in the relationship and find a way to make it work, then it is most likely not a Requirement. Try applying the test question for a Need below.

    B. Test Question for a Need:
    Would you experience discontent or an "issue" each time _____ occurred or did not occur?

    If you answered "yes," then this issue is most likely a Need.

    C. If your list item does not meet the test for a Requirement or Need, it is most likely a Want.

SECOND PRINCIPLE OF CONSCIOUS DATING:
Learn How to Get What You Want

6

In this chapter we will focus on your relationship attitudes and beliefs, identify effective dating strategies, and gain insight about how to date to get what you want. You will discover how to consciously find the love of your life.

RADIANT REDHEAD SEEKS REMARKABLE MAN!

Cathy's heart was pounding. Her stats and photo would soon be visible to millions of other online singles.

Cathy knew that she was not ready to search for her life partner. The grief and anger following her divorce were raw. Still, she did want to have fun. She was ready to get out there and live her life to the fullest, while remaining single and keeping her boundaries around sex and emotional involvement.

Cathy was not ready for a committed relationship, but she wanted to date and have fun.

Cathy was ready to focus on the *Second Principle of Conscious Dating: Learn How to Get What You Want*. She was ready to look at her *adaptive choices*, meaning her attitudes, skills, and strategies—all the things that she could do to live the life she wanted as a successful single person. But how would Cathy get over her fear of dating again?

On New Year's Eve, Cathy's friends invited her to a big bash downtown. All dressed up in a flowing turquoise silk skirt, she joined a married couple and her two single girlfriends. As midnight approached, someone turned on the big-screen TV. The ball would drop in ten minutes.

That's when Cathy's mind flashed an epiphany: What you do at midnight New Year's is what you'll do the entire year. She grabbed her purse and, like Cinderella, she darted out of the room.

I am seeking a passionate and spiritual man for a deep friendship, and possibly more.

Cathy rushed home and turned on her computer. Her headline came to her first:

"Radiant Redhead Seeks Remarkable Man!"

She wrote the rest of her profile in an intense and focused flurry:

I'm a tall and stylish forty-year-old redhead with sculpted cheekbones and a radiant smile. One word that best describes me: joyful! I love music, movies, and dining out with my family and friends, as well as evenings in with that special someone. I also adore long hikes, slow dancing, luxurious naps, and anything chocolate. I am Christian, divorced, no children. I am seeking a passionate and spiritual man for a deep friendship and possibly more. You have no addictions, love to cook and travel, laugh heartily, and simply enjoy life.

Cathy attached a photo of herself on the beach in a one-piece bathing suit, her red hair blowing in the breeze. Cathy's attitude about dating was: I want to have fun. She also wanted to learn more about herself and relationships.

* * *

WHAT YOU BELIEVE, YOU CAN ACHIEVE

Like Cathy, we all have fears and self-limiting beliefs, but many of us are unaware of them. Attitudes are internal beliefs that create your experience of yourself, of others, and of life. The way that you see things can be self-fulfilling: it will be true because you hold these beliefs and allow them to come true. Attitudes are influenced by your personality and experiences. We all have attitudes. Some people think the world is a safe place. Others believe it is unsafe. Some people feel good about themselves. Others feel flawed and inadequate. Positive attitudes are productive; negative ones are unproductive. You can consciously choose the attitudes that serve you, and let go of the ones that sabotage you.

Very often, we hold onto certain attitudes without even realizing it. How do you feel about dating? How does this affect the way that you might present yourself to potential partners? Many of us have been conditioned to respond to certain situations in a traditionally masculine or feminine way. For example, a common saying among singles is "men use love to get sex, and women use sex to get love." Some women believe that men only want "one thing" and that they are not really interested in commitment. Many of these women are not conscious about their beliefs, so they go about meeting just those kinds of men. It is interesting to note that when men are dating, they often want to feel attracted first and have good sex before they become invested in pursuing an ongoing relationship. And women are often more security-minded. They don't just want to jump into bed. They're more conscious about their selection. It's a more conscious process for them, which is good. However, it is easy for a man to interpret a security-minded woman's attitude as trying to "trap" him into commitment too soon, and it is tempting for a woman to interpret a man's "fun first, commitment later" attitude as not being serious.

I realize that I'm generalizing, but if we understand these common attitudes, we can read other singles more accurately. This is the kind of knowledge that will make you more conscious of your attitudes so that you don't fall into a dating trap (see Chapter 3).

Many singles believe: "Men use love to get sex, and women use sex to get love."

Our beliefs and attitudes affect our reality. Being single provides an opportunity to address attitudes that can spoil your future success. I encourage you to take this self-test to assess which self-limiting beliefs you might be holding onto.

WHAT ARE YOUR RELATIONSHIP BELIEFS?
We all have fears and self-limiting beliefs. Check the ones below that fit you. When reading each one, do a "gut check," and if you experience the slightest physical or emotional reaction, it most likely applies to you.

ABOUT SELF:
_____ 1. I'm not good enough

_____ 2. I don't deserve love

_____ 3. I don't deserve to be happy

_____ 4. I'm not _____ (attractive, successful, young, rich, thin, etc) enough.

_____ 5. I'm too _____(old, unattractive, dysfunctional, late, unsuccessful, etc)

ABOUT DATING:

_____ 6. All the good ones are taken

_____ 7. I have to take what I can get, or be alone

_____ 8. My ideal partner doesn't exist or is already taken

_____ 9. There is no such thing as a soul mate or true love

_____ 10. I must be "realistic" in my expectations

ABOUT RELATIONSHIPS:

_____ 11. I will be rejected if I ask for what I want or say no

_____ 12. I will be abandoned if I care too much

_____ 13. I will hurt the one I love

_____ 14. I will be smothered or controlled

_____ 15. I will lose myself

_____ 16. I will be hurt if I trust

_____ 17. If you really know me, you won't like or love me

How do you feel about dating? How does this affect the way that you might present yourself to potential partners?

CHOOSING EFFECTIVE BELIEFS AND ATTITUDES

Letting go of self-limiting beliefs and adopting productive attitudes is very challenging to most singles. Dating and relationships can trigger these issues quite strongly. When you are aware of your unproductive attitudes, you can consciously choose productive ones.

So how exactly do you choose productive attitudes? Well, the first step is to be conscious of the negative beliefs you hold, which continue to harm you. Pause now and take a look at how you answered the questions above in "What Are Your Relationship Beliefs?"

How do you feel about yourself?

How do you feel about dating?

How do you feel about relationships?

Your beliefs and attitudes affect your outcomes. If you believe that you do not deserve to be happy, you won't be happy. If you expect less, you will get less. If you believe that all men/women are greedy/selfish/demanding (fill in the adjective), they will be. It's up to you to be conscious of your attitudes and change them! This is about "retraining" yourself to think differently. If you clearly identify your attitude as counterproductive, you can consciously choose to adopt and practice a positive replacement. The trick is to stay aware when the old belief shows up and to focus on your positive replacement.

When you are aware of your

unproductive attitudes, you can

consciously choose productive ones.

For example, let's say you are aware that you anticipate rejection so you don't pursue other singles that attract you. You believe "nobody who I'm interested in would go out with me." You can choose to replace that belief with "I'm a good person and anyone would be lucky to hang out with me. There's no harm in asking, and if they don't want to go out with me, then they're missing out on a good thing." If you are aware of your pattern and you know when it is likely to show up, you can watch for it when it occurs and consciously choose your positive replacement. Refer to the Conscious Dating Plan Exercise in Chapter 7 for more about changing unproductive attitudes.

To be successful in a career, we know that we need education, training, experience, and effort. Why do we expect it to be any different in a relationship? Mating is an ancient drive that ensures survival of our species, and we seem to take it for granted that we know how to do so without a manual. However, getting together is not nearly as much a challenge as staying together. Staying together depends upon you being clear about what you want, and your ability to acquire the knowledge and skills to make it happen over time.

Getting together is not nearly as much a challenge as staying *together.*

YOUR CONSCIOUS DATING STRATEGY

You will now embark on a series of four steps to finding your life partner:

Conscious Dating Step #1: Scouting

Now that you have identified your self-limiting beliefs, it's time to focus on your dating skills. How do you find your life partner? Well, the first thing you need to do is Scout. This is the process of finding someone to meet.

Singles can Scout in many ways. You go to the grocery store and look at the men and women in the aisles. You check out the people in line at the post office. You read personal ads. Friends and family members can Scout for you by introducing you to eligible partners. You can wear a button that says "Single and Available" to encourage people to notice you and approach you!

There are many possible strategies for finding people to meet. To be a conscious single, you need to choose the ones that are effective for finding potential partners who meet your requirements. You need to identify the places and activities where you can meet potential partners. I call these "attraction venues." The more aligned the venue is with who you are and who you are looking for, the higher likelihood of success. I identify at least four levels of attraction venues. Since "birds of a feather flock together," the higher the level, the more aligned the participants will be:

- **Level One**: public settings, such as the post office and grocery store

- **Level Two**: generic singles settings, such as singles events, personal ads, and the Internet

- **Level Three**: special interest activities, such as a ski club, ball room dancing, or yoga class

- **Level Four**: highly aligned communities in which you share important values, goals, and/or passions with everyone there, such as religious communities, social activist groups, and spiritual organizations

---

Scouting is the process of finding someone to meet. Where are you going to go to meet someone?

With the help of her coach, Cathy was figuring out where she might Scout. No, she wasn't ready for a committed relationship, but she didn't want to waste her Friday nights on guys with whom she had nothing in common. Since arriving in Cincinnati, Cathy had only spent time in Level One and Level Two venues.

The day after Cathy's "Radiant Redhead Seeks Remarkable Man!" went online, her inbox was filled with messages.

* * *

Seth was on a mission to find the love of his life. A gay man living in Manhattan, Seth had been in and out of short-term relationships, along with having a string of one-night stands. Meeting men at the bar (Level One) was not working. Seth's first move was to place a personal ad online (Level Two). He marked his calendar to attend a relationship seminar series at his local bookstore (Level Three). He also decided to take a course in photography—one of his passions—at a local art college (Level Four).

Conscious Dating Step #2: Sorting

Sorting is the process of quickly determining if there is enough in common to pursue getting to know someone. This means that the person is lined up enough with your Requirements that you would like to get to know him/her better.

Sorting can occur by reviewing someone's online profile or by having a five-minute conversation. Let's say that you're at a singles party, and you are working the room. You have five-minute conversations with six or seven eligible people there. This means that you are getting enough information to determine if there is enough interest and compatibility for you to choose to spend more time and get to know any of them better.

Sorting is the process of quickly determining if there is enough in common to pursue getting to know someone. Sorting is generally a five-minute conversation!

Seth, in New York City, took his dating "assignments" very seriously; he knew that his life partner would be his "degree." He Scouted by posting his profile on three online matchmaking services. Within twenty-four hours, Seth's mailbox had twenty new messages. It was time to Sort! Seth spent the next two nights up late, reading through each message, and asking himself, "Does this man sound serious about having a long-term relationship, or does he seem like a player?" He replied to the ten men who seemed the most sincere and authentic in their initial introductions.

Speed dating is one structured method of Sorting. I sometimes hold seminars with singles in which we set up a mock session of speed dating to practice a Sorting skill that I call the "Power Introduction." I divide all the singles in half and line each group up on opposite sides of the room. Each person has five minutes to practice the Power Introduction with his/her potential date. This is enough time to determine if there is enough in common to pursue getting to know the person.

The Power Introduction begins by introducing yourself effectively and authentically. I encourage everyone to be honest, friendly, engaging, and self-disclosing. You can learn a lot about people in a very short amount of time by their reaction to you if you are authentic with them! Then I give a two-minute warning, before each person decides if it's a green light (go!), yellow light (maybe; need more info), or red light (pass). I ask all participants to end by giving the other person a compliment, then disengaging gracefully. After this, it's time to move down the line.

Screening is the process of collecting information about whether your requirements would be met with someone.

Conscious Dating Step #3: Screening
Screening is the process of collecting information about whether someone meets your requirements. That's why it's critically impor-

tant that you know what your requirements are (Chapter 5), so that as you get to know somebody, you know which questions to ask. You know what to look for, so you can determine if your requirements might be met. Remember: if one requirement is not met, the relationship will not work. It's going to fail. Screening can take place in several phone calls over the course of a week, in e-mails, or during a coffee date. You are simply collecting data related to your requirements. If you are serious about finding your life partner, you are not going to get involved with people who are not right for you. You need to stay available, because wouldn't it be a tragedy if you met the right person but you were involved with somebody else?

Seth knew that he wanted his partner to be college-educated. He also knew that he wanted to find someone in his age range—not over forty years old. After staying up very late that first night to Sort through many potential partners online, Seth wrote back to ten men. His tone was serious and formal.

After briefly meeting these men in person in public places to Screen them, Seth could ask himself if he wanted to see any of them again. He figured he could collect all the information he needed in sixty minutes or less, and was determined not to spend any more time than he had to with anyone not 100 percent aligned with his requirements.

Over the next two months, Seth sometimes had as many as three dates in one day: a lunch date, a dinner date, and an after-dinner date. Seth believed in giving everyone a fair chance, and in keeping all his options open. During every date, Seth studied each potential partner seriously and genuinely, taking mental notes. After two months, he had had almost forty dates!

The train doors opened and Seth raced up the stairs. His date, Max, was a forty-year-old waiter who wrote in his profile that he'd been sober for ten years and meditated every morning. Max was waiting for Seth at a sidewalk table. The men shook hands. Seth was caught off guard: this guy was good-looking! Max was six feet tall with dirty blond hair and bright blue eyes. His muscles bulged out from his tank top when he grasped Seth's hand.

"I got here a little early and ordered a sandwich," Max said.

"Great!" said Seth, but really he thought it was a little rude.

Seth had arrived right on time; the fact that this guy ordered before he got there wasn't thoughtful. Seth made a mental note: having a respectful and considerate relationship was one of his Requirements. He could easily spot self-centered men with big egos, since he'd been with them before.

Seth asked Max about his job.

"I've been a waiter since I was sixteen," Max said. "But I don't want to be a waiter for the rest of my life. I'm planning to go back to school next year."

"Awesome!" said Seth. "Which school?"

"Oh, I don't know, maybe a community college. I'll probably look into it this summer."

Seth made another mental note: he, too, had big dreams, and knew that they took lots of planning. He needed to be with a partner who really followed through with his dreams. Being with someone who was able to support himself financially was another big requirement for Seth in a relationship.

"Are you from the city?" Seth asked.

"Actually, I'm from Cleveland, where my family lives. But they don't really support my lifestyle, if you know what I mean. I haven't seen them for years."

"Intense," said Seth. "I have yet to come out to my family. But

we're very close. I see them at least once a month."

Seth continued to take mental notes: the fact that Max was estranged from his family was another red flag. He knew that he had A LOT of work to do with his own parents, but he valued his family and wasn't just cutting all ties with them.

Forty-five minutes later, as he marched back to the train, Seth thought about Max. Wow, he was gorgeous. Seth imagined meeting up with him again at a bar, and going back to his place. But he stopped himself. He'd been there, done that.

He took a deep breath and cleared his head. Max did not meet his requirements: in just one sixty-minute lunch date, Seth was able to Screen and get enough information to figure out that this guy was not a good match.

If you are serious about finding

your life partner, you are not going to get involved

with people who are not right for you.

You need to stay available, because wouldn't it be a

tragedy if you met the right person but you were

involved with somebody else?

Screening can also be done completely by e-mail or telephone. You don't have to leave the house. You don't have to meet anyone in person. And you certainly don't have to get involved with anyone! If you are going to meet in person, I recommend that you make it a coffee date in a public setting and limit the time to less than an hour. That way, it's not really a "date." A date is when two single people spend time together (hang out). They typically are either in an ongoing relationship with each other, or getting together with that intention. It's important to make the distinction between "dating" and "screening." Screening is more like a job interview! If this person isn't a fit, you will most likely not pursue an ongoing relationship with him/her.

When Screening, believe what people say about themselves. If you're collecting information on the phone, and someone says, "Well, I'm not really good with money," believe him/her! People often tell you outright what it is you need to know.

> *Cathy wrote back to ten of the twenty-five men who had contacted her, and exchanged phone numbers with eight of them. She had brief conversations with each to Screen them. She eliminated one man because he was still involved in a nasty divorce battle and another because he was recently evicted from his apartment. Her conversation with a geology professor was so awkward—he seemed to be lacking some social skills—that she bumped him off her list too. She was most looking forward to her coffee date with a successful entrepreneur who made her laugh during their brief telephone chat.*

Screening is more like a job interview than a date!

Conscious Dating Step #4: Testing
While Screening is simply collecting information (which may or may not be valid!), Testing means experiencing your requirements being met with a potential partner.

When you Test, you are spending time with someone to determine if the information you have so far is real or not. Let's say that you're an avid tennis player and you decide that one of your requirements is that your partner play tennis too. You might Scout for potential partners at the tennis club; you would Sort by quickly determining if they are single and play tennis, and you might Screen by talking with them in person or over the telephone. Testing would mean actually playing tennis with them to experience your requirement being met or not.

Just because you both play tennis doesn't mean the requirement is met and you would make good partners. What if they played so aggressively or obnoxiously that you wouldn't want to play with them? Information alone is not enough to determine if a requirement is met. You need to verify the information and gain experience and knowledge that your requirements are going to be met *before* getting involved.

A key part of Testing is that you're doing this with a detached mindset. That means you're prepared to say no if it's not working after your first initial meeting. If this person can't play tennis, why should you pursue him/her further? All too often, I see singles sell themselves out by being too tolerant or too forgiving. (Remember the Scarcity Trap in Chapter 3, when you believe there is a limited supply of possible partners, and therefore have to take what you can get or be alone? Unfortunately, when you expect less, you get less.)

Testing means that you experience your

requirements being met before getting involved with

a potential partner.

If you fall into the Scarcity Trap, you will probably practice what I call "Screening In." This means that you're always giving people second chances and the benefit of the doubt, desperately searching for reasons why a relationship could work. Alternatively, "Screening Out" is the practice of identifying the reasons why a relationship would not work. Those who "Screen In" say, for example, "Oh, maybe he's just having an off day; let's meet again and play tennis another afternoon." If there's no potential there, why give this person more chances? Further Testing often reinforces what you first learned about this person. Those who "Screen Out," on the other hand, immediately reject a date within moments, often because they are afraid of being rejected themselves. I knew one man, for example, who ruled out any woman who was ten pounds overweight, although he had weight issues himself. When screening, use your requirements as your primary decision-making tools and don't be tempted to "screen in" to make the round peg fit the square hole, or "screen out" too quickly because you're afraid of being hurt.

Testing only takes a few dates, being conscious to keep your boundaries and observe carefully to learn whether a potential partner truly meets your most important requirements. This is your chance to audition him/her and save yourself a lot of heartache down the road by being prepared to say "no" early in the game if this person is not 100 percent what you want and need in a partner.

YOUR CONSCIOUS DATING STRATEGY IS:

Step #1: Scouting

Step #2: Sorting

Step #3: Screening

Step #4: Testing

Seth's date tonight was with a thirty-one-year-old African-American accountant who described himself as "a centered, mature, masculine guy with Southern values who tries to live a simple/drama-free life; passionate about friends, dance, and good communication." They were going to meet at a classy Thai place uptown for dinner. Seth closed his eyes and smiled. He'd never enjoyed school assignments this much!

There is an abundance of dating resources out there today —such as dating services and personal ads— but these Scouting tools are only effective if you know how to use them.

PUTTING YOUR TOOLS TO USE

If you've dated a lot and are feeling cynical, I want to help you. I want you to understand yourself, your life, your relationships, and the dating process. You have gained a lot of important relationship knowledge so far in this book. You have become clearer about your relationship attitudes and beliefs so that you can make choices aligned with your goals. It's clear you are open to learning new skills. Now it's time to get into action!

One venue that many singles have taken advantage of in the past few years is online dating. Over forty million Americans look at online dating sites each month.[1] Indeed, this is a revolution in the way people meet and court one another. There is an abundance of dating resources out there today—such as dating services and personal ads—but these Scouting tools are only effective if you know how to use them. Conscious Dating strategies will greatly enhance your success. Remember, if you do what you've always done, you'll get what you've always gotten. ✀

CONSCIOUS DATING PLAN EXERCISE NO. 6:

Please refer to Chapter 15 to write your answers.

Where will you look for your Life Partner?

Are you ready for a committed relationship right now? Or do you need more time? (Refer to Chapter 9: "Be Ready and Available for Commitment.")

Are you going to date recreationally, or are you seeking your life partner?

Who will Scout for you?

What Level Two, Three, and Four venues will you choose?

To refresh your memory, here are examples of the venues:

Level One: Public places, such as the supermarket, the post office, an art or wine festival

Level Two: Generic single setting, such as singles bar or event, personal ad

Level Three: Settings in which you share a strong interest with everyone there, such as a ski or bike club, yoga class

Level Four: Settings in which you share important values, goals and/or passions with everyone there, such as your church, service club, personal growth venue

What are your Sorting strategies?

What are your Screening strategies?

What are your Testing strategies?

Note: These questions might be best answered with the help of a coach. If you find these questions challenging, please consider taking our Conscious Dating Relationship Success Training for Singles (RESTS) program.

THIRD PRINCIPLE OF CONSCIOUS DATING:
Be The Chooser

Do you take the initiative to go after what you want? Or do you find yourself reacting to people and circumstances? Learn how to take responsibility for the outcomes in your life by becoming The Chooser rather than playing it safe and limiting yourself to only what's in front of you.

MAKING THE FIRST MOVE

Seth looked inside the folder labeled "Chooser." After browsing through hundreds of online profiles of men who live in New York City, Seth had chosen three men and composed notes to them. Sending e-mails to complete strangers made Seth nervous. All through his twenties, he had been the follower in relationships. Upon turning thirty, however, Seth had vowed to be more proactive in his life. And now, he was.

Being The Chooser means taking initiative and responsibility for your outcomes: you are in charge of creating what you want in life.

When you're single, you may feel insecure and self-doubting. You may have developed attitudes, beliefs, and behaviors that have led you to feel unsure or anxious about being assertive. You may have been conditioned to please others, or never received permission to take risks. You may feel powerless about influencing your outcomes, so you submissively let others make the choices. You may be so afraid of failure that you don't even try.

When I first started leading singles groups in the 1990s, I saw how many singles lacked the skills and attitudes needed to go after what they want in life. This is what inspired me to come up with the expression "Be The Chooser." I first included this term on an audio tape I recorded, "Finding the Love of Your Life and the Life that You Love." Everyone who attended my events got a free copy of this tape, in which I talked about how you, as a single person, could have a successful life partnership and the kind of life that you wanted. But it seemed that what singles really responded to was when I talked about being The Chooser. So many people came back to me and said, "I must have listened to that tape twelve times in my car. I hear your voice in my head, saying, 'Be The Chooser!'"

You may have been conditioned to please others, or never received permission to take risks. You may feel powerless about influencing your outcomes, so you submissively let others make the choices. You may be so afraid of failure that you don't even try.

ARE YOU A CHOOSER OR A VICTIM?

As children, choices were made for us and we had little power over what happened to us. This is normal for children, but when we take this attitude as adults, I call it being a "victim." The opposite of being a victim is to be "The Chooser." In my own life, I've forgotten this fact many times when I was impulsive or reactive. Taking responsibility for our failures and our pain can be challenging. I have wanted to blame my boss, my ex-wife, the other driver, and my parents. Have you?

I've had many wake-up calls that taught me to realize that acting out of ignorance or impulse doesn't absolve me of responsibility for making a bad choice. When I was sixteen and a new driver, I got a ticket for making a U-turn across a double-yellow line. I told the cop honestly that I didn't know it was against the law, and felt it grossly unfair that he ticketed me anyway. I fought the ticket in traffic court and lost. My only defense was "I didn't know! I didn't mean to break the law!" The judge told me ignorance was not an excuse for breaking the law. That was one of my first wake-up calls that as an adult, I would be held accountable for my choices even if they were unconscious. What a scary thought.

Unfortunately, we live in a victim culture. It's usually the other guy's fault that we go to war, get into a car accident, lose our money in stocks, or get a divorce. While victim-hood might make us feel better and in the right, it also makes us helpless and perpetuates our problems.

What do you want? A fulfilling life and relationship? A loving family? Success in your work? Peace in the world? I've learned that to get what you want, you must be The Chooser. Being The Chooser means taking the initiative to create what you want, taking full responsibility for your outcomes, and making your choices mindful of their long-term consequences.

If you believe you don't have a choice, you won't. If you shove responsibility for your choices and outcomes outside of yourself, the Law of Attraction (see Chapter 10) will surely repeat the lesson over and over until you get it. Very often, we are not aware of the range of choices available to us. We are often unaware of our power to choose and of the true power of our choices. We might make choices unconsciously, reactively, or impulsively. We might be unaware of the long-term consequences of our choices.

Choosers know what they want and how to get it.

Choosers take responsibility for what happens and

know they are in charge of their lives.

Choosers know what they want and how to get it. Choosers take responsibility for what happens and know that they are in charge of their lives. Being a Chooser takes a certain amount of confidence and effort, but anyone can be one! Finding the love of your life is not about hoping to be picked. You need to know yourself so that you can be The Chooser, rather than waiting to be chosen. Being The Chooser means taking initiative and responsibility for your outcomes: you are in charge of creating what you want in life. You do not restrict yourself to what or who chooses you.

A.I.M. TO BE "THE CHOOSER"
Step 1: Be AWARE that you have choices
You are never stuck! You always have choices, even if you don't know what your choices are. Don't allow impulse or lack of information to result in a poor choice.

Step 2: IDENTIFY your choices
Always assume there are more choices than you are aware of, and seek to identify a variety of the choices available to you, mindful that "you don't know what you don't know." Identify productive choices and don't settle for unproductive choices.

Step 3: MAKE productive choices
Use all the information available to you to make the best choice

possible to achieve the outcome you desire. Evaluate a choice based upon the likely long-term consequences of that choice.

Finding the love of your life

is not about hoping to be picked. It is about

knowing yourself so that you can be The Chooser,

rather than waiting to be chosen.

I confess that every week I tune into reality TV shows, watching as, say, the lovely glowing twenty-something blonde chooses which men to keep on the show and which ones to eliminate. It doesn't matter if it's a man or woman waiting for that rose; regardless of the gender, everyone hopes to be "the one." How many of these singles have fallen into the Fairy-tale Trap? As you will recall from Chapter 3, the Fairy-tale Trap is when you believe that finding your soul mate will just happen. You passively expect your ideal partner to magically appear and whisk you off to live happily ever after—with no effort at all on your part! This is the opposite of being The Chooser.

I want to emphasize here that it is NOT true that some people are born Choosers while others are not. Rather, being a Chooser is something that you DO. If you are holding onto certain behaviors or attitudes that prevent you from being a Chooser, you can change them. Robert F. Bennett, a U.S. senator from Utah, summed up what being The Chooser means:

> Your life is the sum result of all the choices you make, both con-sciously and unconsciously. If you can control the process of choosing, you can take control of all aspects of your life. You can find the freedom that comes from being in charge of yourself.[1]

If you want to be The Chooser, here are some things you have control over and can DO:

- **Be Creative**: Seek new ideas and opportunities beyond the immediate past and present.

- **Be a Risk-Taker**: Accept rejection and failure as part of life; don't take it personally.

- **Be Assertive**: Ask for what you want, and say "no" to what you don't want.

- **Be Proactive**: Don't merely react to events, or habitually wait for things to happen.

- **Be Goal-Oriented**: Clearly define and vigorously pursue your goals.

- **Assume Abundance**: Believe there will always be plenty of opportunities and resources.

- **Be Positive**: Always anticipate success.

* * *

The last time we saw Angela, she was figuring out exactly what she wanted in a relationship. Her friend Gretchen had helped Angela clarify her Requirements. In the meantime, Angela had been chatting with Jerry, a man she often saw in the gym, and had accepted his dinner invitation.

The day of her date, Angela had a grin pasted to her face. For months, she and Jerry had been checking each other out at the health club. But Angela knew that flirting with Jerry would have been a mistake. She had taken a risk by accepting his dinner invitation.

Angela was very clear about her goals. Yes, she was dating again, but recreationally this time, keeping her boundaries around intimacy and emotional commitment. She wasn't ready for commitment and didn't want to jump into a mini-marriage again. Her future vision still included a life partner, but not until her son had left for college. Rushing into another committed relationship would be unfair to him, and probably to her too.

I WANT TO BE THE CHOOSER, BUT...

Seth skimmed over the notes he had sent the men. He had sent one note to an actor whose ideal partner was "very secure in himself, enough to kiss or fall asleep on my shoulder while riding on the subway train." He had sent another note to a Latino singer who echoed some of Seth's requirements in his profile when he said he was "looking for a man who is willing to communicate his feelings, who is tender, honest, and passionate about life."

But the one man whom Seth was most eager to hear back from was a thirty-five-year-old lawyer whose headline read, "Complete Guy Looking for the Same." This man wrote in his profile that he was "definitely ready to move on to the next stage." Seth was in the same place. Yet Seth felt a pang of vulnerability: what if this guy didn't write back? He exhaled, telling himself not to take rejection too personally if the lawyer didn't reply.

Seth looked out the window, recalling his past five years of dating in Manhattan. At age twenty-four, Seth had finally admitted to himself that he was gay. Still, he had lacked the self-esteem to pursue the kind of relationship he wanted or to even know what that was. He had been the kind of guy who waited to be approached at a bar. He had lived in fear: whenever a man took him home, he dreaded that in the morning his date would kick him to the curb. Seth had not sought out men in places where he might share mutual interests—like an art lecture or an exercise class—and had limited his search to bars. He'd had a hard time saying no to men who were obviously bad news.

But all that was changing now. When Seth and his last boyfriend had moved in together, the emptiness had really eaten Seth up. This boyfriend, gorgeous and wealthy, was a magazine and commercial model who often whisked Seth off to Atlantic City. Yet his boyfriend was also emotionally reserved, and controlling about with whom Seth spent time. Just days before Seth's thirtieth birthday, he had told his boyfriend that he was moving out.

Seth had realized that he deserved to be in a lifelong relationship that was respectful and loving. He truly believed this could happen if he became more assertive and proactive. Now, when he approached a man and was rejected—for example, by sending a kind note online and not receiving a reply—he didn't let it get him down. He didn't need someone else's approval. He now knew that he could take care of himself and say "no" without fear and guilt that he would hurt someone.

When you resist being The Chooser, you risk ending up in relationships that are not right for you because you are merely reacting to the people who choose you.

When you resist being The Chooser, you risk ending up in relationships that are not right for you because you are merely reacting to the people who choose you. Being The Chooser is about choosing how you want to be. It means asking yourself, "How do I want to show up in the world?"

Seth's date, Jeffrey, was waiting for him in front of the upscale Thai restaurant. Jeffrey had short cornrows and clear hazel eyes. He stood up and warmly shook Seth's hand. Seth felt so welcomed that he laughed out loud. They were seated at a corner table near the window.

Jeffrey started asking questions: "Where did you grow up?" "What's your family like?" "What kind of exercise do you enjoy?" "What do you do to maintain a balanced life in New York City?" Seth liked Jeffrey's confidence. Seth felt open and trusting as he explained that his Korean parents were very conservative and

Christian. He had come out to his two older brothers, but not to his parents.

"I'm in the same boat!" Jeffrey said. "My older sisters know that I'm gay, but I'm in no rush to tell my parents. They are strict southern Baptists."

Seth added that he was very close to his family and took the train to visit them at least one weekend a month in New Jersey.

"I just bought my parents tickets to New York," Jeffrey said. "They're coming to the city for their first time this spring."

Seth was impressed. This was a man who seemed to be very close to his family, like him.

Being "The Chooser"

is about choosing how you want to be.

It means asking yourself,

"How do I want to show up in the world?"

The two men talked about living in Manhattan. Jeffrey practiced yoga. Seth told him that his dogs really kept him centered. He loved taking them to the dog run at least twice a day, and cuddling with them every night in bed.

"I dream about getting a dog," said Jeffrey. "But I have two roommates and they're against it."

"You'll have to join me at the dog run one day!" Seth said, feeling uninhibited.

"Great!"

Seth appreciated how assertive Jeffrey seemed to be. Like Seth, he initiated dialogue and seemed to be a risk-taker. Seth was feeling really comfortable on this date—that is, until he started asking more questions about Jeffrey's living situation.

"I have an unusual setup with one of my roommates," Jeffrey said. "I'm just going to be clear and hope it doesn't turn you off."

"Go on."

"When he moved into our apartment last fall, we started sleeping together. It's just a physical thing, if you know what I mean—"

Seth shook his head.

"We're just meeting each other's needs, but we're open to dating other people. We're not really together."

"That sounds confusing," Seth said, imagining that if he and Jeffrey ever dated, they'd always have to go to Seth's place to prevent any awkward or jealous feelings from the roommate.

And who was to say that Jeffrey didn't really have feelings for his roommate? Seth was very attracted to Jeffrey, and it seemed like they had a lot in common. But certainly, Jeffrey was involved with someone and not truly available. Despite Jeffrey's assurances, Seth was feeling very uncomfortable.

"It's not going to work for me," he said. "I'm ready for a committed relationship with someone who is also ready and available."

Seth took a deep breath. "It's not going to work for me," he said. "I'm ready for a committed relationship with someone who is also ready and available. I'm not comfortable with your situation."

"Thanks for the honesty, man," Jeffrey said. "I'm sorry it's not going to work out."

Seth took another sip of tea, proud of himself for listening to his own needs and for being assertive. He said to himself: "I'M THE CHOOSER!" He was choosing to say no to an unavailable man, and yes to what he really wanted.

But back home, Seth fell onto his sofa with a feeling of defeat. This dating thing was exhausting. Could he really keep up with it? He pulled his laptop off the coffee table and logged on. There was a reply from that lawyer he'd written to!

"Hey Seth! Great to 'meet' you. Thanks for writing. I'm having a quiet night at home with my dogs. To share a little more about the kind of guy I'm looking for: he is career-oriented and fun to be with. A sense of humor is a must. I strongly believe in the law of attraction. I know that whoever I'm with needs to feel positive about life. On that note, I don't have a specific type—let the chemistry be the judge of that. I look forward to hearing your thoughts."

Within moments, Seth's dinner date faded from his memory. He clicked on the reply button.

* * *

It is not a lack of talent or a genetic malfunction that prevents us from being Choosers. Rather, we have learned, or internalized, a set of attitudes, beliefs, and behaviors. When you were a child, the adults around you had all the power. Your parents were in charge and made all the decisions for you. So, as you grew up, you had to learn how to be responsible and make choices for yourself. As a child, you might have been punished for making your own choices. No doubt you were conditioned to be a certain way and to have certain values. However, as an adult, you can choose which attitudes and behaviors you want to internalize.

I have a friend whose life is a great example of being The Chooser.

Bonnie Bernell, a successful, happily-married psychologist, is the daughter of a former fashion model and a strikingly handsome physician. Bernell, who is now in her mid-fifties, struggled for years before choosing to love herself as a large woman. As an adult, Bernell chose not to let her parents' attitudes about how she should look affect her self-esteem. She wrote a celebratory book of strategies that large women have found effective to handle challenging situations: *Bountiful Women: Large Women's Secrets for Living the Life They Desire.*

As a Chooser, you need to hold true to yourself and stand up for what you want in your life.

Perhaps there is still some part of you that wants Mom or Dad to make the choices for you so that you can be carefree and untroubled. That part of you lets the boss hire you or fire you. That part of you lets somebody else ask you out or break up with you. Sometimes, the kid in us feels inadequate, or fears failure. It can be scary to stand up for yourself. Other times, peer pressure is so great that it shadows our decision making. Everyone around you has opinions and will express them generously: "You should really date this man/woman. He/she is perfect for you!" Your friends and family will often disagree with you. As a Chooser, you need to hold true to yourself and stand up for what you want in your life.

ARE YOU THE PURSUER OR THE PURSUED?
Some of us find it more comfortable and socially acceptable to be The Chooser in certain situations, such as with friends or at work. It might be clear-cut and easy for some of us to invest our money in certain stocks, for example, but challenging to approach an attractive woman and ask her out. Some of us might be very assertive

when it comes to playing tennis, but giving a man our phone number is unthinkable. I know many women who are successful, decisive, powerful executives in the workplace, but when it comes to intimate relationships with men, they find it very difficult to be assertive. Fearful of coming across as "unfeminine," they are submissive. I recall one client, for instance, who was very successful as the president of her Silicon Valley company. But in her relationships, she had a hard time standing up for herself and played a whiny victim. When we enter the arena of intimate relationships, we also cross over the threshold to emotionally complicated issues of gender roles, self-esteem, and sexuality.

Some of us might be very assertive

when it comes to playing tennis, but giving

a man our phone number is unthinkable.

Traditionally, there are "masculine" and "feminine" styles of being The Chooser. These do not necessarily match with being a man or a woman. As part of my Ph.D. studies, I took a class in gender differences and was amazed to learn how few real differences there really are. (But you wouldn't know this by reading John Gray's *Men are from Mars, Women are from Venus*!) In their book *Same Difference: How Gender Myths Are Hurting Our Relationships, Our Children, and Our Jobs*, Rosalind Barnett and Caryl Rivers challenge the Mars and Venus theory of gender relations. They say that overall, men and women are much more alike than different, and will be harmed if they buy into gender myths. Drawing on years of exhaustive research, Barnett and Rivers reveal how a toxic mix of junk science, pop psychology, and media hype has profoundly influenced our thinking and behavior. This has caused us to make poor decisions about how we choose our mates. The time has come, argue the authors, to liberate ourselves from biological determinism. Barnett and Rivers make a plea to end sexual stereotyping so that women and men may realize their destinies as full human beings.[2]

One scientifically proven gender difference is that men, by nature, are more promiscuous. This means that men are more sexually interested and motivated. Most men will find it very hard to say no to sex. Women, on the other hand, have a lot more to lose when it comes to sex because they can get pregnant. Most women will turn down an offer to have sex if they do not want to.

The stereotypical male Chooser is the pursuer, while the stereotypical female Chooser is the pursued. The stereotypical male Chooser picks an attractive prospect and pursues by initiating conversation, winning favor, and getting the date. This man is like the hunter, and he appears powerful and in charge. The stereotypical female Chooser sends subtle nonverbal signals to an attractive prospect and appears submissively receptive to the responses. Women have been taught to avoid aggression and boost the male ego; their survival and the future of their children have depended on this in the past. So women often appear passive and subordinate, although they can still be quite powerful and in charge indirectly.

As a man, it took me a while to understand the feminine Chooser style. My first lesson came during my first marriage. My ex-wife was very good at saying no. Her initial response to just about anything that had not been initiated by her was resistance. It's a very powerful position! You can stop traffic and win political causes with resistance. I also like to compare the feminine Chooser style to the martial art aikido. In aikido, you use your partner's motion against him/her. A man might look like the pursuer, but the woman actually determines whether this relationship will go further.

Another significant aspect of the feminine style is giving hints, clues, and glances. Most men have not been trained or taught to read that kind of language. My second wife was an extraordinarily feminine person. If she wanted a glass of water, she would say, "You know, I'm thirsty." I thought she was simply complaining about being thirsty, and it took me a long time to realize that she was indirectly asking me to get her a glass of water. In her feminine style, she was giving me an opportunity to be her hero. Still, I spent a lot of time in the marriage lamenting, "Just make a direct request. Don't make me mind-read!"

Our challenge is to learn how to relate to each other

as equals as we develop our own unique blends

of masculine and feminine.

Media hype has profoundly exaggerated the masculine and feminine styles, causing some singles to make poor decisions when trying to find a partner. TV makeover shows reinforce the myth that a woman must have a "perfect" body and face if she is going to find a man. (The American Society for Aesthetic Plastic Surgery reports that in 2003, nearly 8.3 million surgical and nonsurgical cosmetic procedures were performed. That is an increase of 293 percent since 1997.[3])

But men have not had it easy either. Many men today have been raised by single mothers and lack strong male role models. This is reflected in many current television sitcoms that portray men as lazy, foolish boobs who are dependent on smart, competent women. That view is at odds with the 2003 National Study of the Changing Workforce, which found that in dual-earner couples—the dominant family form in the United States—men's housework chores and child care have increased steadily since 1977.

Both men and women know what their traditional, stereotypical roles are; however, most of today's singles don't subscribe to these roles. So, we are often unclear about what to do or expect. Today, traditional gender roles don't work well for either gender. In recent generations, women's roles have been greatly expanded beyond being wives and mothers. They expect and deserve equality with men. And, in order to compete with men in the workplace and succeed, women have discovered that they must be more "masculine" and less "feminine."

Regardless of whether you prefer to be receptive or proactive, being The Chooser means making your own choices.

Some men still prefer to pursue their partners in a traditionally masculine way, like hunters or warriors, while others are uncomfortable being so aggressive. Some women still prefer to bat their eyelashes to make a man feel like a hero, while others prefer to be dominant. In today's world, men and women are free to determine the relationship style that fits them. Still, some men and women wish to be equal, to be involved in relationships where neither party is dominant or submissive, the pursued or the pursuer. This requires that we be aware, intentional, and authentic. These skills must be learned and practiced. We are redefining today's gender roles, which can be confusing. I believe that all of us have masculine and feminine sides. Our challenge is to learn how to relate to each other as equals as we develop our own unique blends of masculine and feminine. Regardless of whether you prefer to be receptive or proactive, being The Chooser means making your own choices.

A Strategy for Being The Chooser:
THE RULE OF THREE

You may have heard that the third time is the charm, and while that has certainly been true for me in my own relationships, I'm not recommending getting divorced twice to find your life partner. The Rule of Three for Conscious Dating is one strategy you can use to be The Chooser. It means that when meeting someone attractive to you, it takes at least three contacts to determine mutual interest and comfort to proceed further.

In the real world of singles, the most anxiety-producing situation occurs when you spot someone attractive to you whom you would like to meet. This is so stressful that an entire industry caters to singles to help them with this—for a price. Save your money, use the Rule of Three, and be The Chooser. Here is an example:

> Let's say you are attracted to the teller at the bank. You could flirt, deliver your best pick-up line, and ask what time he/she gets off. But you wisely anticipate that the person might be uncomfortable with that approach. So, what do you do? Try the Rule of Three:

CONTACT #1: You smile, make eye contact, introduce yourself, ask his/her name, make small talk, pay a compliment, anything you would do to be friendly with anyone in any setting.

The purpose of this first contact is to walk away having left a positive impression.

CONTACT #2: Return to bank within a day or two. Now that you are on a first-name basis, you can start with small talk and add some personal sharing about something important to you related to your Requirements, such as your children or work. Notice his/her reaction: is it positive, negative, or neutral? Having revealed something specific about yourself, you then ask him/her about the topic (for example, "Do you have kids?").

You are seeking to do three things at this step:
- *Discover whether you have anything in common, especially an important Requirement.*

- *Confirm your attraction and interest after discovering some thing real about this person.*

- *Leave another positive impression, this time based upon something real about you.*

CONTACT #3: Return to bank in another day or two. Talk a bit further about what you have in common. Toward the end of the transaction say, "I really enjoy talking with you, and it seems that we have a lot in common. Would you be interested and available to meet for coffee sometime?"

Notice the above is a clear statement about you, and asks about his/her *interest* and *availability*. Asking in this way is typically construed as friendly, nonthreatening, and respectful. You are giving him/her room to decline easily and gracefully.

Most people would be flattered and positive. Don't worry about the people who take you the wrong way; they are simply screening themselves out. You're just being authentic, benign, and innocently friendly. It is very helpful to be unattached to the outcome. He/she can accept or not; you will be fine either way.

ALTERNATIVE #1: If asking so directly is not your preference, you can give the person your business card and say, "I really enjoy talking with you, and it seems that we have a lot in common. Here is my card. I would love for you to call or e-mail if you are interested and available to meet for coffee sometime."

ALTERNATIVE #2: You can repeat Contact #2 as many times as you like to build more comfort and learn more about each other before you decide to try #3.

ALTERNATIVE #3: The Rule of Three for Conscious Dating can be applied to any social setting such as a party, except you would use intervals of fifteen to thirty minutes instead of hours or days.

Initiating contact with people who are attractive to you is essential to being The Chooser. In doing so, remember how important it is to be authentic—especially with your bank teller, because he/she already knows more about you than most of your friends and family!

HOW CAN YOU BECOME THE CHOOSER?
As you know, Choosers define their own styles, preferring, for instance, to initiate or be receptive when meeting someone. Choosers know themselves well and have figured out which dating strategies work for them. Choosers initiate contact with prospective partners.

"We choose our joys and sorrows long before we experience them."

—Khalil Gibran

I acknowledge that all of us have limits to our choices. For example, if you're gay, you can't wake up one day and decide to be straight. One of my favorite writers, Khalil Gibran, said, "We choose our joys and sorrows long before we experience them." Still, we all have tremendous freedom in our lives. We can decide what kind of work we'd like to do, what kinds of friends to make, and what kind of partner we'd like to have. In short, we have the freedom to ask, "Who am I?" "What do I want?" and "How do I want to show up in the world?"

To be The Chooser, you need to break free of your conditioning. You need to take risks and go beyond your comfort levels. Every moment of the day, you need to make honest choices to satisfy yourself, not just others. Being the Chooser is a mind-set and a way of living. You are the pioneer of your life! ✀

CONSCIOUS DATING PLAN EXERCISE NO. 7:

Please refer to Chapter 15 to write your answers.

What are your obstacles?

We all have obstacles that prevent us from being Choosers. All of these obstacles have been learned, and they can be un-learned. When reading each obstacle, do a "gut check," and if you experience the slightest physical or emotional reaction, it most likely applies to you. Make a check mark next to the ones that apply to you.

_____ "I'm not good enough" (Having low self esteem)

_____"It won't happen for me"; "I can't" (Having limiting beliefs and attitudes)

_____"I must avoid rejection" (Needing to be accepted or conforming to social pressures to feel worthy)

_____"I don't know how" (Lacking creativity, information or skill)

_____ "It's not ladylike"; "It's not gentlemanly" (Adhering to gender roles)

_____ "I need approval"; "I don't want to hurt anyone" (Needing to please others)

Remember: you can choose which attitudes you want to internalize. You are not stuck with them. Perhaps you won't feel it right away, but if you continue working on this, you will internalize new attitudes and they will become natural to you.

Now, go back to the above exercise and compose an affirmation for each obstacle so that it will no longer be in your way.

For example:

I must avoid rejection, can be changed to, "I am The Chooser in my life. If someone rejects me, he/she is doing me a favor."

Instead of I'm not good enough, you can say, "I am OK as I am, and I deserve to be happy."

Instead of "It won't happen for me," you can say, "It only takes one, and I'm the one."

FOURTH PRINCIPLE OF CONSCIOUS DATING:
Balance Your Heart with Your Head

When you experience chemistry with someone, is it like an irresistible magnetic force that causes you to leap eagerly into a relationship? While chemistry and attraction are important for a sustainable relationship, this chapter will cover how you can experience these feelings while staying in touch with reality.

FALLING IN LOVE

At the next red light, Angela checked herself again in the rearview mirror. She was on her way to meet Jerry for their first dinner date. Her new silver earrings glistened in the evening light. She smiled at herself, feeling positive and excited. The first time Angela had spotted Jerry in the sauna at the gym, she'd been drawn to him. He was over six feet tall, with well-defined biceps and salt-and-pepper hair. She loved guys with deep voices, and she appreciated how thoughtful Jerry seemed. Sometimes, for example, he took the empty treadmill next to Angela and asked her questions about her job and her son.

Still, for months, Angela had kept her distance because she was in a relationship. Now that her ex was history, Angela had a new surge of energy and excitement. This week, in fact, she'd joined her sixteen-year-old son on three mornings to run around the local track. Before work, she had taken the time to write in her journal, envisioning herself as a freshman in college again and dancing away her weekends with fun and lighthearted guys. At age forty, however, she was aware that she'd have to keep some of that infatuation in check. Every time she and Jerry ran into each other at the gym, the attraction was strong and she had to remind herself to take a deep breath.

Angela imagined that she was a teenager again, dancing away her weekends with fun and lighthearted guys.

But Angela trusted herself, and the fact that she had some rules helped. First of all, she had decided that she would not sleep with any man until they'd gone out for at least a few months (and if he slept over, her son would be at his father's house). Secondly, she would not make herself vulnerable right away by being exclusive and seeing a man every day in the beginning. Lastly, she would not isolate herself as she had with her ex-boyfriend. Instead, she would use her support community of friends to help her stick to her goal of dating nonexclusively and giving herself some time before she got involved in another relationship.

After parking her car, Angela ran a comb through her light brown hair. She wondered if Jerry would be waiting for her at the bar.

IT'S HOT AROUND HERE!
Jerry was waiting for Angela at the bar—along with two glasses of red wine. He stood up to greet her and said, "You look lovely!"

Angela laughed. "I guess this is the first time you've seen me in anything but my gym clothes, right?"

Angela took the stool next to Jerry, which felt very close. In fact, she was so close that she could see a small razor cut on his face. Angela almost wanted to reach out and touch it, but held back. She reminded herself about her boundaries. They talked until their table was ready. Jerry wanted to know who Angela worked with in her social services job and whether she enjoyed it. She told him about the youth intervention projects for which she had recently been awarded some grants, and he seemed impressed.

"Have you been dating much?" Jerry asked.

"My last relationship ended recently, so not much," Angela said. Sometimes she had a way of spilling her guts to strangers, so it felt good to pace her conversation with Jerry.

Over dinner, Angela noticed herself laughing easily. Jerry didn't seem to take his eyes off her, which made her feel attractive. She found him to be very gentlemanly; from the way he held his salad fork to the way he refilled her wine glass. There was no doubt that he was sincere and romantic. But could he meet Angela's requirements?

She found him to be very gentlemanly;

from the way he held his salad fork

to the way he refilled her wine glass. There was

no doubt that he was sincere and romantic.

But could he meet her requirements?

You recall that in Chapter 5, Angela had worked hard at defining her requirements. She knew, for example, that she and her partner would value telling each other the truth and doing their best to do so. No matter how much she was in love, it wouldn't work any other way. So, when Angela asked Jerry about his ex-wife, she was pleased how openly he talked about their conflicts and divorce years later. She asked him about his hiatus from his job, and was also impressed by the fact that he was going back to school to earn a second master's degree.

When the check came, however, Angela suddenly panicked. The date was almost over. Would he try to kiss her at the car? She felt such chemistry, but did he?

What does it mean when our palms get sweaty, our cheeks are flushed, and we're suddenly breathless? Are they reliable guides?

What does it mean when our palms get sweaty, our cheeks are flushed, and we're suddenly breathless? Should we follow these reactions or ignore them? Are they reliable guides? Arthur Aron, a professor at the State University of New York at Stonybrook, has explored the dynamics of what exactly happens when two people are falling in love. Even the simple action of looking into each other's eyes has a power of its own, as proved in his experiments with two complete strangers. For ninety minutes, Aron asked numerous strangers to disclose intimate details about themselves such as their most embarrassing moment, how they would feel if they lost a parent, and what they liked about the other person. At the end, they were asked to stare into each other's eyes without talking for four minutes. The results were amazing in that many of the couples confessed to feeling deeply attracted and close to the other person. Two of his subjects even married six months afterward!

Our physical reactions might include increased heart rate and blood pressure; feeling warm; sweating; tingling skin sensations; or sexu-

146

al arousal. These chemical reactions are both involuntary and strong, leading to powerful feelings of attraction. They are actually driven by:

- pheromones (chemicals emitted to attract a partner)
- oxytocin (acts on the hypothalamus to produce emotions)
- PEA or phenylethylamine (a natural amphetamine)
- dopamine and norepinephrine (natural mood enhancers)
- testosterone (increases sexual desire)

Lust is driven by the sex hormones testosterone and estrogen. But testosterone is not confined only to men. It has also been shown to play a major role in the sex drive of women. Helen Fisher, author of Anatomy of Love and a professor of anthropology at Rutgers University, says that these hormones "get you out looking for anything." [1]

Have you ever fallen in love and had

a friend or family member ask, "Are you crazy?"

or "Are you blind?"

Falling in love involves phenylethylamine (PEA) or the "love drug," which gives us that euphoric high when everything feels so wonderful. This person can do no wrong. Have you ever fallen in love and had a friend or family member ask, "Are you blind?" Well, yes, you really were blind. And almost no one could reason with you about the relationship at that stage of the game, because PEA was pouring out in large quantities. PEA is what causes you to be less likely to be aware of the faults of the other person. When we meet someone to whom we are sexually attracted, our bodies respond by releasing these neurochemicals that can leave us sputtering, incoherent, and breathless.

Infatuation is when people fall in love and can think of nothing else. Some of the neurotransmitters—natural mood enhancers—I mentioned above play an important role. For example, dopamine is also activated by cocaine and nicotine. Norepinephrine, also known as adrenaline, is what gets our heart racing and our bodies sweating. Sometimes, we lose both our appetite and sleep, preferring to spend hours at a time daydreaming about our new lover.

Attachment is what takes over after the infatuation stage if a relationship is going to last. If we stayed in the infatuation stage forever, how would we ever get any work done? Attachment is a longer lasting emotional connection, and is the bond that keeps couples together when they go on to have children. Oxytocin is one of the important hormones released by the nervous system in the attachment stage. It is also released by the hypothalamus gland during childbirth and also helps the breast express milk. It helps cement the strong bond between mother and child. And it is released by both sexes during orgasm, and is thought to promote bonding when adults are intimate.

In Chapter 2, "What Do We Really Want?" I mentioned Pat Love, author of *The Truth About Love,* who explains that one of the physical benefits of intimacy is oxytocin. Not only is this "cuddle drug" the same hormone secreted by nursing mothers and after orgasm by both partners, it is released in good and healthy relationships in the presence of our long-term partner. Oxytocin is what makes us feel connected and blissful just being with him/her. The more sex a couple has, the deeper their bond becomes. After you have sex, the risk is high that you're going to feel like a couple. All those chemical reactions are leading up to this. When I talk to singles about using their heads, I often use this as an argument for putting off sex until you know what you are getting into.

So when we talk about "attraction," "infatuation," or "following your heart" after meeting a potential partner, we're actually talking about reactions produced in our brain. These reactions made us feel more alive and excited than almost any other time in our lives. It's like the rush of adrenaline you might feel when skydiving or riding a roller coaster. Sometimes these feelings are so extreme that we become addicted to them, and move from relationship to relationship to recapture and sustain them. Many singles, overwhelmed by these feelings, interpret them as "love" or a sign that the relationship is meant to be. Most of us would agree that, on an intellectual level, this is not the kind of love we really expect to last. After all, these phenomena occur prior to really knowing and building a relationship with someone.

EMOTIONAL CHEMISTRY

The theory of emotional attraction that makes the most sense to me is Harville Hendrix's concept of the imago. According to Hendrix, we have an unconscious image or "imago" of our ideal partner. This imago is composed of the positive and negative characteristics of our parents or early caretakers. Hendrix theorizes that because we are seeking to emotionally heal and complete ourselves, we are unconsciously attracted to potential partners who match our imago. For example, someone who grew up with a critical parent might unconsciously choose a critical partner in the hope of finally winning approval. Our imago match is best suited to help us finish our unfinished childhood business because of our partner's resemblance to the people who had the heaviest impact on our early development.

Another factor in emotional chemistry is the "rebound effect." We will often be attracted to people who remind us of past partners or have traits that were missing in past partners. This effect is so strong that divorced singles are often advised to wait TWO YEARS after their divorce is final to make another partner choice. Moving too quickly into your next relationship almost guarantees that you are making an unconscious choice driven by past experience and greatly colored by your last relationship, which may or may not work for you in the long term.

USING YOUR HEAD OR LOSING YOUR HEART?

The ink was barely dry on Mark's divorce papers when he started to date again. Although he felt ready for action, everyone

149

around him thought he was rushing. One of his friends kept leaving messages on his answering machine: "C'mon, Mark, give it some time!" Recently, one of his coworkers handed him the book How to Survive the Loss of a Love. He had read one chapter every night with a box of tissues next to his bed, and then decided he'd been sad long enough.

Thirty-five-year-old Mark felt that he'd already spent the last two years of his marriage grieving as well as bickering, and was ready to move on. The divorce papers were signed, and he had his daughters, ages eight and ten, every other weekend. This gave him lots of free time for his new life as a bachelor.

A successful business manager in marketing, word seemed to pass quickly through Mark's circles that he was single. The fact that he got together with friends for drinks every night also sped up the process. Mark was a good talker and had always made women laugh easily. His bureau at home was decorated with a number of women's phone numbers written on cocktail napkins.

But it was Stacy, an administrative assistant who worked down the hall from him, who really caught his eye. A stunning blue-eyed blonde, she smiled at him in the elevator. Before the doors opened, Mark passed Stacy his card.

"I'd love to see you sometime," he said.
When she nodded her head and smiled again, he knew that she would call shortly.

Two nights later, Mark waited for Stacy at a cozy bar in downtown San Francisco. When she walked in wearing a low-cut silk dress and heels, he whistled under his breath. He couldn't resist kissing her on the cheek.

They sat in a booth together, their legs touching. This was hot!

"So, how old are you?" Mark asked.

"Guess!"

He looked her up and down, guessing that she was about ten years younger than he. "Twenty-five?"

Stacy shook her head.

"Twenty-four?"

She shook her head again. Mark swallowed hard. Gosh, just how young was she? "I give up," he said.

Stacy raised the fingers on both of her hands and flashed them twice in the air. Twenty.

"Wow, Baby!" said Mark. "That makes me fifteen years older than you." He didn't add that, technically, he could be her father.

Mark wasn't sure what he wanted in a girlfriend, but knew that he felt crazy just sitting next to her.

Still, there was a certain maturity about Stacy that made Mark forget their age difference. Raised by a single mom in Nebraska, Stacy had graduated from high school at sixteen and earned a bachelor's degree in business from the University of Nebraska. She'd paid for college by modeling for fashion catalogs. She had moved to the San Francisco area the previous summer and landed a job in three days. She lived with three roommates, was a vegetarian, and liked to go out dancing. Mark really wanted to get Stacy in bed with him. He couldn't think straight.

Stacy was five-foot-eight and had a very slim waist, a large bust, and long thin legs. Mark wasn't sure what he wanted in a girlfriend, but knew that he felt crazy just sitting next to her. He couldn't remember feeling like this before, unless he counted junior high school. Moreover, Stacy seemed a world apart from Mark's uptight thirty-six-year-old attorney ex-wife.

That same night, Mark took Stacy home. They never actually fell asleep, they were so busy. Mark called in sick the next day, but Stacy had to go into the office. Mark thought he was in love. His attraction to Stacy felt so instantaneous that he figured he had to be following his heart.

Within one month, Mark had invited Stacy to move in with him. Mark's oldest daughter, Katherine, did not seem pleased by the new living arrangements. "Dad, she's only ten years older than me! How embarrassing!"

"I know, Honey—"

"She better not come to my soccer games!"

"But she's part of our family now—"

"Not mine!"

The situation was awkward for everyone, especially Stacy, who felt like an outsider and somewhat guilty and responsible. The honeymoon was over quickly and the conflicts began. But Mark didn't know what else to do other than muddle forward and try to make it work.

Running on adrenaline and hormones, he didn't realize that he had rebounded into a "mini marriage" (refer to Chapter 9). There was no gradual, conscious process of getting to know each other and determining if this might be a good long-term relationship choice. Mark did not stop to think about who he was—as a recently divorced father of two young girls—or what he wanted for the rest of his life beyond his attraction for Stacy. It never occurred to him to even think about whether he was ready for a committed relationship.

Rather, Mark was so hungry for companionship and good sex and so terrified of being alone that he had jumped at the chance to be exclusive with a young and beautiful woman. Now everyone was miserable.

* * *

We all love the feeling of being attracted to someone and the excitement that comes with it. This experience is similar to being intoxicated on drugs or alcohol. I'm not saying these feelings are wrong, but they need to be tempered with using your head. It's not either/or. My position is that you can have both: using your head as well as your heart is still exciting!

Ask yourself, "When is the soonest

that I should have sex

with a new person I'm dating?"

There are many strategies for managing your physical and emotional attractions. One of the best boundaries you can have is around physical intimacy. Give yourself time to know this other person as a human being. After you're groping each other, it's going to be hard to backtrack and enforce boundaries that have already been crossed. Ask yourself, "When is the soonest that I should have sex with a new person I'm dating?" You want to stay as objective as possible without your emotions and hormones getting in the way. A lot of singles I work with say, "Two to three months." It's crucial to define the amount of time you need to get to know somebody without getting physically involved, and to stick to that.

LOVE VERSUS ATTACHMENT

For most people, when you have sex with someone, you feel like you're a couple now, and you start getting attached. It is easy to confuse love and attachment. We easily attach to both people and things. Think about how you feel about your car or your favorite clothes. Sex is engineered to create attachment; that's the way we're wired. If you're going to consciously Scout, Sort, Screen, and Test, you need to maintain your physical boundaries. Alcohol and drugs can influence us to lose our boundaries, as well. Unfortunately, there's no drug that will help us stay conscious, so what should we do?

Let's assume that you're dating someone and feeling really love-struck, but you want a reality check. Of course, you're going to have blind spots because you're high on the "love drug." You're not going to be thinking or seeing things accurately. Have your friends and/or family meet this person, and listen closely to what they say. They can give you an accurate read on this person and help you see things that you might not be allowing yourself to see. Or, find a relationship coach who can give you a reality check and help you be more objective.

Have your friends and/or family

meet this person and

listen closely to what they say.

Writing things down is another way of managing your reactions. This is why the exercises at the end of every chapter of this book are so important. This is also why it's imperative that you write down your Requirements. Try writing down the things that work— and don't work—for you about your new flame. What do you look forward to every time you see this person? What do you appreciate? What are the red flags? What are the drawbacks? It's easy to overlook the negative aspects, but when you write them down, they have more reality. It's not as easy to forget the downside if we externalize our thinking and put it in writing.

What do you look forward to

every time you see this person?

What do you appreciate? What are the red flags?

What are the drawbacks?

WHAT ABOUT CHEMISTRY?

On the flip side, one very common question that singles ask me is, "Can chemistry evolve over time?" Let's say you're getting to know someone who appears to meet your Requirements, but the chemistry is not quite there for you. Well, chemistry is not something that you can control. I advise singles to take their time and see what happens. Often, it turns out that you might not have a lover, but you now have a good friend.

REQUIREMENTS IN ACTION

Let's say that you're at a speed-dating event and you have an eight-minute conversation with this really attractive man/woman. You go home and just can't get your mind off of him/her. You call all your friends to gush, feeling like an animal in the wild. Helen Fisher, a professor of anthropology at Rutgers University and author of *Anatomy of Love*, says this is not as farfetched as it may seem: "I think that you can fall in love with somebody in much less than eight minutes of conversation, but eight minutes will do. I think we are animals that were built for love at first sight. Within the animal community, it's my guess that this brain circuitry for attraction, it can be very spontaneous and we've inherited that and indeed you see evidence of this."

But how do you know if this eight-minute love-fest is real? We all want to tiptoe through the tulips and feel good, but the danger here is that we often choose either our head or our heart. Chemistry is not something that you can control. It's either there or not there. But you can use your feelings of attraction as radar. This is how we identify somebody to Scout, Sort, and Screen. It's a given! If you weren't attracted, you wouldn't be interested in them in the first place. To identify who to scout, follow your feelings of attraction. But when you're engaging them, use your head as well as your heart.

When I was first getting to know Maggie, we discovered the book *Intellectual Foreplay: Questions for Lovers and Lovers-to-Be* by Eve Eschner Hogan. We wanted to be conscious and take things one step at a time, and this book was a great asset because it's filled with open-ended questions that couples can ask each other to find out whether this romantic partner is "the one." Intellectual Foreplay includes guidelines for working with a partner's responses, and to help prepare couples to have fulfilling relationships. As you might recall from the Introduction, Maggie and I developed a routine of talking on the telephone in the evening and taking turns asking each other questions from the book. It was enjoyable to see that the more we tested each other's realities, the more excited we were about being together. Also at the time, both of us had worked hard to clarify our own Requirements. I can't stress this enough. Just making a list won't do; you've got to refine your Requirements and be committed to them, or you are not going to be happy.

How do you know if a Requirement is met?
Follow these three steps:

1. Review your Requirements.

Remember that Requirements are not just an abstract list of ideas or values; they are so big, and so core, as to be absolutely real and unambiguous. If you are unsure, have to think about it, or believe it is possible to live without it in a relationship, it is NOT a Requirement. A Requirement is so core to who you are and what you need that you would have to leave a relationship if it were not met. When this much energy exists around something, it tends to force or drive events. If you are ambivalent about whether a Requirement is being met, just give it time. If it is not being met, the issue will get larger and larger until it eventually breaks the relationship up, regardless of each partner's wishes.

2."Operationalize" your Requirements.

This means that you are specific about what the Requirement means behaviorally. What would need to happen or not happen for it to be met? Events such as "monogamy" and "loves children" are unambiguous. Traits, values, ideas, labels, etc. such as "romantic," "integrity," and "trust" are too vague.

3. Be aware of your experience of your Requirements with this person.

What matters is that the Requirement is met in a way that works for you. You can rationalize and argue "trust," but what matters is that you have the experience of trust that is important to you in a relationship.

When we put language to Requirements, we are really trying to describe and be conscious of something we must experience in a relationship for it to work for us. This can be subjective, but in the end that is all that matters. You might ask, for example, "If I have trust issues, then isn't it my 'stuff' and not about my partner?" But ALL Requirements are about YOU, and it is largely up to you whether they are met or not. Early in a relationship, it is not always clear if a Requirement is met or not. If you are single and screening a possible partner, or in a pre-committed relationship, and you are not sure if a Requirement is met, you can choose to give it more time. While you might feel a sense of urgency, the reality is that there is no emergency and no need to hurry to make a decision about a relationship. If you give it more time and you are STILL unsure, then take that as a "no."

If you are ambivalent about whether a Requirement

is being met, just give it time.

If it is not being met, the issue will get larger and

larger, until it eventually breaks the relationship up,

regardless of each partner's wishes.

YOUR HEAD CAN HELP YOUR HEART

Being conscious and using your head allows you to get what you really want in your heart. I once worked with a couple who were considering getting married, but had a concern about alcohol. He liked beer, and would have one after work every day, and drink the equivalent of a six-pack with his friends on the weekend. He had never had any negative consequences due to drinking beer, such as DUIs, problems at work, etc., and insisted that his level of beer drinking was not a problem in his life. However, she was an adult child of alcoholics, and experienced anxiety and stress every time he opened a beer. She agreed that he probably did not have a problem with his drinking, but it was very hard for her to be around him when he drank. She accepted responsibility for the issue and tried to adjust and accept his beer drinking. He did not want to give up beer, and she agreed that he shouldn't have to. After months of struggling back and forth with this issue, she decided it was a Requirement for her to be in an alcohol-free relationship, and broke it off with him. He was not wrong for liking beer. She was not wrong for needing an alcohol-free relationship. In their hearts, they really wanted to be together and tried to make it work, but it never really did. Over time, she became clear in her head that, despite stemming from a dysfunctional childhood, this issue in the relationship was related to a Requirement that must be met for her to be happy and fulfilled. She made a conscious choice with her head that will allow her heart to get what she really wants and needs.

What is the likelihood that our chemistry and unconscious attraction will result in good relationship choices? The failure rate of relationships suggests that the odds are low. In this chapter, you have learned some important skills to balance your heart with your head. We can use our physical and emotional reactions to potential partners as useful information. Being clear about our Requirements and performing reality checks will allow us to make conscious relationship choices. ✗

CONSCIOUS DATING PLAN EXERCISE NO. 8:

Please refer to Chapter 15 to write your answers.

Is it really love?

> 1. Recall the last few times you were infatuated with someone and jumped into a relationship.
> • How long did the infatuation last for you?
> • How long did the relationship last?
> • What broke up the relationship?
> • What did you learn from that relationship?

> 2. Who in your life, whose judgment you trust, will you use to get a reality check when you are infatuated with someone?

> 3. What is the minimum period of time you will date somebody before being physically intimate? How will you keep this boundary?

FIFTH PRINCIPLE OF CONSCIOUS DATING:
Be Ready & Available
for Commitment

Although you—along with every other single—want to be in a relationship, that doesn't necessarily mean you are ready for one. In this chapter, you will analyze your own relationship "readiness" and choose an aligned dating strategy. Also, you will learn that there are at least three forms of dating relationships: recreational, committed, and the mini-marriage, and discover what each means to your future relationship success.

ARE YOU THE CHOOSER OR THE CHOSEN?

Every Wednesday night at nine o' clock, you will find me sitting in front of the TV set with my family, all of us looking like deer caught in headlights as we watch The Bachelor. As a relationship coach, the plethora of dating reality shows evokes a combination of horror and fascination in me. On one hand, these dating reality shows are really "un-reality." A single guy is dating a large group of attractive women with a camera following his every move, shopping for his life partner on TV, and proposing after just six weeks. On the other hand, a show like The Bachelor actually involves a very conscious process. As the contestants spend time together, their methods parallel my Four Steps for Conscious Dating; Scouting, Sorting, Screening, and Testing, which I detailed in Chapter 6.

In the dating reality shows, the producers are responsible for scouting the potential partners, so it shouldn't be a surprise that the success rate of these couples is very low. (As I write this book, only one couple from all these reality shows is still together.) Still, I think these shows are wonderful illustrations of how to consciously screen and test potential partners. Moreover, the Bachelor and the Bachelorette featured on these shows typically are clear examples of singles who are ready and available for commitment.

This chapter is about the Fifth Principle of Conscious Dating: "Be ready and available for commitment." While I don't recommend that you go on a reality show to find your life partner, I do encourage you to watch some of these shows as an exercise of self-reflection. As you watch the show, ask yourself, if, when you're dating, are you more like the bachelor/bachelorette, or the contestants? Are you the chooser, or the chosen? Do you date with such empowerment that you can vote off the man/woman who doesn't meet your Requirements? Or are you vying for attention and acceptance? The attitude of the bachelor/bachelorette as The Chooser is one that I would like to see in all singles.

Do you date with such empowerment

that you can vote off the man/woman who doesn't

meet your Requirements? Or, are you vying for

attention and acceptance? The attitude of the

bachelor/bachelorette as The Chooser is one that I

would like to see in all singles.

I also think these reality shows reflect a dating trend. The process of finding a life partner is looking more like buying a house or choosing a job. We are making relationship choices more carefully and thoughtfully, which is much better than the alternative! Another aspect I appreciate about the reality dating shows is that you can see Requirements popping up all the time as the most important reasons for contestants getting voted off as incompatible.

Like the bachelor/bachelorette, most singles don't want to be alone. So we date seeking a committed relationship. Yet many of us confuse wanting a commitment with being ready for one. We all want to be with a partner, but, for a variety of reasons, we might not be ready. And often, we are unaware of our lack of readiness. When our dating strategy doesn't align with our readiness status, we unconsciously set ourselves up for failure. In the end, this complicates our lives and the lives of our dating partners.

Like the bachelor/bachelorette, most

singles don't want to be alone. So, we date seeking

a committed relationship. Yet,

many of us confuse wanting a commitment with

being ready for one.

ARE YOU READY?

Angela, the forty-year-old divorced mom of a teenage son, could not get her mind off Jerry, who had taken her out to dinner last Friday. She wanted to dive headfirst into dating him, but reminded herself that she was committed to keeping all her options open. She was going to date recreationally this time, not commit herself after just one dinner.

At work, Angela was glowing. She must have been sending out some strong "available" vibes because in the office cafeteria, Michael, who worked on another floor, approached her. He asked Angela if he could join her at a table where she was eating the special-of-the-

day by herself. Angela didn't think anything of it. She figured that he was just looking for some familiar company—until he asked her if she would like to go out for dinner with him some night.

She almost said, "Are you kidding me? I've got two dates in one week!"

But she held her breath and kindly responded, "Yes, that would be nice."

So, right there, in the middle of the cafeteria, Michael wrote down his phone number. They planned to meet at Lo Coco, a new French restaurant downtown, on Friday at 7 p.m.

"What do you mean I have to be ready?"

So, how do you know if you're ready for a committed relationship? This is a novel idea for many singles. When singles hear this question, they often respond by protesting, "What do you mean I have to be ready?"

What I mean is, if you were to meet your soul mate today, would you be ready and available to enter into a relationship with him/her? Do a self-study by looking at different areas of your life to judge your relationship readiness. You might start right now with the Relationship Readiness Quiz at the end of this chapter. This will give you a quick look at how ready you are for an intimate relationship. Are you ready to be close to someone, or are you carrying some baggage from your previous relationships? Are you experiencing a lot of fear or anger? Are you legally ready to be in a serious relationship with someone? Is your life in transition with a change in career or a return to school?

If you are ready to find your life partner, I suggest that you return to Chapter 6 to review the skills you learned; Scouting, Sorting,

Screening, and Testing potential partners until you find someone who is highly aligned with what you are seeking. This means staying available and not entering "mini-marriages." Often, we are so focused on the goal of having a relationship that we are blind to those things that might interfere with our readiness. Many of us focus on the relationship we want with someone else rather than honestly looking at ourselves, our life situations, and the relationships we already have in our lives. Often, we are not conscious about whether or not this relationship might be a good long-term choice or, if it is, whether we are setting ourselves up for success or failure by getting involved at this time in our lives. By exploring yourself first—your physical health, mental health, emotional health, work or career situation, lifestyle, finances, family—you will discover how ready you really are for a relationship.

By exploring yourself first—your physical health, mental health, emotional health, work or career situation, lifestyle, finances, family—you will discover how ready you really are for a relationship.

Assessing your readiness means making choices that are aligned with where you are and what you want in your life. Every choice has a consequence, and you need to make choices consciously, using your best judgment of what the consequences might be. I refer to this process as "intentionality." For example, if you choose to have unprotected sex, you also choose the consequences that might follow, whether you chose with conscious intention or not, whether the consequences are desirable for you or not. Also, just because you want something doesn't mean you're ready for it. Is an adolescent ready for sex and possible parenthood? Are you ready to date just after separating from a long-term relationship because you don't want to be alone? Is a lottery winner ready to play the stock market just because he/she has the money in the bank? You get the picture.

Single adults often think they're ready for sex because they want to have sex. You meet someone and really click together; the chemistry is buzzing. You want to sleep together. Does that mean that you're ready? Sex breaks down a lot of boundaries very quickly, and most of us lose our objectivity and clarity about what we really want when physical intimacy comes into the picture. So if you're going to have a conscious relationship with someone, you probably need to get to know him/her better and decide the future potential of the relationship before having sex. I'm not saying that singles should be alone until they're ready for a committed relationship. No way! Who wouldn't want all the benefits of a relationship? That is, regular sex, companionship, security, having somebody there for you. But you need to have some boundaries to set yourself up for long-term success.

Your dating journey is one of the most important journeys you'll take in life. You can approach it randomly and make lots of mistakes. Or, you can do so consciously and navigate those roads as best as possible.

I like to compare finding your life partner to taking a cross-country road trip. There are two ways you can approach this trip: spontaneously jump in the car and go, or map out your journey with a detailed itinerary. If you just jump in the car, it's going to be quite an exciting adventure. You might run out of gas. You might get lost. If you plan out your trip consciously, you're going to have various maps in the glove compartment, reservations at motels along the way, a few credit cards, and, most importantly, a plan. You can have adventures and minimize problems that could spoil your trip. Your dating journey is one of the most important journeys you'll take in life. You can approach it randomly and make lots of mistakes. Or, you can do so consciously and navigate those roads as best as possible.

MEETING THE GROPER

Angela found Michael waiting for her in the restaurant lobby at seven o'clock sharp. He was holding a bouquet of pink and red flowers. She thanked him. She waited for him to say something about how she looked—this red silk dress was a far cry from her usual office attire—but he merely commented on how nice the weather was.

Seated at their table, Michael talked about his work as a computer programmer in Raleigh, a job he had held for the past thirty years since graduating from college.

"At last, here's a man with a job!" Angela thought.

Still, when Michael told her that he'd been working at their company for last three decades, she wondered if he was stuck in a rut. Always wanting to learn something new and branch out, Angela was the kind of woman who liked the challenge of getting promoted or relocating if her present job got too dull.

Michael talked and talked during the entire dinner. He also kept his eyes on his food and rarely looked at her. Angela figured that he was anxious. Still, when it was time for dessert, Michael didn't stop talking. He told Angela that he'd been married once before, but had no children. He told her about fixing his cars and hunting on weekends. When Angela tried to tell Michael about her own son, he actually interrupted her to get the bill! By eight o'clock she was more than ready to go home.

167

After walking Angela to her car, however, Michael leaned over to kiss her on the mouth.

Angela pulled away. Boundaries had always been challenging for her, but it was about time she stood up for herself.

"I'm going home now," she said.

"Oh, c'mon, don't I even get a good-night kiss?"

Michael leaned into her, his hands wrapped around her shoulders.

"Excuse me—" Angela said, gently pushing him away.

She got her keys out. He knew nothing about her—so what right did he have to kiss her? In her mind, he was no longer "Michael." Now, he was "The Groper."

The next morning, Angela got up early and wrote in her journal about her date with Michael. She was proud of herself for dating again, and especially for keeping her physical and emotional boundaries with "The Groper." After an hour with him, it was evident that he was not the kind of man she wanted to date, even short term for fun. Wow, in the past it took her weeks and months to make a decision like this!

* * *

The next morning, Angela's phone rang. It was Jerry, the gorgeous man from the health club who had taken her to dinner last Friday. Jerry said: "There's a new French place downtown, I'd love to take you to—"

Angela couldn't believe that Jerry—just one night after The Groper—wanted to take her to the same restaurant! No, she was not going back there. It would be too strange.

"Jerry," Angela said, "this might sound unbelievable, but I actually ate there last night."

"Wow, I'm impressed," Jerry said. "It only opened two weeks ago."

Angela continued: "One of my favorite restaurants is this little Mexican place around the corner from the post office. The food is delicious and this sweet grandmother-type from Merida runs it."

"I love Mexican food," Jerry said. "That sounds fabulous."

Angela was relieved that Jerry was receptive to her idea. She hung up the phone all jittery. First, she had stood up for herself and chosen the restaurant where she wanted to eat, and second, Jerry had welcomed the change of plans with enthusiasm. Angela wondered if this was a sign that she was going to take more responsibility for her life. In her head, she could hear her friend Gretchen, urging her to "Be The Chooser."

As Angela showered and dressed, her heart beat quickly. Maybe midlife dating wouldn't be the pits after all.

* * *

Now that we've covered relationship readiness, it's time to look at the three forms of dating relationships: recreational, committed, and the mini-marriage. The purpose of recreational dating is to have fun and satisfy your social needs when you don't want, or when you're not ready for, a committed relationship. The purpose of committed dating is to find your life partner. The mini-marriage is a hybrid of these two.

* * *

RECREATIONAL DATING

Most singles who want a relationship think they are ready for one. But after some self-examination, many of us realize that we are not truly ready. By "truly ready," I mean there are no barriers or obstacles in your life that prevent you from proceeding forward into a committed relationship. Again, the Relationship Readiness Quiz at the end of this chapter should give you a clear picture of your level of readiness. If you're not ready, it's more appropriate to stay single and get involved in recreational dating. This is a win! You can be single and still have relationships; you're just handling other business in your life before committing yourself exclusively. Many singles have told me, "If I'm not ready for a relationship, then I don't want to date at all." I tell them: this doesn't mean that you have to be alone. Get out there and have fun while keeping clear boundaries.

On the other hand, other singles have told me, "But if I don't date seriously, how will I find my soul mate?" It is not impossible to find your soul mate by dating, but if you're involved with someone, even if (in your mind) it's not long term, you will be unavailable to meet the one for whom you're really looking. Wouldn't it be a tragedy if your soul mate passed you by because you were casually involved with someone else? It can be challenging to keep your boundaries around a recreational relationship. I recommend that singles keep four guidelines in mind as they date for short-term fun:

1. *Be clear that you are not looking for a committed relationship.* This means saying to your date something like, "I'm working full time and I go to school full time. I don't have a lot of time for a relationship, but I'd like to hang out and have fun with you." It might be hard to say this because you feel like no one will want to go out with you. True, some people might be looking for a more permanent relationship. But if you're not ready for permanence, then it's better not to go out with them.

2. *Do not be exclusive.*
Exclusivity is a form of commitment. It's really hard to put boundaries around a relationship and keep it casual and fun if you are exclusive with one person. People sometimes feel threatened if you are not exclusive with them. They think that you are just a "player," but it's much easier to maintain your availability

for your life partner or to work on your own life and self-development if you are not exclusive with somebody. For recreational dating to work, you must keep the mind-set that you are single.

3. *Set a time limit.*
Set up a time limit so you see the light at the end of tunnel. You might need six months to finish school, or to finalize your divorce, or to find a new job. Know that you are not going to be single forever.

4. *Enjoy being single.*
Simply enjoy the fact that you are single at this time in your life and can do whatever you want, whenever you want. You are not accountable to anyone but yourself. This attitude empowers you, and you'll bring this power—rather than desperation and need—to a long-term relationship when you're ready.

COMMITTED DATING

The journey I describe in this book is a very different one from the kind of dating we see in our current culture. One of the most challenging things about Conscious Dating to find your life partner is simply staying available. But if you're going to find your life partner, you can't be involved with someone who isn't right for you. It's often painful and difficult to say no to another person and walk away. Still, you need to have clarity about what you want in your life and the kind of person who might fit your requirements. Then, you will need to be available when this person comes, and stay single long enough to find him/her!

Committed dating to find your life partner involves staying single and practicing my *Four Steps for Conscious Dating*:

1. **Scouting**: the process of finding potential partners.

2. **Sorting**: the process of quickly determining whether someone meets your most important requirements and has potential.

3. **Screening**: the process of collecting enough information to determine if all your requirements would be met.

4. **Testing**: the process of gaining experience and knowledge that your requirements would be met, *before* getting involved in a "relationship."

When you meet others with intentionality, you do so with clarity about who you are and what you want. You have clear boundaries that keep you from getting involved with people on a random basis just because you are attracted to them and just because they are available. You have committed yourself to attain clarity and stay focused on your goal of finding your life partner. You are not stumbling around in the dark and getting involved with partners who are not good long-term choices for you.

How many of us have made commitments in our life with less than 100 percent of a "yes"? If you commit to take a job and then you decide you don't like it, you can quit, resign, transfer, and just leave it behind you. If you get involved in a committed relationship knowing that 20 percent of it just isn't working, the problems are only going to increase over time. Our high divorce rate indicates that many people in today's world do not take commitment seriously enough. But leaving a relationship after you have made a commitment has high costs. It tends to be an irreversible decision; you can't go back to your life exactly the way it was before, especially when there are kids. So we have to take our relationship choices very seriously.

I believe it's completely possible for you to find a relationship in which all your requirements are met. This doesn't mean that the relationship is going to be trouble-free. All relationships have challenges, but with a good long-term partner choice, the problems are solvable and you have a good foundation to build on.

MINI-MARRIAGE

A mini-marriage is when singles get together and become an instant couple. There is no gradual, conscious process of getting to know each other and determining if this is a good long-term relationship choice. Singles fall into this dating pattern when they don't want to be alone and have not assessed their relationship readiness.

The mini-marriage shows up mainly in the date-to-mate trap, which I discussed in Chapter 3. You assume that "dating" is how you are going to find your life partner, so you date and become an instant couple. You try on this relationship as if you're trying on a new dress or suit. If it doesn't work, then you will just break up. So it becomes a mini-divorce. You see it everywhere: two people are in a hurry to get into relationship start dating each other and "Bang!" they are a couple. They act like a couple. But because they have not done their homework or there are things left hanging, there is excess baggage in the relationship.

A couple in a mini-marriage acts committed. One form of commitment is exclusivity. Say you meet someone for the first time and get very excited about him/her. You meet again, after which you decide not to date anyone else. Other forms of commitment are having sex or moving in together.

Nonexclusive dating means that you consider yourself single and are not accountable to anyone. You know you're a couple when you're planning most or all of your free time with someone and you have expectations of each other to behave as a couple. Often, because you want the benefits of a relationship, you act committed without really being committed or even being ready for commitment.

So we see that, contrary to what many singles might think, there is more than one kind of dating relationship. Your goal as a conscious single is to make relationship choices in alignment with who you are, what you want, and where you are in your life right now. If you are ready for a committed relationship, stay available and Scout, Sort, Screen, and Test to find your life partner. If you are not ready for a committed relationship, date for fun, keep a single mind-set, and assert boundaries to set yourself up for success.

WHAT ARE THE THREE KINDS OF DATING RELATIONSHIPS?

RECREATIONAL DATING	COMMITTED DATING	MINI-MARRIAGE
Readiness status: Not ready for a committed relationship.	**Readiness status:** Ready for a lifelong committed relationship.	**Readiness status:** Readiness is unclear. You might want to test-drive a relationship to see if it is a good long-term choice. Or, this relationship might be "the one night stand who never left."
Purpose: To have fun and satisfy social needs.	**Purpose:** To find your life partner.	**Purpose:** To meet physical, social, and emotional needs prior to a committed relationship, or when commitment is not desired.
Goal: To meet short-term needs while working toward long-term goals beyond the relationship.	**Goal:** To have a long-term, desired future. To find a partner who meets all of your requirements.	**Goal:** To meet short-term needs when you're unclear about the future of the relationship.

Characteristics:

No future expectations.

Open to dating more than one person at a time.

Boundaries must be very clear around involvement, including levels of sex, time, emotional depth, present and future expectations, whether this "friend" will be involved with your children.

Comparable to working for a temp agency in between jobs: enjoying the variety and learning of short-term assignments before deciding your next career move.

This choice is conscious and understood by both parties.

Characteristics:

Presents a paradox: you must remain single to be available to find the partner who is right for you and meets your requirements.

The challenge is to keep attractive potential life partners at an appropriate distance while you are in the process of Scouting, Sorting, Screening, and Testing.

Boundaries gradually decrease as emotional investment increases.

Comparable to interviewing potential employers to find just the right fit of company and job opportunity for your career.

This choice is conscious and clearly communicated to potential partners.

Characteristics:

One or both parties are unsure about the relationship or don't consider it to be a good long-term choice.

One or both parties are not ready for a committed relationship.

One or both parties are driven by need, fear, and unconsciousness.

To most observers, this relationship appears committed.

Comparable to accepting your first job offer just because you really need a job; you avoid the red flags and cross your fingers that it will all work out.

This choice is typically unconscious; both partners are unaware of or do not discuss the above.

GETTING READY FOR WHAT YOU WANT

Most of us dream of meeting our soul mate and living happily ever after, but the reality is that most of us will spend time as single adults. We might want to deny this reality and try to change it as quickly as possible. But if we accept this period in our life as good and necessary, we can use the time to "build it, and he/she will come." In our consumer-oriented culture—in which just about everything is about instant gratification—"readiness" seems to be a foreign concept. There is no shortage of examples illustrating that getting what you want can have undesired consequences: AIDS, STDs, teenage pregnancies, lottery winners who can't handle their money and go broke, or celebrities who can't handle their fame and self-destruct. A successful committed relationship depends on being ready physically, emotionally, financially, legally, and spiritually for the life and relationship you want. ✀

RELATIONSHIP READINESS QUIZ FOR SINGLES

To assess your readiness for a committed relationship, rate yourself in each of the following ten areas. Try to be objective and honest with yourself. We recommend asking close friends and family members for their opinions as well.

Rating Scale: Rate each item on a scale from 0 to 10

8-10: **Good**; this area of my life is strong and would be an asset to my next relationship

5-7: **OK**; this area needs work, but most likely would not sabotage my next relationship

0-4: **Needs Work**; this area could interfere with the success of my next relationship

---

1. I know what I want

I have a clear vision for my life and relationship. I can envision my perfect life in rich detail that feels strong and very real and keeps me motivated.

Self-Rating

_____

2. I know my requirements

Self-Rating

I have a written list of at least ten nonnegotiable requirements that I use for screening potential partners. I am clear that if any are missing, a relationship will not work for me.

_____

3. I am happy and successful being single

I enjoy my life, my work, my family, my friends, and my own company. I am living the life that I want, and I am not seeking a relationship out of desperation and need.

_____

4. I am ready and available for commitment

I have no emotional or legal baggage from a previous relationship. My schedule, commitments, and lifestyle allow my availability to build a new relationship.

_____

5. I am satisfied with my work/career

My work is fulfilling, supports my lifestyle, and does not interfere with my availability for a new relationship.

_____

6. I am healthy in mind, body, and spirit

My physical, mental, or emotional health does not interfere with having the life and relationship that I want. I am reasonably happy and feel good.

_____

7. My financial and legal business is handled

I have no financial or legal issues that would interfere with having the life and relationship that I want.

_____

8. My family relationships are functional

My relationships with my children, ex, siblings, parents, and extended family do not interfere with having the life and relationship that I want.

_____

177

9. I have effective dating skills

I initiate contact with people I want to meet, and disengage from people who are not a match for me. I keep my physical and emotional boundaries, and balance my heart with my head with potential partners.

10. I have effective relationship skills

I understand relationships, can maintain closeness and intimacy, communicate authentically and assertively, negotiate differences positively, allow myself to trust and be vulnerable, and can give and receive love without emotional barriers.

Self-Rating

—————————

—————————

SCORE RESULTS:

80-100: **Green Light** You are well on your way to the life and relationship you really want.

50-79: **Yellow Light** Continue to work on the areas needed and take it slow in relationships while doing so.

0-49: **Red Light** Take a break from seeking a partner, focus on your life and prepare for the relationship you really want.

—————————

Total Score

CONSCIOUS DATING PLAN EXERCISE NO. 9:

Please refer to Chapter 15 to write your answers.

How ready are you?

Now that you have taken the Relationship Readiness Quiz, it's time to write down your results.

1. What is your total score?

2. Did you get a Green Light? A Yellow Light? Or a Red Light?

3. So, what form of dating are you ready for?

If you got a Green Light, this means you're ready to find your life partner. If you got a Yellow or Red Light, this means you should consider short-term recreational dating for now.

Have you ever been in transition—divorce, career change, relocation—and noticed that many people around you are in a similar place? Have you ever observed that when you're feeling particularly negative about life, you seem to attract more negativity? This is the Law of Attraction, and in this chapter you will learn how to use it to attract the partner you want.

Are you single and over thirty? Although we live in a progressive culture, many of us still feel stigmatized if we are not partnered with someone. You might wonder if something's wrong with you. Shouldn't I be in a committed relationship? How can I feel comfortable being single when my friends and family are always asking me if I'm dating anyone? How can I embrace my singlehood when I don't really want to be single? In this chapter, I will show you how the Law of Attraction can help you plant the seeds for the future you want. While you're single you can live the life you want, which will maximize your likelihood of having the kind of relationship you want.

PLANTING YOUR FIELD OF DREAMS
In the 1989 film *Field of Dreams*, Iowa corn farmer Ray Kinsella has spent his whole life searching for his dreams. He feels stranded, having become a farmer only because it allowed him to break away from his father's expectations. While out in the cornfields one day, Ray hears a voice: "If you build it, he will come." Ray interprets this to mean that he should build a baseball diamond on his field, and

he does just that. Indeed, after half a year of working very hard, guess who shows up? It's Shoeless Joe Jackson, who was dismissed from the game of baseball forever during the 1919 Black Sox scandal. Ray's life is forever changed.

When working with singles, I turn the *Field of Dreams* message around to reflect on your life and your life partner. I tell singles, "If you build it, he/she will come." This means that when you develop yourself and live the life you want, you will attract the partner you want.

The Law of Attraction for Singles:

When you develop yourself and

live the life you want,

you will attract the partner you want.

ONE YEAR AND ONE HALF INCH

My own love story—how I met Maggie—illustrates how the Law of Attraction worked for me. As you might recall from the Introduction, before I met Maggie I'd been married and divorced two times. I'd married my first wife when I was a young and unconscious twenty-one-year-old, and I'd married for the second time after ignoring the red flags of a passionate push-and-pull relationship. Still, three children and two divorces later, I was not about to give up finding my life partner.

For years, I worked hard on myself and my career, and was inspired to help singles prepare for relationships in which they set themselves up for success. When I posted my profile on Match.com, I felt a bit awkward since I was a relationship guru for singles in my area. My headline was, "Romantic Single Dad" and my user name was "3DMan," meaning I was three-dimensional in my life as a family man and a businessman and was relationship-oriented. I described myself as a single father who liked to sail, hike, run, and bike. Over the next six months, I went out with a number of women I'd met online but could not imagine myself being in a relationship with any of them.

When I posted my profile on Match.com,

I felt a bit awkward since I was a local relationship

"guru" for singles in my area.

Eventually, I became very frustrated with online dating. But rather than give up, I changed my profile to be very specific—"demanding" might be a better description—even if it meant getting no responses. For one, I wanted to meet a woman who was a helping professional like me. She needed to share my life mission of helping to make the world a better place; love kids; and be oriented toward relationship, family, and community. I wanted to be with someone who was physically active and enjoyed nature adventures; was spiritual but not religious; spoke her truth with high integrity; was responsible; was addiction-free; tolerated and appreciated differences; communicated well; owned her projections; and was ready and available for a committed relationship. I put it all out there and was not going to settle for less! After three months, however, I had no responses. I'd scared them all away! I surrendered and let go of my attachment to finding my life partner and decided that I would focus on my own life, my friends, my family, and my work. In short, I would spend my time and energy building my Field of Dreams.

I let go of my attachment to finding my life partner

and decided that I would focus on my own life,

friends, family, and work.

I had been leading weekly singles groups, and one night a divorced mother of two showed up. Her name was Maggie and she'd read a letter to the editor I had written for the local paper in response to an article about the scarcity of single men relative to single women in Silicon Valley. This was her first time at a singles event since her divorce. However, she did not catch my eye that night because I was focused on leading the group, and because I thought it would be unprofessional of me to date women who were participants of my programs, even if they weren't my "clients." In the meantime, I hired Marvin Cohen, a local graduate student and executive coach, to help me lead singles events. Maggie signed up for the Conscious Dating Relationship Success Training for Singles (RESTS) course with him. (Years later, I'm still teasing Marvin: "You knew Maggie, and you never told me about her!")

I put it all out there and

was not going to settle for less!

After the eight-week course, Maggie decided that she was ready to attract a life partner for herself, so she placed her profile on Match.com. She described herself as a warm-hearted woman, spiritual seeker, single mother, social worker, and amateur musician looking for a life partner. Like me, Maggie was very specific about what was essential to her: giving and receiving love; her family and community; her work in the world; music; and the natural world. Like me, Maggie got very little response to her profile.

Then, one evening, there was an e-mail from Maggie in my inbox. It turned out that although she had been on Match.com all this time too, our search criteria had missed each other. She had specified men who were her age or older (I was a year younger) and I had specified women who were at least five foot two (she is five foot, one and one-half inches). So our profiles had never matched up! Out of frustration due to low response to her ad, Maggie had changed her criteria and widened her search. When she lowered her age bracket by a couple of years, she discovered me. When talking to singles at workshops, this is why I refer to my journey as "One Year and One Half Inch."

Today, looking back, I think that I left "bread crumbs" for Maggie as I focused on creating my life the way I wanted it to be. All these events—the letter to the editor I wrote, the weekly singles events, and the RESTS class—connected me to Maggie and eventually led us together. Honestly, I was in a place of despair when she found me—feeling that I would never find all that I needed and required in a relationship—but with the help of the Law of Attraction, she pursued and found me!

I left "bread crumbs" for Maggie

as I focused on creating my life the

way I wanted it to be.

IT'S NEVER TOO LATE TO DATE

As I pointed out in Chapter 4, being single is an opportunity to seize and not a disease to cure. Many singles feel that their life is on hold until they get into a relationship. But rushing from one relationship into the next is not the solution, nor is living in fear that you'll be single for the rest of your life. It's necessary to take a break and allow yourself to be single to prepare for your next relationship. No, you don't have to live like a hermit. But you can focus on yourself before resuming your search to find a partner. In previous chapters, you focused on your Requirements, Wants, and Needs. You learned how to Scout, Sort, Screen, and Test. Now it's time to see how the Law of Attraction can help you.

* * *

It seemed like one of the craziest things Dorothy had ever done in her life. The weekend after she had dropped by the video dat-

ing office, Dorothy sat down and called all six of her potential matches. Each time she reached a man's voice mail she took a deep breath, trying her best to listen to his greeting, and then said in her most friendly, outgoing voice, "Hi! This is Dorothy! I got your number from—"

The only reason she'd had the courage to call these men was that she'd assured herself this was not about making a lifetime commitment with someone on the phone. Yes, she wanted to find her life partner, but she didn't want to rush into anything. Rather, she was simply giving recreational dating a try. This meant she was going to have fun and be open to dating more than one man at a time. She felt confident that she could maintain her boundaries around intimacy, emotional vulnerability, and future expectations.

One hour later, the banker on her list called her back. She was thrilled, until he kindly told her: "I'm sorry, but I've recently started to date someone seriously and was just about to inform the video dating service. I wish you the best in the future."

Although it was initially disappointing, Dorothy reminded herself that she had five other potential matches.

Dorothy was tempted to wait around all of Sunday to see which men would call her back. But she reminded herself that this wasn't about waiting around for a man. This was about taking part in her own recreational dating "boot camp" so she could move forward with her goal of eventually finding her life partner. She walked to her local bookstore and browsed the self-help section. One book, Excuse Me, Your Life Is Waiting: The Astonishing Power of Feelings by Lynn Grabhorn, focused on the Law of Attraction, which says that "like attracts like."

This was the path Dorothy was taking now: building the life she wanted to attract the partner she wanted. It was a sharp contrast from the last time she was in a relationship some years ago. She had met Sam during a business trip to New York City. After a three-month long-distance relationship in which they had visited each other a few times, he had offered to move down South to live with her. At the time, it had felt like a dream come true. But within a few weeks, their differences had become evident.

This was the path Dorothy was taking now: building the life she wanted in order to attract the partner she wanted. It was a sharp contrast from the last time she was in a relationship some years ago.

Sam was a fifty-five-year-old Jewish man born and raised in the Bronx, never married, and an intense businessman. Dorothy, a Presbyterian, had been born and raised in the South, and she was the divorced mother of two sons. Looking back, she realized that both she and Sam had been desperate to get hooked up before it was too late. But after four months, they had decided to go their separate ways. Still, that was five years ago, and Dorothy had done a lot of personal and emotional growing since then.

During this time, Dorothy had taken numerous workshops with a relationship coach in Houston in which she had learned the basic singles skills of Scouting, Sorting, Screening and Testing. Although Dorothy had done a lot of soul-searching, she hadn't yet put herself out there to meet anyone. Singles bars turned her off. Speed dating was not her thing. Bravely, she had signed up for this video service.

Sure enough, by the end of the weekend, all five men had returned Dorothy's phone calls. All were in their fifties and from the Houston area. They were all very nice on the phone. Still, she was able to sort out three of the five within a few minutes of talking with them. One was a divorced pharmacist with two grown sons who made her uncomfortable by disparaging his ex-wife. Another was a computer consultant who had never married and didn't seem to have a life or interests outside of his work. The third man was a chef at a gourmet restaurant who seemed to have no free time on the weekends. The remaining two men Dorothy felt excited about—a therapist and a business owner. Both, it seemed, had done some self-discovery work on themselves.

From six down to two. Now, Dorothy had some fun and exciting work ahead of her!

* * *

Lynn Grabhorn, author of *Excuse Me, Your Life is Waiting*, has a wonderful way of presenting the Law of Attraction, describing it as a realm of feelings that many physicians, scientists, physicists, and theologians believe is very real. Grabhorn isn't the first to write at length about the Law of Attraction. She puts it this way: if you apply emotional energy to anything, you draw it to you. If you worry about something (getting sick, getting fired), you're more likely to cause it to happen. And if you passionately visualize the job you'd like to have, the mate you'd like to marry ... well, watch what happens. I like to steer singles to this book to help them turn their unconscious feelings into conscious ones and attract the right life partner. Her book, perhaps controversial to some, illustrates how to turn your life around in any facet, whether it's failing health, empty bank accounts, or unfulfilling lives.

Grabhorn says that if we want to turn our lives around, we simply need to "manipulate" our feelings. She explains it this way:

The Law of Attraction—like attracts like—is absolute... No one lives beyond this law, for it is the law of the universe. It's just that we never realized until recently that this law applies to us too. This is the law behind success or failure. It's what causes fender-benders or fatalities. It is, to the point, what runs every waking moment of our lives.[1]

LIKE ATTRACTS LIKE

What, exactly, does "like attracts like" mean? I interpret it as: what's on the inside shows up on the outside. Let's say that you're in the middle of a divorce, but you're eager to find someone because your nights are so lonely. Most likely, you're going to attract others who are in transition too. Or, if you're in between careers or homes, and feeling crazy about all these changes, you will probably find someone who will reflect where you are in your life. If you are aware of the Law of Attraction, it can help you to make conscious choices toward your goal of having a successful life partnership.

Grabhorn writes:

> Relationships ... like everything else in our world are about how we are vibrating. And how we are vibrating is coming from how we are feeling... It's not going to take a genius to figure out that if we're feeling anything other than at peace with ourselves... our vibrations are going to be slicing away at that relationship, no matter how much we're convinced that since there's nothing wrong with us, it must be the other guy's fault.[2]

Grabhorn gives some clear examples about how we are the sole creators of our experiences, "not our partner, not our parents, not even the boss who just fired us:"

> If we are verbally or mentally accusing, berating, or disapproving in any way, we are attracting negatively.

> If we are feeling trapped, ignored or neglected, unsafe, misunderstood, or shortchanged, we are attracting negatively.

> If we race into please, rescue, or placate, we are attracting negatively.[3]

* * *

As you see, the Law of Attraction can work for you or against you. You might recall the Attraction Trap from Chapter 3, when I quoted H. Jackson Brown from *Life's Little Instruction Book*: "Choose your life's mate carefully. From this one decision will come 90 percent of your happiness or misery." If we choose consciously, we can get what we want. If we choose unconsciously, we are going to be choosing a certain amount of misery and possible relationship failure. If you are unconscious, certainly the Law of Attraction will work against you.

The Law of Attraction

can work for you or against you.

LOOKING FOR THE PERFECT PACKAGE

In Chapter 8, you read about Mark, the thirty-five-year-old businessman and recently divorced father of two daughters. Mark was pursuing Stacy, a twenty-year-old stunning blue-eyed blonde. Mark invited Stacy to move in with him, against his daughters' wishes. Mark felt that he'd found his dream woman, and his adrenaline soared in this sexy and passionate affair.

In the meantime, Mark's company was doing very well and he splurged on a weekend place on the coast. Stacy loved lounging there every Sunday and drinking wine by the fireplace. Soon after, Stacy convinced Mark to buy a red Porsche. Mark worked overtime during the week to cover his increasing expenses. Their first summer together, the two of them went to Hawaii for a couple of weeks.

Within a few months, the recession of the early '90s hit and money was suddenly tight. Stacy had gotten used to a luxurious lifestyle with Mark—and budgeting was not part of the deal. She sulked and started to stay out late, supposedly with her girl-friends. Mark now found himself cutting grocery store coupons on the weekend, but he still lusted after Stacy, who was giving him the cold shoulder. In his funk, Mark was forced to look at how empty he felt on the inside. Had he attracted a woman who mirrored what was going on inside him?

In his funk, Mark was forced to look at how empty he felt on the inside. Had he attracted a woman who mirrored what was going on inside him?

Unfortunately, Mark got caught in the Packaging Trap, which you recall from Chapter 3. He objectified his girlfriend by focusing on her packaging, without realizing that he too was being objectified—for his job, money, and car. Afraid to look deeply inside himself, Mark focused primarily on the exterior: making a lot of money, buying a sporty car. Post-divorce, it was natural for him to look for a "packaged" woman. Many of us understand the value of relationships before seeking new ones. Regrettably, Mark was unable to look on the inside—within himself or his girl-friend. Bartholomew spells out "like attracts like"—a situation like Mark's—recently in *Excuse Me, Your Life Is Waiting*:

The law for creating anything is really quite simple. Take good or bad thoughts (meaning positive or negative vibrations), bake with varying degrees of emotion to increase magnetism, and here comes what we've attracted, like it or not. What we have focused on, and how we have vibrated about it, is what we have gotten ... from birth.[4]

Recently I was coaching a fifty-five-year-old single man who was frustrated by his pattern of short-term relationships with women. He and I had an ongoing debate about his weight requirement—no more than five pounds overweight. (I could never figure out how he would measure that!) Body shape was his first and primary sorting tool, as he pursued women with fit and slender bodies—who were usually not attracted to him—and immediately rejected women who were not slender. Still single and nearing retirement age, he was desperate to find a partner. I liked him a lot and wanted to see him happy in a relationship. Our conversations began to focus more specifically on the Law of Attraction, and how his weight "requirement" might be interfering with his success. I reminded him that the Law of Attraction can work for you or against you, and that "like attracts like." If he let go of focusing on weight, he might be opening the door for his soul mate—a wonderful woman who would be attracted to him to whom he too would be attracted.

BE CAREFUL WHAT YOU WISH FOR

I'm not a religious guy, but I believe there are higher forces in the universe that we don't have power over. I think that we can all understand the Law of Attraction, but don't have power over it. It's like gravity: the Law of Attraction is a law of the universe. So, where you put your attention has consequences. The universe will respond to it, and other people will respond to it. In short, your energy follows your attention.

Another way to think about this is: be careful what you wish for. In my own life, I've thought about being a dad since I was a little boy. I was eager to get married and have children, and I was certain that I'd be the kind of parent I did not have as a kid. Moreover, I'd always fantasized about having twins. I don't know where this idea came from, but early on I imagined raising twins. My daughter, who is now seventeen, was born in my first marriage. My ex-wife and I tried to have more children, but she had two miscarriages. Then I got divorced and later remarried. One of the reasons my second wife and I were so drawn to each other was that we both wanted to have another child. She already had two children, but her ex-husband had not wanted more kids. As you can see, the Law of Attraction was working here. We were both on a mission, with like attracting like.

However, by the time my second wife and I got married, she was forty-three years old. We tried conceiving naturally but were unsuccessful. So, we started fertility treatments, leading to IVF (in vitro fertilization), in which the frequency of multiples is very high. Well, we ended up with twins! When my boys were born, I recalled my childhood fantasy and realized that the universe was giving me what I'd wished for.

GETTING WHAT YOU DESERVE

This last aspect of the Law of Attraction is the most controversial one. I've always been fascinated by this challenging statement that I heard attributed to motivational speaker Jim Rohn: "Life doesn't give you what you need; it gives you what you deserve." When I've shared it with others, I'm often taken aback by their protests, such as, "Nobody deserves cancer," "I didn't deserve to lose my job," and "My sister didn't deserve to be widowed with three young kids!" True, events happen in our lives that are out of our control and we feel like we didn't deserve them. But if you are conscious and paying close attention, what might seem random is actually a result of our choices.

While I would not have agreed at the time, I take responsibility for being divorced twice. Being the child of divorce, and valuing life partnerships as highly as I do, it was painful to acknowledge my responsibility in being divorced. The first time I married, I was young, unconscious, and in a hurry. I wanted to grow up fast and achieve my dreams. The second time I got married, I thought that I was older and wiser. But I ignored the red flags in that relationship and then blamed our problems on addiction. Then I realized that I could not be happy or successful if I was a helpless victim of circumstance. It was hard to take responsibility, but when I finally looked deeply into how I caused my divorces, I learned how to have a lasting relationship.

I know that terrible random bad things happen to good people; however, "getting what you deserve" means to me:

- Ignorance or unconsciousness is not an excuse. I am responsible for my choices and their outcomes, whether they are conscious or unconscious, intentional or unintentional.

- Success and happiness are not entitlements. Life doesn't work the way I want, need, or expect it to.

- I don't know what I don't know.

- Therefore, I must take nothing for granted, and put effort into becoming more conscious and continuing to learn and grow.

I've had lots of wake-up calls in my life to show me that I got what I deserved, such as when I crashed my 26 foot sailboat into the rocks of Alcatraz. (I always seem to learn the hard way!) I'd spent months taking sailing lessons and practicing every weekend. I'd studied the tides of the San Francisco Bay and mapped out the best route and times to sail. I planned exactly what time to leave the Marina to catch a very powerful ebb tide that would sweep me out the Golden Gate. I thought I had everything worked out.

I planned my departure for nighttime to catch an unusually strong four-knot ebb tide that would sweep me from the South Bay out the Golden Gate. It was the most exhilarating sailing experience of my life. When I reached San Francisco, I turned the tiller and my bow was dead on the Golden Gate Bridge. Normally it takes eight hours to sail from the South Bay to San Francisco, but I did it in four. My sails were filled with wind and although I knew that Alcatraz was on my right, I didn't worry about it. I had everything worked out, right?

What didn't occur to me, though, was that currents and tides don't go in a straight line like streets on a road map. It's not like the currents in the Bay will go north toward San Francisco, and then hang a left to the Golden Gate like a road. I was ten feet away from rocks of

Alcatraz when I realized that I was caught in a current stronger than the wind in my sails. I tried to start the motor, but it was too late.

Did I want to crash into the rocks of Alcatraz? Absolutely not! I'm an intelligent guy, and I'd planned out every detail. Did I deserve to crash? Now that I know what I know, I *did* deserve to crash. I could blame it on the current. But I was inexperienced and did not realize that currents to do not follow a straight line like a road. I had to take full responsibility for my decisions, whether I wanted to or not. The most important lesson for me in this situation was: I finally understood that I needed to give up my ego-driven illusion of competence and control.

I'm not saying that anyone deserves to get cancer, lose a job, be a victim of a felony, or get into a car accident. I believe that the important principle here is that as adults, our life is largely self-determined, and we must take responsibility for our choices and outcomes. Many events are out of our control. But when it comes to choices that we make in our lives, the Law of Attraction plays a big role. When it comes to our choices, we often get what we deserve—not what we need, want, or expect.

Our life is largely self-determined, and

we must take responsibility

for our choices and outcomes.

I think that every choice has long-term consequences, like lining up dominoes and then tipping the first one so they all fall. We can go out and have casual recreational sex without thinking about the long-term consequences. But what if the condom breaks? What if that one-night stand turns into a stalker? Tipping the first domino results in the last domino falling, whether you are aware of it or not. One of the biggest problems in our culture is our resistance to taking full responsibility. Therefore, it's also one of the biggest problems in our relationships. ✄

CONSCIOUS DATING PLAN EXERCISE NO. 10:
Please refer to Chapter 15 to write your answers.

What will you build so that he/she will come?

1. Construct a personal ad

I want you to construct a personal ad, just as I did when I met Maggie. You don't have to run the ad or place it online, but it's important that you write a very specific personal ad. Instead of trying to market yourself, try to be demanding!

2. Network with your friends, family and people in your life

Choose five people in your life who are closest to the life partner you seek. They might be young or old, or people you're only remotely acquainted with. Who are these people? How do they resemble your ideal life partner? Who do they know that would be good for you to meet?

3. Make a list of your "Shoulds"

Sit down and make a list of ten things that you know you "should" do. What are they? Narrow this down to your top three most important goals.

4. Now make a list of what might be interfering with these goals.

Write them out in terms of consequences, like this:

If I continue to _____, the Law of Attraction will _____

For example:

If I continue to overeat and gain more weight, the Law of Attraction will bring me a partner who also lacks impulse control.

If I continue to watch too much TV, the Law of Attraction will bring me nobody/a coach potato.

5. Now turn the above into positive statements, like this:

If I _____, the Law of Attraction will _____

For example:

If I stop overeating and lose twenty pounds, the Law of Attraction will bring me a partner who is healthy and attractive.

SEVENTH PRINCIPLE OF CONSCIOUS DATING:
Gain Relationship Knowledge & Skills

In Chapter 6, you gained the necessary attitudes and skills to find a relationship. Now we will focus on what is needed to keep a relationship. You will also gain more relationship know-how so that you can improve your success in all your relationships.

I JUST WANT TO BE HAPPY!

We all want to be happy, but we don't seem to know how. We are often isolated—we're alone at home watching television or perched in front of our computers—rather than making new friends or working on our present relationships. In our consumer-oriented, immediate-gratification society, we often expect everything to come to us with ease. Our deep friendships and family ties will just happen, our loving bonds with our children are effortless. That's how the media present it, anyway. We seem to feel entitled to be able to buy and get what we want with little effort on our part. We have been conditioned that happiness comes from the outside: by having enough money, the car we want, the job we want, the partner we want. Then, when we get what we want, we find that we aren't happy! But because of this externalized, entitlement mind-set, our relationships are not working.

The truth is that if our current relationships are not working right now, this is a daunting forecast for how our future relationships will turn out. I can't stress enough how important it is to work on your current relationships—with friends, family, co-workers and acquaintances—so that you can set yourself up for success when you meet the love of your life. Sometimes we believe that the road to happiness is to find the right partner who will bring what we want into our lives. Nothing could be further from the truth.

Look around and take an assessment of your present relationships. What are your relationships telling you about yourself? At this point in your life, do your relationships bring you happiness? If you're not happy, it's time to stop blaming others. How do you get along with your parents? Your children? Your friends? Your coworkers? These relationships are the true mirrors into your well-being. If you can learn from your existing relationships while you're single, you will set yourself up for success when you find your life partner.

Look around and take an assessment

of your present relationships.

What are your relationships

telling you about yourself? If you're not happy,

it's time to stop blaming others.

SECRETS OF HAPPINESS

I'd like to share with you my own Ten Dirty Secrets of Happiness. They're not really secrets; feel free to pass them on! I refer to them as "dirty" because many of us (consciously or unconsciously) want to believe the promises of television commercials and don't want to look at the reality. These "secrets" are contrary to the messages found in the entertainment media.

1. If you want a partner, be a partner
Many of us have a wonderful and romantic vision of the life partnership we want. But the reality is that great relationships require a

lot of self-work and effort. If you feel like you are putting more effort into a close relationship than your partner, friend, or family member, you're probably doing it right. The good news is that you can live your Vision; the challenge is that the effort must come from *you*.

2. Your journey is your destination

We tend to focus on goals and results, which works well in many areas of our life, but not so well in our relationships. Chances are you will always be striving toward the relationship you really want and will never "arrive." We need to be present in the moment because this life is all we really have. Similarly, our journey with the people in our lives is all we really have. Are you present with your friends? Are you present with your family members? Learning to be present with yourself—and those close to you—so that you can appreciate the journey is the path to happiness.

3. Your journey is always longer and harder than you expected

We are an impatient culture and most of us want immediate results. We look around and other people seem to get what they want so easily, and we wonder why it has to be so hard for us. When you're in a bind with a friend or family member, do you hang in there for the journey, even when the going gets tough? Truly accepting this principle is a necessary step toward happiness in your present relationships. And this will lead to happiness in your future.

4. Have goals while letting go of your outcomes

While having goals and wanting results is natural, letting go of outcomes seems to be a necessary ingredient to happiness. This means being able to "go with the flow," be flexible and creative, and view mistakes and failures as necessary learning opportunities. Notice what happens when you find yourself in a conflict with someone close to you. Do you view this as an opportunity? Or, do you find yourself wanting to run far away? Notice what your response mirrors about your relationships. Success and happiness comes from a yin/yang balance of ambition and acceptance, assertion and tolerance, firmness and flexibility, choice and fate, having goals and letting go of outcomes.

5. Grow up and take responsibility

I highly recommend a book on this subject—Dr. Frank Pittman's *Grow Up! How Taking Responsibility Can Make You a Happy Adult.* It does an excellent job of explaining how we have become a society of victims, narcissists, and adolescents, and what to do about it. He writes: "...Happy grown-ups take responsibility. They take responsibility for their bodies, their characters, and their relationships. They own their lives and they own up to the choices they make. Finding the responsible thing to do is the lifelong quest for grown-ups. And it leads to real, grown-up happiness..."[1]

Notice how often you take responsibility when your present relationships aren't going as you'd like them to. What does this show you about how you might handle conflicts when you are with your life partner?

6. To be happy you must grow; to grow you must stretch

Our human nature is to have an inner conflict between comfort and challenge, between growth and inertia. Balancing these opposing forces within us is an ongoing effort. When we lean too far toward comfort, we risk stagnation, complacency, inertia. Too much challenge can lead to stress and burnout. Our culture overvalues comfort and undervalues effort. Are you willing to stretch yourself beyond your comfort level, even when it's scary?

7. To get it, you have to give it away

This is a paradox that challenges the "Me" generation. We are much more motivated to "get" than to "give," which wreaks serious havoc in our relationships. When we focus on giving and let go of keeping score, we have a chance of finding happiness in our life and relationships. If you can practice this now, you will set yourself up for a very happy and fulfilling life partnership.

8. What goes around comes around

There is a consequence for your every choice and action. Of course we want our choices to be successful and get us what we want, and we resist acknowledging the possibility of undesired outcomes.

While this may seem simple and obvious, look around you to see just how much we are suffering: the spread of AIDS, multiple divorces, children without homes. These situations happen when people go after what they want and ignore consequences. In your present relationships, do you take responsibility for your actions? Do you pay attention to the consequences?

THE 10 DIRTY SECRETS OF HAPPINESS

> **1. If you want a partner, be a partner**
>
> **2. The journey is the destination**
>
> **3. The journey is always longer and harder than expected**
>
> **4. Have goals while letting go of outcomes**
>
> **5. Grow up and take responsibility**
>
> **6. To be happy we must grow; to grow we must stretch**
>
> **7. To get it, you have to give it away**
>
> **8. What goes around comes around**
>
> **9. The truth will set you free**
>
> **10. Our relationships are our mirrors**

---

9. The truth will set you free
Most of us struggle with a dissonance between what we want and what we have, the way things "should" be with the way things are, what we want to believe and the reality. When we can let go of our fears and ego enough to accept the truth about ourselves, life, and relationships, we open the door to the possibility of happiness. What is the reality about your present relationships? Have you let selected friends get very close to you, or do you shun intimacy?

10. Our relationships are our mirrors
The most honest and genuine definition of intimacy is: "Into me I see." This can be quite challenging and uncomfortable, as we will

experience the parts of ourselves that we don't like—what I refer to as our "shadows"—as well as what we want to see. Happiness in a relationship means learning to use the relationship to learn and grow, which means taking full responsibility and even embracing our shadows when they are reflected back to us. How do you see into "You" right now? What are your relationships showing you about yourself?

YOU DON'T KNOW WHAT YOU DON'T KNOW

You'll notice that many of the Ten Dirty Secrets of Happiness are attitudes or beliefs. Attitudes are internal beliefs that create your reality; the way you see things and your internal state of "being." Attitudes are influenced by your personality and experiences, and can be positive and productive, or negative and unproductive. You can consciously choose the ones that serve you and let go of the ones that sabotage you. For example, you can criticize a friend for being immature, or you can see that this relationship is actually a mirror of yourself. You can continue to hold others responsible for the misfortunes in your life, or grow up and take responsibility. This is in no way a comprehensive list about how to be happy, but it's a way of showing that our mind-set about life greatly affects our intimate relationships.

Our mind-set about life greatly

affects our intimate relationships.

Growing up, we learn certain knowledge and skills from our parents, caregivers, and siblings. By the time we're adults, the outside world—teachers, friends, movies, television, books, and our own experiences—has added immeasurably to our knowledge and skills. Yet many of us still struggle to learn what we need to find happiness and fulfillment in the most important area of our lives—our relationships. I believe that the key to successful relationships lies in what you don't know, because this is where there are gaps in your knowledge and skills. But I always tell singles: "You don't know what you don't know."

How can you gain these relationship skills? It all starts with being conscious of your blind spots in your present relationships. What are your attitudes and beliefs in your close relationships right now? When you fail to learn from your past, you're doomed to repeat it. Being open to learning right now is a good place to figure out what you need to know so you'll be ready when you meet your life partner.

When you fail to learn from your past, you're doomed to repeat it.

I have young twin boys who are continually showing me how our attitudes affect our outcomes in life. The other night we had sweet potatoes for dinner, a side dish that we have not had for a long time. When I put their plates in front of them, the boys protested immediately, "That's yucky!" Upon seeing something new and strange, their attitude was that it must taste awful. This belief is not based upon experience or facts. (They apparently didn't recall that we had some for Thanksgiving!)

I told them, as I always do, "Why don't you try it?"

Both boys tried the sweet potatoes. One twin, quickly letting go of his negative attitude, responded: "It's good!"

But the other twin, refusing to let go, began to gag. "I'm going to throw up!" he cried dramatically. I pointed out to him that he was making himself throw up, but he refused to let go of his belief about sweet potatoes being "yucky."

As you might recall, I have a teenage daughter, and she too shows me the importance of certain attitudes. One of our ongoing struggles is that whenever I try to tell her anything, I hear three words in response: "I KNOW, DAD!" She's learning about the world and about herself right now, and she feels like a young adult. But I stress to her how important it is to have an open mind to learning more. Notice the difference between "I already know all this!" and "I'd like to learn how to do this." If you can have an open mind, be a conscious student, and practice the skills spelled out here, you will learn the relationship skills to be successful in your life partnership.

LEARN THESE TOP 10 RELATIONSHIP ATTITUDES!

Relationships are complex and require a variety of skills. If you're not competent in these skills in your present relationships, then your life partnership isn't going to work. It took me decades to really get all this. Our current relationships are a true reflection of our future relationships, so if you focus on the present, you'll set yourself up for success when you meet the love of your life. Just remember that you can choose your attitudes—and that skills are learnable!

Our current relationships are a true reflection of our future relationships.

HERE ARE MY "TOP 10 RELATIONSHIP ATTITUDES:"

1. Have goals while letting go of attachment to outcomes

Happiness comes from accepting what is and letting go of outcomes. Go ahead and have goals, but watch how unhappy you are when you get too attached to them. Acceptance is a necessary relationship attitude. Hold your intentions and know that the outcomes will be exactly as they should be. Contentment comes from truly accepting what is. Notice if you hold onto certain attachments right now in your present relationships.

2. Strive to live and "be" in the present

"Being in the present" presumes an understanding that relationships only occur in the present. This means that true connection happens only in the present; life and experience happen only in the present. There are only three waking states of mind: the past, present, and future. If you are conscious, you'll notice which state you're in.

Notice when you are truly in the present, you feel relaxed and calm. Moreover, being present means that you are not judging what is happening at that moment. Say that one of your close friends is acting distant: does this trigger you to react? If so, you are judging the present moment by unconsciously comparing this situation to past hurts or future expectations. You might feel anxious, angry, or afraid—and being aware of those feelings will prepare you for your future relationship with a partner. If you want to be happy in life, live in the present!

3. Love, accept, and trust yourself

This is a radical attitude for most of us, since it presumes that you understand the Law of Attraction (Chapter 10), which says that what you resist will persist. Let's say that you get into an argument with a close friend and go home feeling very angry. You can hold onto that rage, or you can shift your attitude and think, "What can I learn from this? Here's somebody I care about, and somebody who cares about me. How can we resolve this and reconnect?" If you love, accept, and trust yourself, every interaction becomes a learning opportunity.

This also means that you understand that people are different. I love Mr. Rogers' quote, "You're special just for being you." Differences can be threatening if you're insecure. Sometimes we handle our discomfort with differences by wanting others to be like us, or wanting to be like everyone else. Mr. Rogers knew that kids resist feeling special because they fear that something might be wrong with them if they're different. Accept others for who they are, and appreciate yourself for who you are. This will be a true asset when you meet your life partner.

4. Focus on connection, not results; a partner is someone to love, not an object or goal

This presumes an understanding that you want to create a life and relationship that fits your Vision. This is not about winning a prize or achieving a goal. It's about connecting to another human being, and a fulfilling relationship comes from deep connection. Remember the Packaging Trap (Chapter 3), in which you focus on outside packaging—such as someone's body, looks, job, wealth, material possessions—and overlook the reality of the person inside. When we are unconscious, we either focus on ourselves—me, me, me—or our partner, you, you, you. But the true magic is in the connection of both people. Take note of your connection with the people in your life right now, such as friends and family.

5. Strive to be authentic; be fully honest with yourself and others, aligning your words, values, and actions

This is my definition of integrity. When you observe people, you can guess what kind of relationships they have. For example, on one of the recent episodes of The Bachelor that I've been tuning into, the "bachelor" makes it clear over and over that he just wants to be with a girl who likes to have "fun." You can imagine how authentic his relationships will be. If we are unconscious, we feel like we have to put on a show and appear a certain way. But if we are conscious, we are real, honest, and assertive. We love and accept who we are and do not look for appreciation or approval. Are you being authentic in your relationships right now? Or are you playing a role or putting on a show?

6. Strive to live life with intentionality and make conscious choices

In my own life, I've had a lot of wake-up calls and surprises. Each time I got divorced, for example, I asked myself, "How did this happen?" Well, I created the mess by ignoring red flags. Intentionality means that you make your choices conscious of their consequences.

What kinds of choices are you making in your present relationships? Your choices determine your outcomes.

7. Strive to take risks, overcome fears, and stretch your comfort level to reach your goals

It is human nature to stay with the status quo and be comfortable. Stretching takes a lot of effort and can feel scary, but we've got to stretch ourselves if we are going to succeed. In order to grow, you need to take risks. You will run into obstacles and feel afraid; friends and family will disagree with you. But happiness does not come from getting approval from others or from hiding and playing small. Watch what happens when you take risks and play large with the people close to you! This will prepare you for taking risks when you meet your life partner.

8. Assume abundance and opportunities will appear for you

So, often we fall into negativity: "I'm too old," "All the good men are taken," "There are not enough compatible women out there for me." The scarcity mind-set is poison! The Scarcity Trap (Chapter 3) results in relationship failure because there is a temptation to settle for less. Unfortunately, it's a self-fulfilling prophecy, because when you expect less, you get less. The Law of Attraction (Chapter 10) assumes abundance.

9. Take responsibility for your outcomes by taking initiative in your life and relationships

You are a responsible adult. You know that your outcomes are largely your own creation. When we are unconsciously reactive, we are not accountable for our actions. This is the whole challenge of growing up: kids don't want to take responsibility, but you know they've grown up when they do. Being a Chooser (Chapter 6) means knowing what you want and how to get it. Are you The Chooser in your present relationships? Do you take initiative for creating your life the way you'd like?

10. What others judge about you is about them; strive to let go of what others think and not take it personally

To truly understand relationships, you know that others have their own baggage and often project their stuff onto you. The phenomenon of projection is that we assign our own thoughts and feelings onto someone else. Maggie and I go through this all the time at home. She's very sensitive to changes in temperature, and we're always going back and forth about turning the heat up or down. She'll say, "I'm freezing! Aren't you freezing?" Either the kids or I will say, "No, I'm just fine." But she can't understand it: "What do you mean? It's freezing!" She's cold and she is sure that we should be too. But her experience is not ours. Once you understand this phenomenon, it's easier to allow for differences and remember that the human experience is an individual one.

* * *

You recall Dorothy, who at age fifty-five signed up for a video dating service for the first time in her life. On Sunday afternoon, Dorothy drove into downtown Houston to meet her date, Richard, a fifty-nine-year-old divorced businessman, for coffee. On the phone, Richard had suggested dinner, but because this dating adventure was new and a little intimidating for Dorothy, she had felt more comfortable meeting him for the first time in broad daylight at a busy café.

Dorothy had been impressed by Richard's profile because they seemed to have a few things in common. He also had two sons, and he had been divorced for almost twenty years. He was also born and raised in Houston. And a statement he'd made in his profile—that he did not drink alcohol and preferred to be with an abstinent partner—made Dorothy wonder if he might meet one of her Requirements. A member of AA since her divorce, Dorothy had not had any alcohol in two decades. She felt like it would be very difficult for her to be in a relationship with a man who drank, even if it was only occasionally.

"Hello!" Richard greeted Dorothy with a warm hug just inside the café entrance.

"Hello!" she smiled at him, immediately comfortable with his friendly manner.

They followed the hostess to a booth. From the corner of her eye, Dorothy took in his salt-and-pepper hair and long legs. When they sat down, she was pleased to see how his gray-blue eyes sparkled. They gave her the impression that he took care of himself. This was affirmed when he ordered herbal tea instead of coffee.

"I have to admit," Richard began, "this video dating thing is rather new for me."

Dorothy laughed. "You're kidding me! I'm not quite a pro yet either."

Dorothy was impressed by Richard's openness right off the bat. Also, something about him—maybe it was his gentlemanly style and deep voice—reminded her of her first long-term boyfriend following her divorce, whom she still pined over at times. He was the man who had introduced her to AA and led her on her road to self-recovery. Their relationship—emotionally open and available—had been such a welcome contrast to Dorothy's marriage. It seemed so long ago that he had been transferred to another city and they'd gone their separate ways. If she had known then that she would still be single today, she probably would have moved with him.

Indeed, her date also attended AA meetings regularly, and it surprised both of them that their paths had not crossed before. Dorothy noted to herself that this was a man who seemed to take care of himself, which fit right into her Requirements for a partner.

LEARN THESE TOP 10 RELATIONSHIP ATTITUDES!

1. I will be happy by having goals and letting go of attachment to outcomes

2. I strive to live and "be" in the present

3. I love, accept, and trust myself

4. I focus on connecting, not results; a partner is someone to love, not an object or a goal

5. I strive to be authentic; being fully honest with myself and others, aligning my words, values, and actions

6. I strive to live my life with intentionality; making choices conscious of my goals and consequences

7. I strive to take the necessary risks, overcome my fears, and stretch my comfort level to reach my goals

8. I assume abundance; all the opportunities and resources that I need will appear

9. I take responsibility for my outcomes by taking initiative in my life and relationships

10. What others judge about me is about them; I strive to let go of what others think and not take it personally

IT'S TIME TO LEARN EFFECTIVE RELATIONSHIP SKILLS

It's so important that you use your present relationships as learning laboratories. I'll say it again: your current relationships reflect what your future relationships will be like. So, if you focus on what your relationships are like right now with your friends and family, you will set yourself up for having a healthy relationship with your life partner.

Think about one of the most recent

problems you had

in a relationship, say,

with a close friend or a parent or a child.

Ask yourself, "What was it that I needed

to learn right then?" "What was this teaching me at

that moment?" Notice how your own attitudes and

skills are being reflected back to you!

Relationship skills can be taught and learned. To be successful, each skill requires certain attitudes and choices. You need to "be" as well as "do."

The following table of selected relationship skills is broken down into three sections: Social Effectiveness Skills apply to everyone; Dating Skills are specific to singles seeking a partner; and Intimacy Skills are specific to an intimate relationship. This is a starting point, so feel free to add skills to the above lists or change categories for certain skills. Remember that to be successful, you must have positive and productive attitudes while you practice each skill.

RELATIONSHIP SKILLS FOR SINGLES

SOCIAL EFFECTIVENESS SKILLS	DATING SKILLS	INTIMACY SKILLS
1. Initiating contact 2. Self-introduction 3. Power introduction 4. Making conversation 5. Eye contact 6. Nonverbal communication 7. Being the "Chooser" 8. Proactive assertiveness 9. Reactive assertiveness 10. Maintaining self-integrity 11. Awareness of opportunities 12. Seizing the moment 13. Staying present 14. Owning experience/judgment 15. Understand/own projections 16. Working the room 17. Disengaging 18. Community/network 19. Supportability 20. Variety of relationships	1. Keeping sexual boundaries 2. Asserting proactively 3. Communicating expectations 4. Being reality-based and grounded 5. Allowing things to evolve naturally versus forcing 6. Scouting/sorting/ screening/testing 7. Having patience, delaying gratification	1. Recognizing commonalities 2. Accepting differences 3. Being authentic 4. Telling microscopic truth 5. Appreciating, showing gratitude 6. Having intention versus attach-ment 7. Being tolerant and nonjudgmental 8. Being emotionally available 9. Owning fears, "stuff"

FACTS, JUDGMENTS, AND FEELINGS

A necessary skill is to be aware of the difference between facts, judgments, and feelings. It's so easy to confuse these three things, but if you want to make better sense of your reality and communicate effectively, you need to separate them.

For example, let's say you go to see a movie with your friends and on your way out, you say, "That's the greatest movie ever made!" But your friends disagree with you: "No way! It was very corny." Rather than seeing that they have a different experience, you react: "What do you mean? That's the greatest movie!" You don't realize that you actually have a judgment. While you may have a strong belief, it is not a fact. It would be more effective to state, "In my opinion, that was the greatest movie ever made!" and allow others to have a different reality.

Another example might be a man who answers a call from an ex-girlfriend while he is out on a date with a woman for the first time. They chat for a few minutes, and when he hangs up, his date is furious: "How rude! Don't you ever do that again! I'm so upset!" She allows her judgments and feelings to dominate rather than addressing the facts of the situation and her needs. She could have said: "I notice that you took a call from your ex-girlfriend during our dinner. If we are going to date, I would like your full attention. Next time, I'd appreciate it if you let your voice mail answer your phone."

* * *

As Dorothy and Richard continued to talk, a couple of things made her feel cautious. A successful businessman—Richard owned and ran numerous office supply stores—he told her that he planned to retire in a few years.

But when Dorothy responded enthusiastically and asked him what he planned to do, he said, "I have no idea."

No idea?! Since Dorothy had been working for so many years to learn about who she was and what she wanted in life, certainly she wanted to be with someone who was on the same path. Still, she wondered if she was being a little harsh. It was only their first date, after all. Maybe Richard didn't feel ready to open up and reveal all his future dreams.

She felt another red flag as they talked about dating. Although Dorothy didn't reveal that Richard was her very first date, she did say that she'd joined the dating service less than a month ago.

Richard added, "Finding a woman by the end of the year is my goal! I sure don't want to grow old alone."

Dorothy didn't want to grow old alone, either, but look at his attitude! Finding a woman was his goal, as if she were a trophy. Was Richard looking for a lifelong partner, or just a woman to crawl into bed with at night?

"I don't think anyone wants to grow old alone," Dorothy agreed, trying not to be reactive. "Yet, I would rather be alone than settle for a situation in which I was unhappy."

Richard nodded and said, "I just can't tell you how much I miss coming home to a woman! Night after night, I walk into a dark house, and it just eats at me."

Dorothy leaned over the table, ready to point out to Richard how desperate he sounded. Instead, she took a sip of ice water and kept her thoughts to herself. Her objective here was not to correct Richard. Being authentic to herself, she knew that she wanted to be with a man who shared her vision for a committed relationship.

"A penny for your thoughts?" Richard said.

"Oh, I was just thinking about how men and women in our society often relate to each other."

"What do you mean?" Richard asked.

"I think that, in part due to the influence of the media, men and women often objectify each other by focusing on the outside package, whether it's about one's age or one's looks."

"I'm following you," Richard said, "In my own past, I feel like some women have focused on the material things about me, like my business or income, rather than getting to know the real me. For example, I've dated a couple of women who were definitely attracted to me because I earned over two hundred thousand dollars a year, owned a house, and vacationed in Hawaii."

"And did you feel that you were objectifying these women, too?" Richard's chest jutted forward. "Perhaps I was," he admitted. "Both were much younger than me and very attractive–they had previously been models."

Richard looked away from the table, as if he were envisioning those young beauties again. The expression on his face made Dorothy feel defensive.

Then Richard looked back at her. "Neither relationship lasted more than a few months. We really didn't have much in common, and it was clear that we didn't share the same values."

"I think it's normal to respond eagerly when we feel attracted to someone," Dorothy said, feeling less defensive now that Richard was opening up. "That chemistry thing is very powerful, if you know what I mean."

They both laughed out loud.

Dorothy wanted to ask Richard more questions–previously, had he only been looking for a certain package in a woman? Was he still in that mind-set? But she felt careful about getting TOO personal TOO quickly, since this was only their first date. Dorothy was well aware of the fact that she herself could fall into a sort of Scarcity Trap. There were days when she felt like she was get-

ting too old, and her supply of possible partners was running out. But then, she caught herself. No, she was not going to settle for less just so she wouldn't be alone.

After chatting for over an hour, Richard asked Dorothy if she wanted to share some dessert. They decided on cheesecake. In between spoonfuls, their conversation grew lighter. At 5 p.m., they rose from the table and walked outside. Dorothy thanked Richard and added,

"I would love to take you up on your original offer for dinner some night!"

"I'd be delighted," Richard said.

Although she felt cautious—there were some red flags about Richard—it also seemed too early to judge. Getting to know him a little better seemed fair, and she had really enjoyed their conversation.

Getting back into her car, Dorothy smiled. She was proud of herself for passing her first day of relationship boot camp. ✂

CONSCIOUS DATING PLAN EXERCISE NO. 11:

Please refer to Chapter 15 to write your answers.

What are your relationship challenges?

1. How can you identify your relationship challenges? First, let's return to your past: and think about any relationship conflicts you can recall. They might have happened with anyone and in any time frame: a lover, parent, sibling, or neighbor.

2. Off the top of your head, make a list of five relationship conflicts that you recall. For example, *I'm feeling let down and disappointed because last night's date didn't call me the next day.*

3. A conflict is actually unskilled communication. It points to a place where you might be challenged. To identify the actual conflict, you might need to look back at the list of relationship skills above. Identify where your challenge is/was. The challenge might be: *I did not overcome my fear and call him to express what a great time I had.*

4. Write down which relationship skill was in deficit. What does this skill look like? How do other people do it? The skill here is: *I don't wait by the phone. I strive to take risks by initiating phone calls.*

5. Now choose one skill and practice it in your existing relationships. Once you're conscious, you can do it simply by choosing to do it.

EIGHTH PRINCIPLE OF CONSCIOUS DATING:
Create a Support Community

Most likely you are reading this book because you want to share your life with someone. You do not want to be alone. We all survive and thrive in relationships; we cannot be successful or happy if we are alone. Having a support community will help you on your journey toward a successful life partnership. Let's find out how to do that together.

MATCHMAKER, MATCHMAKER, MAKE ME A MATCH...
Amanda, one of my good friends for years, calls me every time she meets a man and feels that the love bug has bit her. We are very close: I stayed by her side when she went through a bitter divorce and again when she had a breast cancer scare. She supported me through my custody battle and gave me her blessings after she met Maggie. So, when Amanda calls me and tells me that she has met someone special, she knows that I will be honest with her. I make it my personal mission to meet this guy and screen him. The way I see it, guys know other guys, and I don't want her to find out the hard way what I can discern in the first five minutes of talking to him.

To be successful in any area, you need to have other supportive people in your life.

To be successful in any area, you need to have other supportive people in your life. I believe that women, but especially single women, need at least one (preferable more than one!) close, male friend. This is a guy who will scout for you, find good men for you to meet, and then help you screen. Along these same lines, all men need good female friends (which can sometimes prove hard for men). A man's female friend can be his best scout. Women tend to trust the judgment of other women, and if another woman introduces you, she might be more comfortable with you and think you must be OK.

* * *

Dorothy recently signed up with a video dating service and gone on a coffee date with Richard, a divorced fifty-nine-year-old businessman. Now Dorothy was planning to meet Richard for a dinner. Wow, another date with him! It almost made her forget that she was middle-aged.

Dorothy was isolated in her personal life and knew that it was time to allow a friend deeper into her life to support her as she dated again.

Still, Dorothy was feeling overwhelmed. Over the past week, she had been working on her Requirements and Life Vision. She felt ready to share them with a close friend. Karina—her office assistant who had originally helped Dorothy write her dating profile— seemed like the perfect confidant. Dorothy had always felt fond of her young and attractive coworker, and was ready to open herself up to a new friend. Dorothy was isolated in her personal life and knew that it was time to allow a friend deeper into her life to support her as she dated again.

Karina offered to come over that very night. After pouring some tea, the two women got down to business. Dorothy pulled out a folder from her file cabinet and sat down next to Karina on the sofa. This would be the first time that she would share her Requirements out loud, and she knew that her feelings and tone of her voice would reveal the truth. Was she sincere? Was she excited?

Dorothy cleared her throat and started to read:

"Our relationship is addiction-free, and neither of us smokes or drinks alcohol.

"My partner has no young children.

"My partner and I make every effort to communicate deeply and respectfully with each other.

"My partner and I are present and supportive to each other.

"My partner and I share dreams to grow emotionally together, to travel around the world together, and to share lots of cozy and warm evenings.

"My partner and I are physically compatible, and able to satisfy each other.

"My partner and I are committed to each other sexually, emotionally, spiritually, and physically.

"My partner and I live in a financially responsible way together."

When Dorothy was done reading, Karina applauded. "Bravo!" Dorothy felt good about her Requirements, but Karina said that she wanted to play the devil's advocate to test whether they were really nonnegotiable.

"What if a guy met all of your Requirements, but he just wasn't very good in bed?" Karina asked.

"Out of the question!" Dorothy said, laughing. "I'm not expecting him to be some hot rod on wheels, but still, I want to be with a man who is sensual like me."

"Fair enough," said Karina. "What does 'financially responsible' mean to you? Let's say that you meet a man who's retired and living grandly off his savings—"

"That's fine, as long as he has the savings to do it. I just don't want to be with a man who spends frivolously and expects me to support him until death do us part."

"So, if he overspent while you were together, you would probably break it off."

"Yes, I would," Dorothy said. "It's not that I'm materialistic, but I want to be with a man who is responsible with money." Dorothy felt much clearer and more certain about what she wanted. Now it was time to figure out how to get it.

Even as Neanderthals and Cro-Magnons,

we were social beings who survived and thrived by

belonging to a community.

WHERE IS YOUR COMMUNITY?

Look around you and see if you can find some examples of real communities in which people are supporting each other. Do you belong to a local church or synagogue? Do you volunteer for a local group that, say, serves elders or youth in need? Even as Neanderthals and Cro-Magnons, we were social beings who survived and thrived by belonging to a community. Technological advances allowed us to increase our mobility, and we left our communities to travel the world. Eventually we became a mobile society, choosing where to live and work, and with whom to live. We no longer limited ourselves to the locations and people we inherited and grew up with. We are now a highly fragmented society with a large percentage of first- and second-generation immigrants. Fewer and fewer people choose to live and work in the communities in which they grew up. Yet this mobility has not made us any happier.

Moreover, we seem to have lost the art of community in our culture. The number of adults in the United States who live alone has doubled since 1960, and is now over 25 percent of our population. Many of us grow up without a real community or built-in support system. Maybe our parents divorced, or we moved often. This further increased our feelings of being fragmented and forced us to place our social and emotional support needs on our primary relationships. But this is a lot of weight for one relationship, and under this much pressure, it will collapse. A single relationship, no matter how compatible, cannot meet all of our needs.

A single relationship, no matter how compatible, cannot meet all of our needs.

The complexities and conflicts of any relationship—whether it's a partner, friend, or family member—can prove to be challenging. But if you are not learning how to relate with friends and family, then you're going to end up playing this out in a life partnership. So, you might as well learn how to handle these challenges when you're single. Your social environment largely determines how your love relationship will turn out, so it makes sense to build your support system now as part of preparing for, finding, and keeping a successful life partnership.

While most singles have friends and family, this is not a large enough support community. Building a network of close, mutually beneficial relationships requires time, effort, and intention. In today's society, the closest example of this kind of support system is the community that exists in most church or temple environments. These characteristics include:

1. geographical proximity

2. shared values, beliefs, and goals

3. intergenerational membership

4. ongoing shared activities

5. a contribution of time and resources by all members

6. mobilization in times of crisis and need

A community with the above characteristics can be found or created outside of religious institutions. It can be as close as on your block or in your neighborhood. Today, there are a number of intentional communities left over from the 1960s, and in Israel, people on "kibbutzim" still thrive. A kibbutz is a communal living arrangement that is organized through a form of town hall-style democracy.

Your social environment largely determines

how your love relationship will turn out,

so it makes sense to build your support

system now as part of preparing for, finding and

keeping a successful life partnership.

The members of a community, like a kibbutz, contribute what they can and receive the support they need. A single male member might volunteer to fix the plumbing of an elderly female member, who happens to think of a friend of her granddaughter whom he might like to meet. Only in a community does this kind of spontaneous, mutually supportive relationship develop.

At this point in the chapter, I'd like

you to pause and ask:

Do you have friends or family members who have

the kind of life partnership that you'd like to have?

Name three examples.

BREAKING OUT OF ISOLATION

Isolated singles often find each other and become isolated couples. When they have children, they become isolated families. Relationships survive and thrive in a community, but tend to shrivel and die in isolation. How does this isolation contribute to the high failure rate of relationships today? By deepening your connection with others and expanding the circle of people with whom you connect, you improve the quality of your life and relationships. A support community can meet your social and emotional needs while you are single. You can then allow your community to support you in finding and having a successful life partnership.

Relationships survive and thrive

in a community, but tend

to shrivel and die in isolation.

ASSESSING YOUR COMMUNITY

Take a look at your own community, and notice that you can divide people up into three categories: acquaintances, friends, and intimates.

Acquaintances are people you meet in specific settings, such as at work, church, or school. These are people you know and like; you relate to them in these certain settings, but they don't know other parts of your life. You might feel close to them, but have not socialized outside of the setting in which you know each other. For example, your acquaintances typically have never seen the inside of your house, or ridden with you in a car. Many of us confuse our acquaintances as friends.

---

1. Acquaintances are people you know in certain settings—such as work or church—but they have never seen the inside of your house or ridden with you in a car.

2. Friends share interests with you—such as sports or entertainment—but there are limits to the relationship, and you tend to lose touch with them when you move.

3. Intimates are your best friends, your inner circle who know everything about you and stand by you in times of need.

Friends share interests with you and spend time with you. You socialize with them, say, by going out for drinks or to the movie theater. Your friends tend to be narrowly defined by their interests: you have your tennis buddies, drinking buddies, and dancing buddies. You might feel close to them, even go on vacations with them, but your connection is a social one with boundaries around closeness. You wouldn't invite your tennis friends over to open gifts with your family on Christmas. You wouldn't want them seeing you looking your worst in a hospital room. You would hesitate from lending money to or borrowing money from friends. And when you move, you tend to lose touch with your friends and make new ones.

Intimates, on the other hand, are your inner circle, your family by choice. These are the people you rely on when you are most vulnerable. You share your joys and sorrows with your intimates. You invite them to share Thanksgiving with you. (Friends are the ones you'll go out with the next day.) They are your best friends, close family members, and the people in your closest circle. There are not many boundaries with your intimates; they know your secrets. Most of all, you are there for each other. You'd fly across the country if an intimate was very sick in the hospital. He/she would fly across the country for you. Intimates are at your wedding and holiday dinners. If you move, you tend to stay in touch with your intimates. If you're going through a rough time—divorce, health issues—your intimates stand by you. Unfortunately, in today's isolated society, it's common for many of us to have no intimates.

WHO WILL YOU PROMOTE? WHO WILL YOU DEMOTE?

I want you to pause here and do this simple exercise to assess your current community of relationships. It is time to evaluate your support system. Begin by writing down the names of at least ten people in your circle of friends. As you write down each name, use the above definitions to determine whether each person is an acquaintance, friend, or intimate.

Now it's time to take a closer look at each person and ask the following:

1. Does this person drag me down, hold me back, or drain my time and energy?

2. Does this person support my goals and hold me up during hard times?

Decide who in your life you're going to promote and who you're going to demote. This might seem cold, but you need to disengage from the people who are unproductive for you. This is not about being selfish or hurting anyone. If you have a friend or intimate who doesn't support your goals—and prevents you from having the life you want to have—this isn't a win-win situation. It's one thing to spend your days taking care of an elderly parent. But it's not acceptable to be "taking care of" an able-bodied friend who drains your time and energy.

On the other hand, is there anybody on this list whom you can allow deeper into your life? Perhaps it's time to choose a productive relationship and lower some boundaries so that this friend can enter your inner circle. Maybe it's time to bring this person closer to you for a more meaningful, mutually beneficial relationship.

I've always believed that "birds of a feather flock together." Being with people who support you will help you achieve your goals and probably attract similar people. And, chances are that these friends will know somebody who is good for you to meet. As you recall from Chapter 10, the Law of Attraction is absolute: like attracts like.

Challenge Question:

Here's a question that might help you

figure out who your true intimates are.

Let's say you just won a weeklong

trip to an all-inclusive resort on the big island

of Hawaii. You can take FIVE people with you, free!

Who would you invite?

CREATE YOUR SUPPORT COMMUNITY

Where can *you* meet potential partners? This is the most common lament I hear from today's singles. In my experience, the singles asking this question are too isolated in their everyday life, and need to focus first on building their community before finding a partner. This problem did not occur in past generations when we lived and worked in a community of family, friends, neighbors, and coworkers, all of whom would typically introduce singles to each other. Without this support system, today's singles increasingly rely on dating services and personal ads. But then where is the community to support, nurture, and sustain these relationships?

In Chapter 4, I wrote about *creating a community*. Without a built-in community, today's singles must intentionally create their own support system. While most singles have friends and family, this is still not a large enough support system. Building a network of close, mutually beneficial relationships requires time, effort, and intention.

Here are some strategies:

1. Research existing communities aligned with your values and interests, such as charitable, service, and recreational groups

2. Explore personal growth and spiritual organizations

3. Check out men's or women's organizations

4. Deepen your connection with your existing friends, coworkers, family, and neighbors by getting together more often

5. Start "people-collecting" by gathering cool people into your life of a variety of ages and genders

---

Without a built-in community,

today's singles must intentionally

create their own support system.

In Chapter 8, you read about Mark, the thirty-five-year-old divorced businessman who was living with Stacy, his twenty-year-old eye-catching girlfriend. These two led life in the fast lane with lots of splurging and traveling. But then the recession of the nineties hit and money was tight; Stacy was not happy about having to cut costs, and Mark was forced to see that all this luxury only made him feel emptier. The week before Christmas things hit a low point, and Stacy moved out. Mark's two daughters were with his ex-wife for the holidays. A few days before Christmas, he was driving around in circles after work, not wanting to go home alone.

When he returned home, the answering machine was blinking, and he hoped the message was from Stacy. But no, it was his cousin, Todd, calling from Los Angeles: "How are you, man? Just checking in about you, we haven't spoken for a while—"

Mark and his cousin had spent every summer together growing up and Todd was the best man at Mark's wedding. Todd was one of Mark's intimates. Mark pulled a cold beer from the refrigerator and sat down on the sofa to dial his cousin's number. It was really good to hear his supportive voice, and Mark was thrilled when he heard that Todd, a social worker, was taking some courses to become a relationship coach.

Mark opened up about how lonely he was feeling. He confessed that he was beating himself up because his life hadn't turned out the way he wanted it to.

"You did the best you could at the time," his cousin said. "I can hear how self-critical you are, but it's time for you to be kind to yourself."

Todd wanted to know if Mark had any plans for the holidays. No; Mark was feeling pitiful and hadn't called anyone. Todd encouraged Mark to call his single friends: he could mull wine with some friends for Christmas, or host a small New Year's party. He could volunteer in a soup kitchen. Or maybe he could get out of town and fly to LA for a cousins' getaway at the beach.

"I'd love that!" Mark said. He didn't have to be alone for the holidays. He and Todd always made each other laugh, and they loved

to surf together. Just because Mark was single again, he didn't have to be alone for the holidays.

---

1. **Tell your friends that you're single and would like to meet somebody.**

2. **Make specific requests.**

3. **Follow up the request.**

4. **Continue to have your friends screen after you meet prospective singles**

IT'S TIME TO ENLIST HELP!

Now that you've figured out who your true intimates and friends are, it's time to get them to work! You can use your community to scout and screen potential partners for you. Remember the Challenge Question above, when you invited five friends to join you for a week-long trip to Hawaii? Write down their names again. These five people might be the best judges for you, to help you scout and screen.

1. First and foremost, be honest with these five friends. Tell them, "I'm single and I'd like to meet somebody." (Notice how different that sounds from, "I'm single and I'm just fine, thank you.")

2. Make requests. This means directly asking for support. You might say, "Do you know anyone that might be good for me to meet?" Remember that because your friends are not you, they can see more objectively. They might be far wiser in attempting to find prospective partners for you.

3. Make specific requests. The above question—"Do you know anyone?"—is very general. Instead, tell your friends that you need a date for a New Year's Eve party; or your company picnic.

4. Follow up the request. Don't just wait by the phone. Ask your friends again.

5. Continue to have your friends screen. Invite your date to go out with your friends. Notice their reactions. Trust their wisdom.

If you get a negative reaction from the people in your life who are close to you, that's a big red flag. This is not an automatic indicator, but it's a very important piece of information.

You now have a better understanding of what a support community is and how to build your own. As you continue to strengthen your relationships-with people who support your life vision and goals-this will help you find your life partner. ✄

CONSCIOUS DATING PLAN EXERCISE NO. 12:
Please refer to Chapter 15 to write your answers.

Who will you invite to your Bachelor/Bachelorette party?

You've learned in this chapter that one of the best ways to meet prospective singles is to enlist your friends' help. So, it's time to host a singles event! Tell your closest four to eight friends that you're hosting a gathering.

Ask your friends to invite one single person to the event to meet you. In other words, the price of admission is: "You must bring somebody good for me to meet." Be specific about your Requirements.

This will be your own personal Bachelor/Bachelorette party! Have fun screening!

NINTH PRINCIPLE OF CONSCIOUS DATING:
Practice Assertiveness

Growing up, most of us were raised to obey others, such as our parents, teachers, and employers. We were also taught that in order to get along in life, we needed to conform. As a consequence, most of us never learned how to be assertive effectively. No wonder it's hard to get what we want in life and in our relationships! But if you can learn how to be assertive, it will be one of the most satisfying assets in your life.

I was recently coaching Maureen, a local store owner and woman in her mid thirties who was back on the dating scene one year after finalizing her divorce. One of her girlfriends had set Maureen up on a blind date with Kurt, a local college teacher in his late forties, and they found themselves laughing and chatting easily within minutes of meeting. Their first dinner together lasted until 10 p.m., and although Maureen knew she should get home to relieve her babysitter, it was wonderful to be getting so much flattering attention that night.

Maureen's heart pounded when Kurt called her the next night to say how much he enjoyed their time together. They stayed on the phone for two hours, and Maureen told him, "Just to let you know, I need to take things slowly." The next day, although Maureen was busy and tired from their late-night conversation, she was also buzzing with this new infatuation. But when Kurt dropped by her store that afternoon with flowers—without notice—and then stayed for over an hour next to the cash register, Maureen felt uncomfortable. Hadn't she been clear when she said she wanted to take things slowly? She had work to do! He should have called first! They'd only been on one date, and he was already acting like her boyfriend!

With Maureen, I helped her identify the interactions that made her uncomfortable. How did she feel when Kurt showed up at her workplace without calling first? What did her body tell her? I reminded her how important it was to listen to her gut. Where did she feel tense or uneasy? Maureen knew that she wanted to take it slow; she was still recovering from her divorce, and her daughter was only four years old. Granted, on her first date, if Maureen had laid out the ground rules right then—"Don't call me; I'll call you when I'm ready"—she might have sounded like a control freak. But now it was time for her to be assertive, and tell Kurt that she needed some space.

They'd only been on one date, and

he was already acting like her boyfriend.

It was time for Maureen to be assertive, and

tell Kurt that she needed some space.

PRACTICE, PRACTICE...

When I say that we need to "practice" assertiveness, I intentionally use the word "practice." For most of us, being assertive takes a lot of conscious effort, and does not come easily. This is why it requires continuous "practice." Let's say that you're a woman out on your first date with an attractive man you met online. You meet at a café on Sunday afternoon, and his first words are: "You are gorgeous!" You feel flattered by the compliment, but as you sit down, you notice that his gaze continually focuses on your chest. He hardly makes eye contact with you. Notice how uncomfortable you're feeling. Do you feel like he's leering? Or undressing you with his eyes? Notice your issues, without judging or second-guessing yourself.

If you are experiencing an interpersonal problem or issue, let yourself be aware of it. An issue is an unmet need. Often in relationships it feels easier to ignore our needs and push them away. But in the long run, that hurts us and causes pain. Notice what happens when you identify your issue. Do you feel self-conscious because this guy keeps staring at your chest? The next step is to communicate your issue. Sure, it might be awkward to say on a first date, "I feel uncomfortable by the fact that you keep looking at my chest," but it's a legitimate boundary. There are many ways to express what you need, such as: "Could you please make eye contact when you talk to me?"

ASK YOURSELF:

1. **How am I feeling?**

2. **What is my issue?**

3. **How can I communicate my issue?**

4. **How does my partner/date respond?**

5. **How do both of us follow through?**

Notice your date's response. Does he apologize? Does he correct his behavior? Does he get defensive? Here, I need to stress how important it is not to minimize your issues and needs. So often, I hear singles with valid issues say, "It's not a big deal" or "It's not worth it." Minimizing lets you avoid a situation for a moment, but it will get larger later. Again, there are no small needs! By avoiding assertiveness, you deny your own needs and boundaries. By not telling or living your truth, you sacrifice an authentic connection with your partner and sabotage the long-term sustainability of your relationship. Your unmet needs will result in your unhappiness. While your first response might be to blame your partner, know that the problem and solution actually belong to you.

HOW TO PRACTICE ASSERTIVENESS

1. Be self-aware: Be aware of your thoughts and feelings, and realize that this situation doesn't work for you.

2. Own your needs, issues, thoughts and feelings: Take responsibility for asserting your needs. Don't expect your date to read your mind, then make the person wrong when he/she doesn't.

3. Be positive: Adopt an attitude that your date/friend means well and might not know this is a problem for you. Be optimistic that by being assertive your need can be met (until the evidence proves otherwise).

4. Communicate effectively: Let your date/friend know your issue; communicate your issue clearly and request what you need.

5. Handle defensiveness gracefully: It's normal to feel defensive when someone corrects your behavior. Have compassion and patience when this happens. Be firm but understanding.

6. Take risks: be prepared to risk conflict—and even the relationship—to resolve the issue and get your need met.

WHAT ARE YOUR BOUNDARIES?

We all have needs and boundaries. A boundary is the line between what is comfortable and what it is not comfortable for you in a relationship. Many of us think a boundary is like a fence or a limit, but this is not just about protecting oneself. It's about being respected, and being respectful. Having boundaries is important in every relationship we have—with family, friends, and children—not just in romantic relationships. Remember the Relationship Readiness Quiz you completed in Chapter 9? I asked you if you initiate contact with people you want to meet, and disengage from people who are not a match for you. I asked you if you keep your physical and emotional boundaries. You might review your answers and reflect upon what your boundaries are.

One of my colleagues, Coach Deki Fox, points out that our relationship Requirements (see Chapter 5) protect our vulnerable selves from harm and optimize the expression of our unique contribution to life.

She says:

> It is easy to be seen in our physical shape because we have the boundary of our skin. Requirements make it possible to define our emotional, mental, and spiritual "skin" so that we can better understand where the boundaries of these subtle bodies end and where touching one another's heart and soul begins.

A boundary is the line between what is

comfortable for you and what

it is not comfortable. It's about being respected, and

being respectful.

The first step to assertiveness is to know your Requirements, Needs, and Wants. As you read in Chapter 5, we are typically conscious of only the tip of the iceberg. Most of us see just 10 percent of our life Vision. But our success and happiness depends on the 90 percent that lies hidden, below the surface.

An unmet need creates an issue.

All of our needs are valid. There is

no such thing as a small need.

The most reliable clue that you are experiencing an unmet need is when you encounter an issue. Issues are unmet needs, and usually appear as physical sensations, such as stress and discomfort. They are also accompanied by negative thoughts.

WHAT ARE YOUR EXPECTATIONS
WHEN YOU'RE DATING?

1. Who will call first?

2. Who will initiate the date?

3. Who decides what you should do?

4. Who will pay on the date?

5. Who will drive on the date?

SAY "NO" TO WHAT YOU DON'T WANT

Being clear about what you require in a relationship is very important. But being clear about what you don't want is just as vital. Let's say, like Maureen in this chapter, you go out on one date and have a great time. You're clear about your boundaries—such as taking it slow—and your date seems to respect them. Based on first impressions, it's looking like your date might be able to meet your Requirements. So, you go out on a second date, and then a third. The third date ends with a long walk around downtown on a warm spring evening, and you find yourself asking your date some important questions about his/her life Vision. This is when you find out that your date is adamant about not having children. While you understand his/her reasons, this is not in alignment with your own life Vision. You want kids.

What do you do? I suggest immediately saying "no" to the relationship in a clear and gentle way. Be clear for yourself and your date that this relationship will not work. Of course, no one wants to reject or be rejected, but you'll be doing yourself and the other person a huge favor by breaking it off now. You are not committed after a few dates! So often, I see singles building up a relationship in their heads after just a couple of dates. It's so easy to make things bigger than they really are because you want to be with someone. But if the alignment is not there, it's so important to disengage.

If you call things off with your date, do it clearly but directly: "I'm sorry, our relationship won't work. Having children and a family is a Requirement for me." We all deserve clear, direct, and assertive communication in our relationships. If your date doesn't seem to hear you—i.e., he/she keeps calling, or sending e-mails—then remember that you have a choice. You don't have to answer those phone calls or e-mails. It's your right to move on and find your life partner.

You'll be doing yourself and the other person a huge favor by breaking it off now.

PROACTIVE ASSERTIVENESS

It might feel scary to put your feelings out there, but being assertive is one of the first steps to building intimacy. Like Maureen, you deserve to be respected, and have the right to ask for what you want. Being assertive requires being conscious of your needs. I'm not talking about being aggressive, but rather self-confident about communicating who you are and what you want. This means stating directly and kindly what you think, feel, and want. Being proactively assertive means that you'll let potential partners know ahead of time what you need. This is not only about being direct about your needs, but also about testing to see if potential partners hear your needs and follow through.

PROACTIVE VERSUS REACTIVE ASSERTIVENESS

What if Maureen had been very clear on her first date with Kurt and

239

told him exactly what "going slowly" meant to her? She could have said gently, "I had a wonderful time tonight, but I need to take things at my own pace. I will call you in a couple of days, all right?" She would have been practicing assertiveness proactively before Kurt crossed her boundaries. **Reactive assertiveness**, on the other hand, is what Maureen did after a two-hour phone conversation the night following her date with Kurt when she said, "Just to let you know, I need to take things slowly." She asserted her needs and boundaries in her moment of discomfort. (And Kurt did not hear her, because he dropped by her workplace the next day with flowers.)

I realize that this might sound a bit businesslike; you might expect to hear about proactive versus reactive assertiveness in a sales meeting, not in a book about relationships. But this works when you're dating, too! When you assert yourself proactively, you say what you need calmly and respectfully in a way that the other person can hear you clearly. If you do not do so, you risk reacting, perhaps aggressively, by expressing your needs to the other person at the moment of conflict when a boundary is being crossed; you might be upset and your adrenaline might be running high. When you are reactive, you're responding to a situation you are experiencing as negative. This is quite a contrast from putting your feelings out there calmly, before the conflict arises.

So, how did Maureen take care of herself? I encouraged her to be assertive by calling Kurt and telling him, "It was great to have that first date with you. As I mentioned, I'm still recovering from my divorce. When dating and getting to know somebody new, I need to take it slow. I was not comfortable when you stopped by my shop with flowers two days after we first met. I need some space now, and I will give you a call in a few days." I reminded Maureen to plan out her request before calling, and present it in a graceful and respectful tone.

I urged her to see if Kurt would honor her request. She was certainly being authentic and asking for what she needed. She let Kurt know exactly where she stood. Would he give her space? That would certainly be good information to learn as they got to know each other. On the other hand, if he argued with her or called again the next day this would certainly be a red flag. In the very beginning of getting to know each other, when singles typically put their best foot forward, it would not be a good sign if Kurt did not honor what Maureen had asked.

ISSUES ARE UNMET NEEDS

What if Maureen had been angry and aggressive? She could have called Kurt and said, "Stop smothering me! I'm not your girlfriend!" Being aware of your boundaries, as Maureen was, says a lot about your needs. First of all, an unmet need creates an issue. Maureen's issue/unmet need was the fact that Kurt did not respect her wish to take things slowly. Conversely, an unmet need might be something your date does not do. (What if Maureen and Kurt went on a couple of dates, and then he never returned her calls?) Remember, all of our needs are valid. There is no such thing as a small need.

Do you have any unmet needs?

Be aware of any stress,

discomfort, or negative thoughts

you might be having in the relationship.

Let's say your friend calls you at 3 a.m. to ask if you'd like to go to the movies the next night. You answer the phone groggily and feel tension building up in your shoulders. Your blood pressure goes up and you think, "How inconsiderate! She could have called me at a reasonable hour tomorrow!" If you were not previously aware that you had a boundary around receiving calls while you slept, your stress and discomfort would literally be a "wake-up call" that this is an issue for you.

STUCK IN THE PAST

Five days after her second date with Richard, Dorothy was on her way to meet Stan. He was the sixty-four-year-old therapist who wrote in his profile he planned to retire the next year and dreamed of doing so with the love of his life.

Like Dorothy, Stan seemed to be an art lover. Although an appreciation of art was not one of Dorothy's requirements—she would not break off a relationship if he didn't join her on weekend excursions to museums and galleries—it was important that she be able to share this with her partner.

When Dorothy walked up to the doors of the Modern Art Museum in downtown Houston, a tall, balding man with hazel eyes waved at her. After kissing her lightly on the cheek, Stan opened the glass door for Dorothy. Although Dorothy had been there a few weeks earlier, she was very pleased when Stan had suggested on the phone that they meet there for their first date. It struck Dorothy as a very romantic idea.

As they ascended the stairs to the second floor, Stan asked Dorothy how long she'd been dating through the video service. "A month," Dorothy confessed, not wanting to reveal that Stan was only her second date. "And you?"

"For almost a year, actually," Stan said. "I have to say, I've been having the most fun I've had since my twenties."

Dorothy was glad to hear that Stan seemed to enjoy being single, and wasn't bitter. But she did wonder how many other women he was dating.

As the two walked through the exhibit, Dorothy was delighted that Stan asked for her thoughts on various pieces. At one point he asked her how the artist's use of lace and human hair might be representative of women. He listened intently as Dorothy talked about her admiration for an artist who used such unusu-

al materials as metaphors for strength and fragility. Dorothy felt like she was sharing a deep part of herself by viewing this exhibit with Stan.

When they stopped at the cafeteria for lunch, their conversation grew more personal. "So, tell me about your sons," Stan said.

Dorothy beamed with pride as she recounted her oldest son's marriage a few years ago, and her youngest son's travels through Asia. Stan did not have any children.

"But my ex-wife and I have remained good friends," he said. "We still get together every week for coffee."

Dorothy nodded her head, but thought this might be a red flag. How odd! To still be involved with your ex-wife after being divorced for ten years, especially when you never had kids together! She wondered what baggage he might be carrying from his marriage. Although it was too early to judge, she thought he might be overly attached to his ex-wife. After spending the last twenty years working through her own issues, the last thing she wanted to do was hook up with a man who was stuck in the past.

After spending the last twenty years

working through her own issues,

the last thing she wanted to do was hook up

with a man who was stuck in the past.

Maybe she was being too judgmental, but as the afternoon wore on Dorothy noticed how Stan brought up his ex-wife again and again. When Dorothy mentioned, for example, that she had recently purchased an electric-hybrid car, Stan told her that he'd helped his ex-wife buy the same kind of car this year. Enough already!

After finishing their coffee, Stan walked Dorothy back to her car. He reached out to give her a hug, but she responded by simply patting his shoulder. Through her body language she made it clear that she did not want any close, physical contact. Her gut was telling her that Stan was not the right man for her. Stan took a step back, a little stunned, and left without a word.

Being a Pleaser often feels safer than being a Chooser. Being a Pleaser might result in short-term, immediate acceptance, but it means risking conflict, disconnection, and unhappiness.

Of course, Dorothy wants to love and be loved. We all want acceptance, connection, and harmony. Assertiveness can feel risky, especially when we assert our boundaries by saying "no." Being a Pleaser often feels safer than being a Chooser. Being a Pleaser might result in short-term, immediate acceptance, but it means risking conflict, disconnection, and unhappiness. Initially, Dorothy was bothered by the fact that her date went on and on about his ex-wife. It might be fine to briefly describe your past relationship, but when first getting to know someone, talking at length about an ex would most likely cause discomfort for the listener. Needs are complex and there are no black and white rules. I'm talking about paying close attention. What if Dorothy had ignored her discomfort when Stan wanted to hug her, and had gone along with him? What would you have done? Perhaps this would have been the easy way out. She would have avoided momentary awkwardness, but this issue would only have gotten larger next time.

NOT READY FOR THAT FIRST KISS

Angela had recently gone out with Jerry, whom she met at her gym. Angela had worked hard at defining her Requirements. She knew, for example, that she and her partner would value telling each other the truth and doing their best to do so. No matter how much she was in love, it wouldn't work any other way. Over dinner with Jerry, she was pleased to see how openly he talked about his divorce, and how much work he'd done to heal. She was also impressed that Jerry had returned to college to earn a second master's degree.

When the bill came, however, Angela suddenly panicked. The date was almost over. Would he try to kiss her at the car? She felt such chemistry, but wasn't sure how far things should go. As Jerry paid for dinner, Angela thought to herself: she wanted to end this date with a physical good-bye, but she did not feel ready to kiss Jerry. She liked him, but kissing would make her uncomfortable. She didn't want to go there yet.

The date was almost over.

Would he try to kiss her at the car?

Outside, Jerry walked her to her car. He asked if he could call her again. "Please!" she said enthusiastically. She felt Jerry leaning into her, with his face close to her mouth. She could have gone along with him, for the sake of not making a scene. But she felt nauseous. She didn't want to kiss him just yet.

"Jerry," said Angela, "I'd love to end this date with a hug."

"My pleasure," Jerry said, gently wrapping his arms around her.

It was a short, warm hug. Jerry did not try to kiss her. She had assertively expressed her needs, and Jerry had respected them.

In response to Angela's issue—wanting to go slowly physically—she had many choices. She could have:

- submissively gone along with kissing Jerry for the sake of peace and harmony in the relationship

- aggressively "acted out" her thoughts and feelings by pushing her date off

- complained like a victim and asked Jerry why he was doing this to her

- been assertive, explained her boundary, and enforced it

As you read, Angela chose the last option. She was not unconsciously reactive—like the first three options above—because a knee-jerk reaction would not have served her needs or the long-term viability of the relationship. Still, if she'd been *assertive proactively*, she could have spelled out her needs—wanting a hug, not a kiss—before the actual moment of parting ways. Being assertive proactively is important when you first start dating someone because it's an excellent tool for testing. What would it have said about Jerry if he'd ignored Angela's request for a hug—and not a kiss—on their date? The goal here is to assert positively and proactively. This is not about blaming or getting upset at the other person. This is simply communicating effectively, one human being to another.

What would it have said about Jerry

if he'd ignored Angela's request for a hug—

and not a kiss—on their date?

In my work with singles and couples, I present them with a "Communication Map," so they can learn how to talk about their Needs and issues, and listen effectively. Let's say that you're on a second date, like Angela, and you want to make it clear to the other person that you need to take things slowly physically. This is your Need, and it's valid simply because you need it. If your Need isn't met, you'll experience an "issue" (or problem) whether you want to or not. Needs cannot be denied. If unmet, you'll experience an issue every time.

To assert your Needs you can go one of two ways: communicate your Need; or hit "The Wall," and let judgment (right versus wrong), defensiveness (such as blaming), or reactive emotions take over. Hopefully, you'll decide to communicate effectively and your partner will be responsive to your needs, especially if there is a hope for the relationship to have a positive future.

When you have a Need arise, beware

of letting judgment, defensiveness,

or reactive emotions take over! Know

that your Needs are valid.

I encourage you to live your own truth by being assertive proactively. Your Needs and boundaries are of utmost important in every relationship you have. The people in my own life whom I most respect are authentic. These are people who tell me what they need and let me know if I'm crossing a boundary. They are genuine and I know where they stand. I encourage you to say "no" to what you don't want, and notice how being assertive will help you get what you want in your life and relationships. ✑

CONSCIOUS DATING PLAN EXERCISE NO. 13:

Please refer to Chapter 15 to write your answers.

How Can You Be More Assertive?

It is time for you to identify social situations and interactions in your own life that might call for assertiveness. Write down a list of any circumstances when you might need to communicate your Needs or boundaries. Here are some examples:

1. On a first date, do you want to pay the bill, split the bill, or be treated?

2. When you give out your phone number, will it be your home or cell?

3. Is there a certain time when you don't want your date to call? (Not after 10 p.m.? Not when the kids might answer?)

4 Do you have boundaries around certain topics of conversation? Such as not discussing sexual preferences or what turns you on, on a first date?

5. Do you have boundaries around physical contact? Such as not kissing on a first date? Not going home with someone?

Now, choose one of your Needs or issues, and create a script to be assertive. What will you say to make it clear that you want to split the bill for dinner on your first date? How will you communicate that you don't want him/her calling your house late?

And lastly, if you know that your date is not aligned with your Requirements, how will you clearly break it off? Write down what you plan to say and remember to practice assertiveness!

Be a Successful Single

It might seem like a paradox: why should I focus on being a successful single when I really want to be in a relationship? In this chapter, you will learn that the best way to find a life partner is to be a happy and successful single.

ARE YOU LIVING THE LIFE YOU WANT?

Being single does not mean you have to put your life on hold. This only leads to unhappiness. The key is living your life fully in the present now, and letting go of attachments to future outcomes.

If you watch reality TV, you might think that every single woman out there only wants to get a husband. But this just doesn't work, nor is it true in real life. I watched Nicole Kidman proudly attend the Oscars with her parents at her side instead of bowing down to media pressure to bring a date. She was a true symbol of a successful single! How can you be a successful single? Start by asking yourself, "Am I happy living the life I want, while I'm single?"

The Law of Attraction (which you read about in Chapter 10) assures that "misery loves company." This means that if you apply emotional energy to anything, you draw it to you. If you are unhappy about your life, you're going to attract more unhappiness. Similarly, success breeds success. To have a happy and successful relationship, you must be a happy and successful single. By living the life you want, you attract the opportunities, people, and resources that align with where you want to go.

Ask yourself: "Am I happy living the life I want, while I'm single?"

Cathy, thirty-eight, had recently moved back to her hometown of Cincinnati following her painful divorce. Cathy felt lonely at times, having left her closest friends in Denver. She shared meals some nights with her father, and sometimes went out to dinner with her work colleagues. She wanted to make new friends, and trusted this would happen if she focused on doing what she loved. She ran around the local track every morning and joined a local book club. Cathy started to work with a coach to live the life that she really wanted.

One night a week, Cathy went straight from work to meet with her coach. Two nights a week, she attended classes to earn the credentials to open a daycare center in her home. She was getting closer to her dream of working with young children. Within a year, she had earned her license and families were signing up their children! Suddenly, her once-lonely home was turned into a joyous, active playground.

SEEKING FROM WANT VERSUS NEED

Cathy's life Vision included being with a life partner, but this was not her sole objective as she worked on her goals. If you're a successful single, you are seeking a partner from "want" and not "need." You do not act out of desperation. If you are unhappy and seeking a relationship as a way out, you will stay stuck. A relationship will just complicate your life and bring more unhappiness.

It is so important to pursue a relationship *while living life fully in the present.* In fact, if you are a successful single living a rich and full life, you most likely will want to be careful about giving up or changing your enjoyable lifestyle for a relationship. And when you do, you might be surprised to experience some grief and sadness about losing the freedom and choices you had as a single. However, you do so willingly because you want to move to the next level of fulfilling your Vision for your life.

Pursue a relationship while living
life fully in the present.

I think that one of the reasons for *Sex and the City*'s popularity with viewers was that it showed single women who were anything but desperate. Sure, they were looking for men, but it was not about survival for them. These were well-dressed, well-paid, sexually gratified women who discarded men when the relationship didn't work anymore. They didn't depend on a man or settle for less. I urge you to look at your present-day life and evaluate where you are. In Chapter 9, you took the Relationship Readiness Quiz. Please pause again and consider:

- Is there anything interfering with your readiness for a committed relationship?

- What issues are you still working on in your life?

- Are you available now, or are you involved with someone?

- If you were going through a divorce at the beginning of this book, is it final now?

- How are you doing financially?

- What demands does your career put on you?

- Do you have stressful family obligations?

- Do you have any mental, physical, or emotional health challenges, such as depression, an addiction, or anxiety disorder?

A year after moving to Cincinnati, Cathy was ready to scout for available partners. Her divorce papers arrived in the mail. Legally, she was free to move on. Through her new business, she had made some close women friends. On weekends, they went out dancing and saw movies together. They talked about real issues, such as relationships.

As you recall, Cathy posted her profile and a picture—"Radiant Redhead Seeks Remarkable Man"—with an online dating service and within days, her inbox was filled with messages. In fact, she got two hundred responses to her profile in just six weeks! Still, Cathy knew that she was not ready for a committed relationship, so she spent the next year working on her personal goals, dating, and having fun. Her days were filled with watching children toddle around her house, preparing bite-sized snacks, and playing silly songs on her guitar. She was laughing more than she had in years!

Her days were filled with watching children toddle around her house, preparing bite-sized snacks, and playing silly songs on her guitar. She was laughing more than she had in years!

In between all this fun, Cathy dated. She found herself drawn to men her age who had also been married before. They seemed to understand what it was like to go through a divorce and move on as a single. She noticed that all the men she attracted were financially secure and were thoughtful about their life goals. Wow, like really did attract like!

Cathy dated two computer consultants, a math teacher, a restaurant owner, an architect, and a woodworker. Cathy was straight-

forward about her boundaries and Needs with these men; she was assertive proactively. For example, on a first date, she drove her own car and split the bill. She also made it clear that she wouldn't be jumping right into bed with anyone.

INVESTING IN YOURSELF

How do you devote time and energy to yourself every day? What are you doing to grow, learn, and build the life you want independent of a relationship? In his book *Keeping the Love You Find*, Harville Hendrix writes that in an ideal society, "singleness would be recognized as a vital stage of the journey to maturation, a time to learn about who we are, to learn responsibility and self-sufficiency, to identify our true desires, and to confront our inner strengths and demons." Hendrix adds: "It would be sorely needed relationship training."

One question that singles often ask me is, "But how do I find the time to invest in myself? I'm working full time, trying to exercise regularly at the gym, grocery shop, cook, and just get enough sleep at night. How can I possibly fit in taking a class? Or meeting with a coach once a week?" Well, you will find the time when you make the time. We all lead busy lives, full of e-mail and phone calls, responsibilities, and work demands. My colleague, Jeff Herring, a nationally syndicated columnist and relationship coach, asserts that more important than "time management" is "action management." He points out that we have only 24 hours in a day and can't change the amount of time we have to work with; however, we can control what we do with our time.

* * *

Mark, the thirty-five-year-old divorced businessman, found his relationship with Stacy, his twenty-year-old eye-catching girlfriend, was getting rockier. Then, the week before Christmas, Stacy moved out. Mark was very down; and in a bad place financially, just trying to make ends meet, although he'd been working over fifty hours a week.

For the holidays, Mark went to LA to visit his cousin Todd, who was back from the Peace Corps after two years abroad. Todd glowed with confidence and told Mark the Peace Corps was the best thing he'd ever done. He spoke about the deep friendships he fostered and his new Argentinean girlfriend.

Mark told his cousin that he'd hit a low point in his life. His bank account was at its lowest. His girlfriend was gone. All of his close male friends were married. He had no close female friends. Todd had a suggestion: maybe he could join the Peace Corps. He'd always been a risk taker!

"You're not only investing in yourself, you're investing in the world!" Todd told Mark over dinner.

"You sound like a commercial, man."

"I'm serious!" Todd said, telling Mark that he'd be perfect for the business segment of the Peace Corps, going abroad for two years to a developing country, having all of his expenses covered.

That night, Mark thought hard: perhaps this was the best way to invest in himself right now. Mark needed the time and space to introspect, and traveling somewhere exotic sounded like a dream.

Mark needed the time and space to introspect, and traveling somewhere exotic sounded like a dream.

HOW'S YOUR SOCIAL LIFE?

Another sign of being a successful single is being truly happy as you are. Are you content with the way your life is right now? Or do you feel that your life needs to change for you to be happy?

Successful singles have rich social lives filled with meaningful relationships and activities.

Successful singles have rich social lives filled with meaningful relationships and activities.

In his book, *Three Minutes of Intimacy: Dance Your Way to a Sensational Social Life*, Craig Marcott encourages people to try dance lessons as a way of diverting their attention from grief, having fun, and getting exercise again. "You don't have to be a Fred Astaire or Ginger Rogers to enjoy dance," he says. How are you dancing your way back to a sensational social life? Are you taking that class you've always dreamed about? Joining your local baseball league? Going to a monthly salon to talk politics?

Instead of putting all my energy into trying desperately to find a partner, I went on long hikes, sailed my boat, and took the kids to the park.

You recall my own search for a life partner online. After posting my profile on Match.com, I went out with about ten women who were all very nice, but I could not imagine myself in a relationship with any of them. I'd spend a lot of time writing e-mails, talking on the phone, and going on dates. But it seemed to lead to frustration. That's when I decided to make my profile very specific—demanding, in fact—so I might attract a helping professional like me, a woman who loved kids and family, was authentic, and communicated well.

I had no responses for months, but did not mope. Instead, I focused on enjoying my own life.

On weekends, I either backpacked in the mountains or took my kids on fun adventures. I also got together with supportive and close friends. Instead of putting all my energy into trying desperately to find a partner, I went on long hikes, sailed my boat, and took the kids to the park. I felt happy and energized. And then Maggie found me!

* * *

Six months after visiting his cousin, Mark was packing his bags and boarding the airplane to San Diego, where he would be trained for three months before departing for the Dominican Republic. He promised to write to his daughters regularly and took a leave of absence from work. During the trainings, Mark felt honored to be surrounded by so many bold and audacious individuals who'd given up their comfortable lives to live abroad for two years. He quickly befriended a man his age from Chicago who was also a divorced father of two. They talked openly about their painful breakups and moving on.

During the orientation, Mark found himself gazing at a young woman with shoulder-length brown hair, gray-green eyes, and a dashing smile. He could hear her laughter from across the room. His hands started sweating when they were partnered up to create a short silent pantomime together. Her name was Miranda: she was a thirty-year-old computer consultant from Boston who wanted to make some radical changes in her life. Just like Mark! Every night at dinner Mark found himself sitting next to her, jumping up to serve her seconds, asking if he could go on evening walks with her. Three months later, however, Mark was off to the Dominican Republic and Miranda was going to Thailand. They promised to write.

THE JOURNEY VERSUS THE DESTINATION
Do you value the journey of finding someone as much as the destination? So often I see singles jump from one relationship right into

another because they don't want to be alone. The process of healing emotionally and re-entering the world of dating again can be challenging. But it is in this journey that you grow and learn from the past so that you can move forward.

Mark had never attempted to date someone through the mail, but this is precisely what happened with Miranda. They wrote to each other on a daily basis, and Mark walked to the post office once a week to mail his thick letters across the world. Mark described helping local families with business development on their farms. He told Miranda about going to the local square every night to listen to music. His Spanish was becoming more fluent, and the Dominican community had welcomed him with open arms. He learned the ins and outs of the Dominican banking system, and explained to his new farming friends how it all worked. His life felt richer than ever. He learned how to scuba dive and windsurf, and ate fresh coconuts and spicy bean dishes.

His life felt richer than ever:

he learned how to scuba dive and windsurf, and

ate fresh coconuts and spicy bean dishes.

Although Mark wasn't digging ditches or planting corn, he was learning a lot—especially about himself. He told Miranda about following the dusty trail every morning to fill his jug with clean water to drink, working together with farmers on their business plans, and reflecting on his own goals. He wrote about his dream to bring a woman into his daughters' lives, an open and genuine woman who shared his values. Mark realized that he was fully responsible for the outcomes in his life, and if he wanted a healthy relationship, it was up to him. As he got intensively involved with the locals, he planned how to live the life he really wanted back home.

One year later, Mark and Miranda were reunited for a three-week vacation in the Yucatan. She decided to ask for a transfer to the Dominican Republic, where she could use her computer skills to help local artisans set up their own businesses. By the time Miranda moved into his two-room cottage near the beach, Mark felt truly content with the person he was.

ARE YOU A SUCCESSFUL SINGLE?

Putting your life on hold while you wait for a relationship to happen only leads to unhappiness. I encourage you to live your life vision and purpose while you are single. The best way to find your life partner is to be a happy and successful single living the life that you really want. You are a successful single when you are truly happy as you are. So, go ahead and pursue your goal of a relationship while living life fully in the present and letting go of your attachment to future outcomes!

You are a successful single when you are truly happy as you are.

Cathy continued to date recreationally for the next year, but as time passed, she knew that she was ready for a long-term relationship. With her coach, she'd worked on being the Chooser and realized that she'd spent too much time simply responding to men's queries online. What would happen if SHE did the choosing? After browsing online and taking notes, Cathy wrote down the names of eight men who might meet her Requirements. Little did she know what special man was in that group!

She and Samuel e-mailed for months, but they were both so busy dating other people that they didn't connect in person. When they met for coffee that spring, there was a spark. Samuel was a forty-five-year-old divorced lawyer with two school-aged children who came from an alcoholic family and had given up drinking fifteen years before. He and his ex-wife had an amicable relationship. Cathy and Samuel continued to see each other every week for a few months, growing closer. Cathy had worked so much on her life Vision—as well as her dating skills—that she knew this love was real.

Samuel was very impressed and supportive of Cathy's coaching experiences and wanted to attend relationship coaching with her. Cathy's coach used a program for pre-committed couples called "Partners in Life" that helped them evaluate the compatibility of their life Vision together, enhance their communication skills, and explore the possibility of building a successful committed relationship with each other. Gradually, they let go of their fears and opened up to each other. Three months later they became so confident of their compatibility and readiness that they decided to get married. The day after Christmas, Samuel presented Cathy with his grandma's wedding ring, which fit perfectly. As did they!

Samuel presented Cathy with his grandma's wedding ring, which fit perfectly. As did they!

Relationship Readiness Assessment For Singles

BECOMING A SUCCESSFUL SINGLE

Below is a seventy-two-item Relationship Readiness Assessment for Singles. This assessment will help you identify specific goals for being a successful single.

Check (✓) each item in the ten areas below that is true for you. Try to be objective and honest with yourself. We recommend asking close friends and family members for their opinions as well.

I	MY VISION, VALUES, AND LIFE PURPOSE
	1. I have a vivid "Vision" of what I want for my life and my relationship
	2. I am clear about my values and live by them
	3. I have clearly defined my life purpose and put it into action daily
	4. I know where and how I want to live
	5. I have written goals and an action plan to help me achieve my Vision
	6. I am living my life fully and in alignment with my vision, values, and life purpose
	Total ✓

II	MY REQUIREMENTS
	7. I know what I will not tolerate in a relationship and don't tolerate these things
	8. I know what I can't live without in a relationship and don't settle for less
	9. I know what values I must share with a partner
	10. I am clear about what personality traits and qualities I most value in a partner
	11. I am clear about what interests/activities I must share with a partner
	12. I have a written list of requirements and will not enter a relationship if even one is missing
	13. I know that only I can be responsible for my own life and happiness
	Total ✓

III	MY NEEDS
	14. I am clear about what I need for a relationship to function for me on a daily basis
	15. I am clear about what I need emotionally to feel loved in a relationship
	16. I am clear about my boundaries and how to enforce them to get my needs met
	17. I ask for what I need and want, and take responsibility for the outcome

	18. I do not expect a relationship to meet all my needs and make me happy
	19. I have a support system to supplement meeting my social and emotional needs
	20. I have inner strength that helps me be self-reliant and proactive about my needs
	Total ✓
IV	**MY RELATIONSHIP HISTORY AND PATTERNS**
	21. I understand what did and didn't work for me in previous relationships
	22. I understand which positive and negative relationship patterns I risk repeating
	23. I am aware of the traits of my parents that drive my partner choices
	24. I am aware of specific traits of my parents in myself
	25. I am aware of habits, patterns, and values I have inherited from my family
	26. I understand my past patterns of choosing partners
	27. I understand my past relationship attitudes, choices, and actions/behaviors
	Total ✓

V	MY EMOTIONAL ISSUES
	28. My past relationship experiences do not impact my present relationships
	29. I have forgiven my parents for my past and present unmet needs
	30. I have let go of relationships that were damaging to me
	31. I have forgiven people who have hurt me
	32. I have sought forgiveness from people whom I may have hurt
	33. I am able to forgive myself for my past mistakes
	34. I trust that everyone does the best they can at all times
	35. I am aware of, and own, my emotional issues when they arise in a relationship
	Total ✓
VI	MY COMMUNICATION
	36. I do not gossip or talk about others
	37. I clearly communicate what I want and need; I don't make people guess
	38. I deal positively with misunderstandings and dis-agreements when they occur

	39. I own my judgments and accept differences with others
	40. I do not get defensive and take personally the things that people say about me
	41. I make requests rather than complain
	42. I regularly practice active listening, give validation, and express appreciation
	43. I am careful about what I promise and keep my word
	Total ✓
VII	**MY COMMUNITY**
	44. I am aware of how I come across and affect others
	45. I am surrounded by caring people
	46. I add value to everyone in my community
	47. I spend my social time with healthy, happy, able people
	48. I have positive relationships with my parents, siblings, children, and ex
	49. I have a close circle of friends and we gather regularly
	50. I take extraordinary care of the people I have chosen to love

	51. I am a member of two or more communities (hobby, spiritual, professional, etc)
	Total ✓
VIII	**MY LIFESTYLE**
	52. I am satisfied with my work/career
	53. I support my present lifestyle and am preparing for my future security
	54. I have no financial or legal problems
	55. I am happy and successful being single
	56. I am living the life that I want as a single person
	57. I am ready and available for commitment
	58. I am healthy in mind, body, and spirit
	Total ✓
IX	**MY DATING PATTERNS**
	59. I take initiative and responsibility for choosing who I want in my life and don't wait to be chosen
	60. I have clearly defined guidelines for sexual involvement that I adhere to
	61. I am authentic and do not present myself inauthentically to attract a partner

	62. I am able to communicate my issues and needs to dating partners
	63. I balance my heart with my head and make careful relationship choices
	64. I do not interpret infatuation, attraction, attachment, and/or good sex as "love"
	65. I do not expect a relationship to "rescue" me from emotional or financial problems
	Total ✓
X	**MY RELATIONSHIP PLAN**
	66. I understand and use the Law of Attraction (like attracts like)
	67. I scout, sort, and screen potential partners effectively
	68. I am clear whether I am seeking a short-term recreational relationship or am ready to seek a long-term committed relationship
	69. I effectively disengage from prospective partners who are not a fit for me
	70. I use my community support system to scout for me
	71. I am actively involved in activities and groups of people highly aligned with me
	72. I am balancing my partner search with investing in myself and living my vision
	Total ✓

CONSCIOUS DATING PLAN EXERCISE NO. 14:

Please refer to Chapter 15 to write your answers.

Are you a successful single?

After going over the above total scores in the Relationship Assessment above, ask yourself the following:

▶ What are your strongest areas?

▶ What areas need improvement?

▶ What do you need to learn more about?

▶ What are the top five items that could most interfere with the success of your next relationship?

▶ Given the above results, what are your top five goals for being a successful single?

1. _____

2. _____

3. _____

4. _____

5. _____

Your Conscious Dating Plan

15

You are now familiar with the principles and strategies of Conscious Dating. You know how to prepare for, and find, your life partner. Now, it's time to develop your individualized Conscious Dating Plan to help you translate your knowledge into action and find the partner you are seeking. Bravo! You're on your way to living the life you really want!

While working through this book, you have been preparing your Conscious Dating Plan by filling in your answers to the exercises here. This is invaluable to helping you get full benefit from the principles and strategies in this book, so please don't skip this part! You will now learn exactly how to use this information to find your life partner.

Sections I-VII below are the different parts of your Conscious Dating Plan, which you have read about in the preceding chapters. Section VIII will help you create a system to implement your plan. It's time for you to put the pieces of the puzzle together to find the love of your life and the life that you love.

[Note: I suggest using a notebook or journal to complete the following exercises.]

SECTION I: WHAT IS YOUR READINESS STATUS?

Are you ready for a committed relationship at this time in your life? The following questions will help you decide whether you're looking for a committed partner or short-term recreational relationships.

Exercise No. 1 [Chapter 1, Page 17]

Are you ready to date?

1. *Have you been hurt in a relationship? How do you think that affects your being single?*

2. *Do you believe that happiness in a relationship is really possible?*

3. *Do you believe that your next relationship can really be your last?*

4. *What do you think a fulfilling life partnership would look like?*

Exercise No. 2 [Chapter 2, Page 40]

What can you do when you're single to prepare to find your life partner?

1. *Imagine that you have $10 billion and ten years to live. Sit down in a quiet place and imagine one hundred things you would want to do in your remaining years.*

2. Don't forget the small things in your list, especially those things that make you feel loved.

3. If you get stuck, put the list down and pick it up again in a day or so.

Exercise No. 3 [Chapter 3, Page 60]

Let's play the Dating Traps Game!

1. Which dating traps have you fallen into?

2. Which trap is your riskiest?

3. If you could give yourself some expert advice, what would you say?

4. What will you plan to do to follow your own advice?

Exercise No. 4 [Chapter 4, Page 82]

How can you turn being single into an opportunity?

1. *At this point in the book, can you come up with at least three things that you've always wanted to do but have not done, due to finances, time constraints, or the fact that you were in a relationship?*

2. *On a scale of 0 to 10, does being single feel like an opportunity to you? (With 10 being very excited and positive)*

3. *If you did not write down a 10, how can you close the gap and be closer to being a 10? Is there something that you let go of or suppressed in your last relationship that you can do now? What have you always wanted to do that you have held back from doing until now?*

4. *Finally, pick one of the three things from Question 1 that you will act on today!*

Exercise No. 5 [Chapter 5, Page 104]

Who are you? What do you want?

1. *Make a list of your last three relationships that did not work out.*

2. *For each relationship, identify the top three reasons it ended.*

3. *Now look back over your list and ask yourself whether each reason was a Requirement or a Need. These test questions will help you determine the answers:*

A. Test Question for a Requirement:
If you fell in love with someone who was very attractive and also independently wealthy—and you really wanted this relationship to work—but _____ was missing, would you stay or break it off?

If it would be possible for you to stay in the relationship and find a way to make it work, then it is most likely not a Requirement. Try applying the test question for a Need below.

B. Test Question for a Need:
Would you experience discontent or an "issue" each time _____ occurred or did not occur?

If you answered "yes," then this issue is most likely a Need.

If your list item does not meet the test for a Requirement or Need, it is most likely a Want.

Exercise No. 6 [Chapter 10, Page 196]

What will you build, so he/she will come?

1. *Make a list of your "Shoulds"*
Sit down and make a list of ten things that you know you "should" do. What are they? Narrow this down to your top three most important goals.

2. *Now make a list of what might be interfering with these goals.*
Write them out in terms of consequences such as:

If I continue to _____, the Law of Attraction will _____

For example:

If I continue to overeat and gain more weight, the Law of Attraction will bring me a partner who also lacks impulse control.

If I continue to watch too much TV, the Law of Attraction will bring me nobody/a coach potato.

Now turn the above into positive statements, like this:

If I _____, the Law of Attraction will _____

For example: If I stop overeating and lose twenty pounds, the Law of Attraction will bring me a partner who is healthy and attractive.

Exercise No. 7: [Chapter 14, Page 267]

Relationship Readiness Assessment for Singles

► What are your strongest areas?

► What areas need improvement?

► What do you need to learn more about?

► What are the top five items that could most interfere with the success of your next relationship?

► What are your top five goals for being a successful single?

1. _____

2. _____

3. _____

4. _____

5. _____

SECTION II: WHAT ARE YOUR STRATEGIES FOR SCOUTING, SORTING, SCREENING, & TESTING?

How will you find compatible people to meet? How will you quickly determine if someone you meet is aligned with what you're looking for? How will you collect and test information about a potential partner before getting involved with him/her?

Exercise No. 8 [Chapter 6, Page 122]

Where will you look for your life partner?

1. Are you ready for a committed relationship right now? Or do you need more time? (Refer to Chapter 9: "Be Ready and Available for Commitment.") Are you going to date recreationally, or are you seeking your life partner?

2. Who will scout for you?

3. What attraction venues will you choose?

Level One: Public places, such as the supermarket, the post office, an art or wine festival

Level Two: Generic single setting, such as singles bar or event, personal ad

Level Three: Settings in which you share a strong interest with everyone there, such as a ski or bike club, yoga class

Level Four: Settings in which you share important values, goals and/or passions with everyone there, such as your church, service club, personal growth venue

4. *What are your sorting strategies?*

5. *What are your screening strategies?*

6. *What are your testing strategies?*

Note: We realize these questions are highly individual and might be best answered with the help of a coach. If you find these questions challenging, please consider taking our Conscious Dating Relationship Success Training for Singles (RESTS) program with one of our trained coaches.

Exercise No. 9 [Chapter 10, Page 196]

What will you build, so he/she will come?

1. *Construct a personal ad*

I want you to construct a personal ad, just as I did when I met Maggie. You don't have to run the ad or place it online, but it's important that you write a very specific and personal ad. Instead of trying to market yourself, try to be demanding!

2. *Network with your friends, family and people in your life*

Choose five people in your life who are closest to the life partner you are looking for. They might be young or old, or people you're only remotely acquainted with. Who are these people? How do they resemble your ideal life partner? Who do they know who would be good for you to meet?

SECTION III: WHAT ARE YOUR BOUNDARIES?

What are your guidelines for sexual involvement? Will you bring your date home? Will you allow your kids to meet your date? What are your expectations for dating? How will you clearly communicate them? How will you enforce your boundaries?

Exercise No. 10 [Chapter 7, Page 142]

What are your obstacles?

We all have obstacles that prevent us from being Choosers. All of these obstacles have been learned, and they can be unlearned. When reading each obstacle, do a "gut check," and if you experience the slightest physical or emotional reaction, it most likely applies to you. Make a check mark next to the ones that apply to you.

_____"I'm not good enough" (having low self esteem)

_____"It won't happen for me"; "I can't" (having limiting beliefs and attitudes)

_____"I must avoid rejection" (needing to be accepted or conforming to social pressures to feel worthy)

_____"I don't know how" (lacking creativity, information, or skill)

_____ "It's not ladylike"; "It's not gentlemanly" (adhering to gender roles)

279

_____ "I need approval"; "I don't want to hurt anyone" (needing to please others)

Remember: you can choose the attitudes you want to internalize. You are not stuck with them. Perhaps you won't feel it right away, but if you continue working on this, you will internalize new attitudes and they will become natural for you.

Now, go back to the above exercise and compose an affirmation for each obstacle so that it will no longer be in your way.

For example:

I must avoid rejection can be changed to: "I am The Chooser in my life. If someone rejects me, he/she is doing me a favor."

Instead of I'm not good enough, you can say: "I am OK as I am, and I deserve to be happy."

Instead of It won't happen for me, you can say: "It only takes one, and I'm the one."

Exercise No. 11 [Chapter 8, Page 159]

Is it really love?

1. Recall the last few times you were infatuated with someone and jumped into a relationship.

- How long did the infatuation last for you?
- How long did the relationship last?
- What broke up the relationship?
- What did you learn from that relationship?

2. *Who in your life will you seek out to get a reality check when you are infatuated with someone?*

3. *What is the minimum period you will date somebody before being physically intimate? How will you keep this boundary?*

Exercise No. 12 [Chapter 9, 179]

How ready are you?

Now that you have taken the Relationship Readiness Quiz, it's time to write down your results.

1. What is your total score

2. Do you get a Green Light? A Yellow Light? Or a Red Light?

3. For what form of dating are you ready?

A Green Light means you're ready to find your life partner. If you got a Yellow or Red Light, this means you should consider short-term recreational dating for now.

SECTION IV: WHO IS IN YOUR COMMUNITY?

Do you have, or are you building, a community that supports you? Are these important people in your life aware that you're actively seeking a partner? Are they clear about what you are seeking, and enrolled in helping you? How can you improve your community's role in supporting you to address your weaker areas as well as finding your life partner?

Exercise No. 13 [Chapter 11, Page 217]

What are your relationship challenges?

1. *How can you identify your relationship challenges? First, let's return to your past: and think about any relationship conflicts you can recall. They might have happened with anyone and in any time frame: a lover, parent, sibling, or neighbor.*

2. *Off the top of your head, make a list of five relationship conflicts that you recall. For example, I'm feeling let down and disappointed because last night's date didn't call me the next day.*

3. *A conflict is actually unskilled communication. It points to a place where you might be challenged. To identify the actual conflict, you might need to look back at the list of relationship skills above. Identify where your challenge is/was. The challenge might be: I did not overcome my fear and call him to express what a great time I had.*

4. *Write down which relationship skill was in deficit. What does this skill look like? How do other people do it? The skill here is: I don't wait by the phone. I strive to take risks by initiating phone calls.*

5. *Now choose one skill and practice it in your existing relationships. Once you're conscious, you can do it simply by choosing to do it.*

Exercise No. 14 [Chapter 12, Page 232]

Who will you invite to your Bachelor/Bachelorette party?

You learned in this chapter that one of the best ways to meet prospective singles is to enlist your friends' help. So, it's time to host a singles event! Tell your closest four to eight friends that you're hosting a gathering.

Ask each of your friends to invite one single person to the event to meet you. In other words, the price of admission is: "You must bring somebody good for me to meet." Be specific about your Requirements.

This will be your own personal Bachelor/Bachelorette party! Have fun screening!

Exercise No. 15 [Chapter 14, Page 267]

Use the items from the Relationship Readiness Assessment for Singles below to identify community and relationship goals.

VI	MY COMMUNICATION
	36. I do not gossip or talk about others
	37. I clearly communicate what I want and need; I don't make people guess
	38. I deal positively with misunderstandings and disagreements when they occur
	39. I own my judgments and accept differences with others
	40. I do not get defensive and "take personally" the things that people say about me
	41. I make requests rather than complain
	42. I regularly practice active listening, give validation, and express appreciation
	43. I am careful about what I promise and keep my word
	Total ✓

VII	MY COMMUNITY
	44. I am aware of how I come across and affect others
	45. I am surrounded by caring people
	46. I add value to everyone in my community
	47. I spend my social time with healthy, happy, able people
	48. I have positive relationships with my parents, siblings, children, and ex
	49. I have a close circle of friends and we gather regularly
	50. I take extraordinary care of the people I have chosen to love
	51. I am a member of two or more communities (hobby, spiritual, professional, etc)
	Total ✓

As you review the two sections from the Relationship Assessment above, ask yourself: "What are the top three issues here that I need to work on?"

SECTION V: HOW WILL YOU STAY ON TRACK?

How will you stay on track with your dating plan? First, glance back at the results you got from the Relationship Readiness Quiz. Which "light" are you? (Green, yellow, or red?) If you are not ready to find your life partner, how will you maintain detachment and stay available? How will you allow yourself to go through the process of finding your life partner without getting prematurely involved with somebody who is attractive to you but not in alignment with your requirements?

Exercise No. 16 [from Chapter 10, Page 196]

Use the section from the Relationship Readiness Assessment for Singles below to identify goals for being a successful single. [Chapter 14]

IX	MY DATING PATTERNS
	59. I take initiative and responsibility for choosing who I want in my life and don't wait to be chosen
	60. I have clearly defined guidelines for sexual involvement that I adhere to
	61. I am authentic and do not present myself inauthentically to attract a partner
	62. I am able to communicate my issues and needs to dating partners
	63. I balance my heart with my head and make careful relationship choices

	64. I do not interpret infatuation, attraction, attachment, and/or good sex as "love"
	65. I do not expect a relationship to "rescue" me from emotional or financial problems
	Total ✓

As you review this section from the Relationship Assessment above, ask yourself: "What is the most important issue here that I need to work on?"

SECTION VI: WHAT IS YOUR EXIT STRATEGY?

How will you disengage from prospects you decide to screen out? How will you break it off with someone who is pursuing you?

Exercise No. 17 [Chapter 13, Page 248]

How can you be more assertive?

It is time for you to identify social situations and interactions that might call for assertiveness. Write down a list of any circumstances when you might need to communicate your Needs or boundaries. Here are some examples:

1. *On a first date, do you want to pay the bill, split the bill, or be treated?*

2. When you give out your phone number, will it be your home or cell?

3. Is there a certain time when you don't want your date to call? (Not after 10 p.m.? Not when the kids might answer?)

4. Do you have boundaries around certain topics of conversation? Such as not discussing sexual preferences or what turns you on, on a first date?

5. Do you have boundaries around physical contact? Such as not kissing on a first date? Not going home with someone?

Now, choose one of your Needs or issues, and create a script to be assertive. What will you say to make it clear that you want to split the bill for dinner on your first date? How will you communicate that you don't want him/her calling your house late?

_____

_____

_____

_____

_____

And lastly, if you find that your date is not aligned with your Requirements, how will you clearly break it off? Write down what you plan to say and remember to practice assertiveness!

_____

_____

_____

_____

_____

SECTION VII: HOW WILL YOU TAKE CARE OF YOURSELF?

How will you take care of yourself during this important journey? How will you maintain balance in your life while striving to be a "successful single"? How will you consistently put yourself first and go after what you really want when there are so many forces—external and internal—attempting to influence you to settle for less?

Exercise No. 18 [Chapter 14, Page 267]

Use the sections from the Relationship Readiness Assessment for Singles below to identify goals for taking care of yourself.

VIII	MY LIFESTYLE
	52. I am satisfied with my work/career
	53. I support my present lifestyle and am preparing for my future security
	54. I have no financial or legal problems
	55. I am happy and successful being single
	56. I am living the life that I want as a single person
	57. I am ready and available for commitment
	58. I am healthy in mind, body, and spirit
	Total ✓

X	MY RELATIONSHIP PLAN
	66. I understand and use the Law of Attraction (like attracts like)
	67. I scout, sort, and screen potential partners effectively
	68. I am clear whether I am seeking a short-term recreational relationship or am ready to seek a long-term committed relationship
	69. I effectively disengage from prospective partners who are not a fit for me
	70. I use my community support system to scout for me
	71. I am actively involved in activities and groups of people highly aligned with me
	72. I am balancing my partner search with investing in myself and living my vision
	Total ✓

SECTION VIII: PUTTING IT ALL TOGETHER

Congratulations! You have been reflecting, dreaming, and thinking as you completed the above exercises in the previous fourteen chapters to identify your goals. Now you are ready to create your own Conscious Dating Plan.

To translate your knowledge in to action and stay on track, it's time to map out your goals, strategies, and action plans. This will ensure that you're on your way to finding the love of your life!

Exercise No. 19

Implementing your Conscious Dating Plan

Step One: *What are your goals?*

> Your goals are what you want to achieve in your life. First, decide how you're going to compile your goals. Will you write them down in a notebook or journal? Store them on your computer?

> Now it's time to compile all the goals you have identified in this book so far. Make sure your goals are PMS—positive, measurable, and specific.

> Example:

> "Contact at least five possible candidates through online personals each week."

Step Two: *What are your action steps?*

This is your detailed plan to carry out your goals (above). Be sure to write down all your action steps, and be creative!

Example:

1. Sign up with at least three Internet dating Web sites, including at least one that qualifies as a Level III or IV attraction venue (e.g. Jdate for Jewish singles, ConsciousDating.org, etc)

2. Make time to browse profiles at least twice per week. Schedule in calendar

3. Ask my best friend to browse profiles to help me scout and sort

4. Get help from my sister (the writer!) to compose an engaging message to send possible candidates that gives them more information about me, personalizing each to comment about what attracted me to their profile

Step Three: *How will you track your progress?*

Use a tracking system on your computer or a calendar to help you stay on track and trigger you to remember to implement your plans.

Set a time and day each week that you will review your goals and action steps. Be sure to space them apart so you don't get overwhelmed.

Example:

1. Create a file for each week. Print out the profile of every possible candidate I contact and put in file for tracking and reference

2. Review progress every Thursday evening after work when I meet with my coach

Step Four: *Get support.*

> When you're doing something new or challenging, get some help. Don't do this alone. Use a buddy, a coach, a mentor, a friend, or a family member to help you stay motivated and on track.

Remember, if you do what you've always done, you'll get what you've always got. Passively reading this book will not work for you. Take this opportunity to create your Conscious Dating Plan and get into action! ✕

Pre-Commitment: Is This "The One"?

Until this point I have focused on you as a single. You should be proud for choosing the path of consciousness to create a successful life for yourself. What happens next when you fall in love and wonder if he/she is "the one"? In this chapter I describe what happens when you, a conscious single, become a couple. Now it's time for you to look deeply at this relationship: will it evolve into a successful long-term partnership?

COMMITTED VERSUS PRE-COMMITTED ... WHAT'S THE DIFFERENCE?

When I travel around the country to give workshops about pre-commitment, I often display one of my favorite cartoons. It's about "The Quigmans," in which Francine is in the foreground with tears streaming down her face. Bob, her husband, is seen in the background throwing his hands up in the air. "You've cried every day since our wedding," he's saying. "I don't believe it's your allergies anymore."

After a good laugh, I explain to my audience that this married couple most likely skipped the pre-commitment stage when they were dating. They did not take the time to see if their relationship would really be a good long-term choice; instead, they jumped right into commitment. Evidently, for Francine, at least, marriage to Bob might not have been a good long-term choice.

So, what exactly does "pre-commitment" mean? I'm very proud of coining this term, since most relationship experts and literature have not yet recognized this stage. The pre-commitment stage is when singles become a couple and they ask themselves, "Is this the right relationship for me? Do I want to make a commitment here?" Pre-commitment is an opportunity for a couple to gain experience and knowledge about their relationship. It is a phase that is used by conscious couples to make a good long-term relationship choice, whether it means staying together and taking the next step toward commitment or un-choosing the relationship because it is not aligned with what one or both partners want for a life partnership.

Pre-commitment is an opportunity for

a conscious couple to gain experience and

knowledge about their relationship.

A few years ago, without any marketing on my part, I started to see a new kind of couple show up in my practice. This couple would announce to me that they had been seeing each other for a while and were thinking of taking the next step toward commitment, and want my help in determining if this would be a good long-term relationship choice for them. Sometimes an individual would consult me for a "reality check," but more often it was the couple. This is the hallmark of the pre-commitment stage: one or both partners are unsure of the future of their relationship, so they're asking themselves, "Is this the one? Should I spend the rest of my life with this person?"

I had not yet come up with the term "pre-commitment," and I wasn't quite sure what to do with these couples. I recall that first couple who came to my office, saying, "We've been dating for three months now, and we'd like to know if we're making the right choice–" I was astounded. I didn't know what to do with them! I didn't have a crystal ball and couldn't find an existing model of helping these clients determine if this relationship was a good long-term choice. They were not a committed couple, and most of my training, experience, and tools did not apply. I didn't even know what to call them; the language of my profession did not seem to recognize this kind of couple.

One or both partners are unsure of

the future of their relationship,

so they're asking themselves, "Is this

the One? Should I spend the rest

of my life with this person?"

Like most other therapists in this position whom I have talked to since, I started working with these couples from a "premarital" perspective, but that didn't seem right to me. In premarital counseling, two people have made a commitment to each other and now are seeking support to get their relationship off to a good start. Since these new couples were not yet committed—and trying to decide whether to take that step—I decided to call them "pre-committed."

Indeed, the pre-committed couple is a phenomenon of our times. The divorce rate and its incredibly high social costs permeate our culture. The marriage rate has declined. I believe these are signs that we are moving toward "quality" over "quantity." But does this mean that fewer people want a Life Partnership? No. The majority of singles still want a committed relationship; however, I think they are becoming better informed consumers who don't want to be sold a lemon. But the desire for committed relationships seems to remain constant.

AM I STILL IN THE TESTING STAGE?

I find that most singles today are more realistic about their futures, but also more skeptical, cautious, and fearful of failure. Are you single and over thirty? Have you let go of that romantic ideal in which you "follow your heart" and plunge blindly into a committed relationship? Most of us want to be in a successful, committed relationship, but we are not sure how to achieve it. Maybe this is why you picked up my book in the first place.

At this point, I'm confident that you are clear about who you are and what you want. You now have the tools to make good relationship choices. In Chapter 11, "Gain Relationship Skills and Knowledge," I wrote about relationship attitudes, and said that you can choose your own attitudes. If you're dating right now, what's your attitude? Are you gaining experience and knowledge as you get to know people? Are you testing the reality before deciding if you're going to become a couple? If so, you are in the testing phase, which I covered in Chapter 6, "Learn How to Get What You Want," and discussed Scouting, Sorting, Screening, and Testing.

A pre-committed relationship is not

the same as a premarital one.

You are not engaged to be married.

Have you found someone you'd like to get serious with? Are you in an exclusive relationship and asking yourself, "Is this the right relationship for me?" If so, you are in the pre-commitment stage, which means that you're really asking, "Should I commit?" Again, if you are in a pre-committed relationship, this is not the same as a premarital one. You are not engaged to be married. Rather, you are asking yourself if you want to commit to this other person. You are at a point where it's still possible to "un-choose" the relationship if you two are not aligned. You know that having a happy and successful life is more important to you than this particular relationship being "it."

TRYING TO "MAKE" THE RELATIONSHIP WORK

What if you are ready to commit, but your boyfriend/girlfriend isn't so sure? When I hear this as a coach, a red flag starts waving in front of me. I've learned the hard way that you cannot "make" a relationship work by yourself. If you came to me and said that you wanted to start relationship coaching without your partner, I would caution you that this is probably a pattern you're starting. As a coach, I would not want you to try to "fix" a pre-committed relationship on your own. Rather, I would work with you to help you see the reality of "what is" and make conscious choices about it.

In a pre-committed relationship,

working too hard to make the round

peg fit the square hole can

be a sign that it is not a good fit.

When a relationship is "new"—as are most pre-committed relationships—this is the time that most couples are most motivated to be together. This is when they really want to experience and enhance the relationship. If someone in this stage doesn't appear to have much energy for doing so during this period, and/or takes a "my way or no way" attitude, it sends up a big red flag. Certainly, this reflects a serious lack of mutuality, flexibility and open-mindedness.

Behavior is not random. Nothing ever happens just once. If your boyfriend/girlfriend is closed to what you're suggesting or rigid to your proposal, I would ask, "Is this part of a pattern?" If you're hearing that things are "Just fine" or "I'm too busy," that doesn't wash well. You better believe that if he/she had a priority in which he wanted his/her partner's participation—such as finances—he/she wouldn't accept a brush-off.

We need to carefully judge when to "work" on a relationship. When you're in a committed relationship, this is a no-brainer. You're going to do what it takes. In a pre-committed relationship, working too hard to make the round peg fit the square hole can be a sign that it is not a good fit.

ATTACHMENT VERSUS LOVE

Have you noticed that it takes a while to get someone out of your system after a breakup? Recently, I was talking to one of our trainers at Relationship Coaching Institute, Lynne Michelson, about this experience. "Singles know perhaps the relationship was not healthy, or that they are better off without the other person, but they still feel hooked," she said. "They might also know their Requirements were not being met, but they cannot get the person 'out' of them."

We talked about how tortuous it is to feel strongly about someone, really want it to work, but choose to let the relationship go because you must. I think that what keeps relationships together and makes breaking up hard to do is more than love; it is attachment.

What keeps relationships together and makes breaking up hard to do is more than love; it is attachment.

What is attachment? We talked about this in Chapter 8. Attachment can mean many things, ranging from emotional affection to physical fixation. Psychologists have whole theories around attachment and identify clinical disorders caused by it. I like to define it simply as a "strong emotional bond." As humans, we get attached. We are attached to objects, such as cars, houses, money, books, and clothes. We get attached to routines, such as washing our hands or reading before bed. We are attached to beliefs, such as killing is wrong. We are attached to sensations and experiences, such as orgasm. We are attached to certain activities, such as work or exercise. And we also get attached to people. In the extreme, our attachment can be an addiction.

Love is a positive feeling toward

something or somebody. On the other hand,

attachment is an emotional need

for something or somebody.

But how are love and attachment different? Love is a positive feeling toward something or somebody. On the other hand, attachment is an emotional need for something or somebody. The major difference seems to be that love is other-directed and attachment is self-centered. So what do you do if you feel attached? Well, you're on your way, because the first step in letting go of an attachment is to be clear about love versus attachment.

WHY ATTACHMENT DOES NOT SERVE YOU:

- Attachment is not love

- Attachment is about me and my needs

- Attachment has consequences: if you continue to pursue a relationship that doesn't work, you're setting yourself up for failure

---

It can be hard to let go of someone if you fear falling into a chasm of pain and emptiness. I urge you to get the support you need to move on and pursue involvement in activities and with people that are productive for you. A coach and/or support group is great for this.

IS THIS THE RIGHT RELATIONSHIP FOR ME?

Most of us want a fulfilling life partnership and have little idea of how to create one. Even couples in successful long-term relationships have little insight into why they are successful. As recently as one generation ago, powerful social and economic pressures brought and kept couples together. For thousands of years, marriage was a contract to create an economic unit for the purpose of raising children and ensuring the survival of the species. Our society has evolved to the point where survival is taken for granted. Instead, it is our desire for love and emotional fulfillment that brings us together. Unfortunately, while we want to be happy, we do not seem to know exactly what we want or how to get what we want.

If you're in the pre-commitment stage, hopefully you are living in the present and focused on your connection with this other person. Hopefully you're not overly attached to a specific future outcome for this relationship, nor wanting to be with this person as some sort of prize. This person seems to fit with your life Vision, and both of you are striving to be authentic and honest.

When you enter a relationship consciously, the pre-commitment stage can enhance your chances for long-term success. It requires a delicate balance of investing in the relationship while staying objective. You need to be prepared to end things if your Vision, Purpose, and Requirements do not align well with the reality. The goal of the pre-commitment stage is to take the time needed to gain experience and knowledge—instead of relying upon hope and potential. This requires patience, awareness, and grounding in reality. You need to be willing to break off the relationship if it's not a good fit even though, as we all know, breaking up is hard to do.

If you think of entering a committed relationship as being like sky-diving, are you going to plan ahead by studying at ground school before putting on your parachute? Or, will you finally be motivated to learn when you are at thirty thousand feet and about to jump? The couples I coach in the pre-commitment stage strive to be conscious and objective about the future of their relationship.

COUPLES WHO ARE PRE-COMMITTED AIM TO:

• become clear about whether this relationship is right for them

• get a reality check

• stay on track with what they really want

• develop strategies for testing and decision-making

• address emotional and compatibility issues

FORCED VERSUS NATURAL

When I speak to singles around the country about pre-commitment, I tell them, "We need to let the relationship evolve as it's meant to be, not force it to be what we want it to be." How do you let a relationship evolve naturally? First, give yourself as much time as necessary. Have enough self-love to not settle! This means asking yourself: What's the minimum amount of time you need before you commit yourself to someone? Only you know the answer to this. Do you need three months? Six months? One year? I've worked with some couples who needed five years before deciding to get married.

> *We need to let the relationship*
>
> *evolve as it's meant to be, not force*
>
> *it to be what we want it to be.*

This question is very similar to asking, "How long should I date someone before I have sex?" Look closely at your own comfort levels, and give yourself the gift of time. I caution you against pressuring yourself into jumping into the illusion of living happily ever after. So often, we want to be ahead of where we are. When we are single, we want to be in a relationship. And when we are in a relationship, we want to be committed and live happily ever after. But the conscious single does not decide to be a couple after two dates.

In a pre-committed relationship, it is best to let the relationship be what it is and evolve naturally rather than try to force it to fit your fantasies and goals. If it's hard to make this relationship work, then it's probably a sign that this is not lined up with who you are and what you what. If you have been conscious and intentional about your relationship, you will be no further than the pre-commitment stage, and while breaking up is hard, the relationship is still reversible. Once a commitment is made, it tends to be irreversible and the consequences run high for breaking up. Unmet Requirements are not justifications for walking away from a committed relationship; the decision to walk away from a relationship is best made before making a commitment.

In a pre-committed relationship,

it is best to let the relationship be what

it is and evolve naturally, rather than try to force

it to fit your fantasies and goals.

It might sound simplistic to make this analogy, but it's like trying on clothes. Either an outfit fits or it does not. If there's a fit and you like the way it looks, then buy it! If it doesn't fit or look good, that outfit will just sit in the back of your closet. No, a relationship is not a commodity, but if a relationship does or does not fit you, it will be obvious.

When a couple comes to me in conflict during pre-commitment coaching, I'll sometimes ask each person, "Be honest with me: Are you trying to make this relationship work, even though you sense that it's not going to in the long run?" If you're trying to "make" it work, you're probably making a mistake. It should not be that hard, especially early in the relationship before dealing with the natural stresses of a committed relationship. If it's that hard, probably there's not enough alignment here. Believe me, I can personally testify that a misalignment has no future—after being in two marriages that ended in divorce.

HE LIKES BEER

I recall one of the first pre-committed couples I ever coached: Brett and Maria were high school sweethearts now in their mid-twenties who lived together. I mentioned them in Chapter 8. They were the "perfect couple" who dreamed about getting married and having children, and their families were very invested in their future together. But there was a problem: Brett liked beer. Of course, the conflict went deeper that that. Maria was the adult child of alcoholics, and every time her boyfriend opened a can of beer, she felt anxious. She had worked on these issues in therapy, but nonetheless she still felt stressed out.

Maria was the adult child

of alcoholics, and every time her boyfriend

opened a can of beer, she felt anxious.

Brett showed no signs of alcoholism, but he liked to drink a beer after work every day, and a six-pack with buddies every weekend. He had never been in trouble with the law and he did not drive while drinking. Brett really wanted this relationship to work, and he'd even tried giving up beer for Maria. But then he felt resentful, because he was giving up something he really enjoyed. Maria, who was also very eager to commit herself to this relationship, tried going into the other room whenever Brett opened a beer. But she could smell the alcohol on his breath, and she saw the empty cans. As their coach, I gave them the space to talk. We worked together for three months, attempting to move forward. I did not have any magic answers, but we looked closely at their Requirements. We talked about whether Brett's beer drinking might be an unsolvable problem. Were they trying to force this relationship to work, rather than letting it evolve?

Were they trying to force

this relationship to work, rather

than letting it be what it is?

In the meantime, Maria was miserable, and three months after we started, she became very clear. "I require an alcohol-free marriage," she said. She knew this was connected to her traumatized past, but was clear that this was a Requirement for her. Rather than force herself to commit to Brett—and lead an unhappy life—she decided that they needed to break up. It was a bittersweet ending. It was heart-wrenching to see this couple come to an end, but I knew they were both now free to have the lives they really wanted.

"We've been dating for two months now and we're

real committed!"... He was way ahead of himself.

GETTING AHEAD OF YOURSELF

I recall this middle-aged man who walked into my office with his girlfriend for pre-commitment coaching and declared: "We've been dating for two months now and we're real committed!"

His girlfriend didn't look so sure. Her expression showed discontent, which this man, in all his excitement, didn't seem to notice. He was way ahead of himself, so eager to make this relationship work. In his fantasy, he was committed: he and his girlfriend were now a "we." But she was shaking her head, and clearly skeptical about all of this.

Singles often become couples very easily and quickly. In your life, were you ever single one day, and in a relationship the next? Many pre-committed couples focus on creating a committed relationship regardless of red flags. Many divorces result from couples trying to fit the round peg in the square hole and "make" their relationship work, even in the face of serious deficiencies. Often, the red flags are waving right in front of our eyes, but we have decided to ignore them. Rather than openly facing what our relationship lacks—and asking ourselves hard questions about what we value—we choose to believe that love conquers all. "Working" on the relationship often seems less painful than breaking up and starting over.

Avoiding commitment does not prevent the pain or costs of a failed relationship.

TRYING TO AVOID FAILURE BY STAYING PRE-COMMITTED

On the other hand, couples who fear failure often seek to avoid commitment by staying pre-committed. While they might feel safe withholding commitment, these couples often act committed by living together, and even having children. Studies have shown that cohabiting couples have lower success rates and higher rates of domestic violence than committed couples.

In the National Crime Victimization Survey, conducted by the U.S. Department of Justice, of all violent crimes committed by intimate partners between 1979 and 1987, 65 percent were committed by boyfriends or ex-husbands. Husbands committed just 9 percent of these crimes. The First Step Family Violence Intervention Center (www.firststepweb.org) has launched a "We Believe in Marriage" campaign, which states that we must take action to clear up the misperceptions around marriage and domestic violence. The center states that research indicates that a healthy marriage is probably the best deterrent to domestic violence. First Step considers its efforts to honor successful marriages and to provide relationship skills a good strategy to help prevent even the first acts of family violence.[1]

Maggie Gallagher, co-author with Linda Waite of *The Case For Marriage*, says that it's "clear that boyfriends are far more dangerous to women than husbands: 55 percent of all violent crimes committed by intimate partners in 1992-93 were committed by current or former boyfriends; husbands accounted for 31 percent of domestic acts of violence against women, and ex-husbands were responsible for 14 percent of such incidents. Even when it comes to murder, killings are more likely to happen to unmarried cohabiters than spouses... Regardless of methodology, the studies yielded similar results: cohabiters engage in more violence than spouses."[2]

PRE-COMMITMENT AND COHABITATION

"When 'living together' waits for marriage, 'commitment' and 'forever' are more likely to be part of the package," says Diane Sollee, MSW, founder and director of the Washington, D.C.-based Coalition for Marriage, Family and Couples Education and director of Smart Marriages.

She was responding as "Dr. Romance"—an advice column at www.smartmarriages.com—to a letter sent to her by a young woman who was thinking about having her boyfriend move in with her. The young woman wrote: "He says it makes no sense to pay rent on two places when he's here all the time anyway. He also says we need to see if we can live together before we get married, and I can see his point."[3]

But she was concerned because her mother had just told her about a study that said couples who live together before marriage actually have a higher divorce rate. One study about marriage and cohabitation, for example, from the Centers for Disease Control in 2002 (yes, the CDC does see marriage as a part of disease control!) showed that unmarried cohabitations overall are less stable than marriages. The probability of a first marriage ending in separation or divorce within five years is 20 percent, but the probability of a premarital cohabitation breaking up within five years is 49 percent. After ten years, the probability of a first marriage ending is 33 percent, compared with 62 percent for cohabitations.

"Dr. Romance" had this to say:

> Your boyfriend is right—you would save money living together. He is using the prevailing logic, that with the current 50 percent divorce rate it makes sense to try things out in advance. But studies have found that cohabitation isn't enough like marriage to be a good test. Cohabitation can also set up a destructive way of thinking: "If this isn't working, we should bail out."

Sollee also urged this young woman to read the research, which shows "that couples who are formally engaged, set the date, and reserve the hall before they move in together improve their odds. Moving in with your 'fiancé' is different than moving in with your 'boyfriend.'"

Many of us have a fear of commitment. It can feel easier to cohabitate without actually committing to each other. This is a "mini-marriage." Many couples feel like they'll minimize emotional risk by not committing. But the truth is—cohabitation actually increases risk! The fact is, you're living together, but your attitudes are leaving the back door wide open (the one with the "Exit" sign above it), which becomes a self-fulfilling prophecy.

David Popenoe, professor of sociology and co-director of the National Marriage Project at Rutgers University, has referred to cohabitation as "the marriage enemy:"

> Hollywood stars are doing it. Most American young people are doing it. Even some politicians now do it. When blushing brides and dashing grooms walk down the aisle today, more than half have already lived together. Cohabitation is replacing marriage

as the first living-together experience for young men and women.⁴

Popenoe acknowledges that living together seems like a good way to achieve some of the benefits of marriage without the risk of divorce. You can share expenses and learn more about each other. You can find out whether your partner has what it takes to be married. If things don't work out, breaking up is easier to do. You don't have to seek legal or religious permission to dissolve your union.

But, Popenoe warns, evidence suggests that living together is not a good way to prepare for marriage or to avoid divorce: "Cohabiting unions tend to weaken the institution of marriage and pose clear dangers for women and children." He says that unmarried couples have lower levels of happiness and well-being than married couples. Between 1960 and 2004, the number of unmarried couples in America increased by nearly 1,200 percent, according to the National Marriage Project.⁴ Moreover, over half of all first marriages are now preceded by living together, compared to virtually none fifty years ago.

"The belief that living together before marriage is a useful way 'to find out whether you really get along,' and thus avoid a bad marriage and an eventual divorce, is now widespread among young people," say Popenoe and Whitehead in their report on *The State of Our Unions: The Social Health of Marriage in America 2005*. "But the available data on the effects of cohabitation fail to confirm this belief. In fact, a substantial body of evidence indicates that those who live together before marriage are more likely to break up after marriage."

The National Marriage Project offers four principles to help guide the thinking of pre-marrieds on the question "Should we live together?"

1. **Consider not living together at all before marriage.** There is no evidence that if you decide to cohabit before marriage you will have a stronger marriage than those who don't live togeth-

er, and there is some evidence to suggest that if you live together before marriage, you are more likely to divorce.

2. Don't make a habit of cohabiting. Multiple cohabiting is a strong predictor of the failure of future relationships.

3. Limit cohabitation to the shortest possible period of time. The longer you live together with a partner, the more likely it is that the low-commitment ethic of cohabitation will take hold, the opposite of what is required for a successful marriage.

4. Do not cohabit if children are involved. Children need and should have parents who are committed to staying together.

FACT VERSUS ATTITUDE

Commitment is both a FACT demonstrated by behavior, and an ATTITUDE consisting of thoughts and beliefs. Saying vows and exchanging rings in front of witnesses establishes the fact of commitment, as does the behavior of staying in an unhappy relationship no matter what. A committed attitude involves thoughts and beliefs to stay in the relationship under all circumstances.

The example of the pre-committed couple above, where the man announced, "We've been dating for two months now and we're real committed," is an example of premature commitment and a misalignment of fact and attitude. They are pre-committed in fact, with a committed attitude. I've worked with many married couples on the verge of divorce where one or both partners had an uncommitted attitude such as "I'm not so sure this is the right relationship for me." In my experience, couples who have a disconnect between fact and attitude rarely stay together.

Making a commitment to a relationship is a serious and irreversible choice, not to be taken lightly or entered into quickly, because you can never go back to the way your life was before. When you are single, dating is your opportunity to explore possibilities. A pre-committed relationship is your chance to fully compare your requirements with the reality. Ideally, you then make a commitment with full consciousness and clarity that this is what you want, accepting all challenges and obstacles as part of the package.

A committed couple has typically performed an identifiable act, symbolic or formal, to become committed; usually, but not always, with the intention of staying together for Life. The fact is: you are married. Your attitudes are aligned. This means that your commitment is explicit, and both of you are well aware of it. In this context, most of us would say there are no exits, and unhappiness alone is not a viable reason to leave the relationship.

Commitment is usually a gradual process, starting with agreeing to the first meeting and the first date, planning future dates, spending time and money together, becoming exclusive, becoming sexually involved, meeting each other's family, spending the weekend together, etc.

If you're in a relationship right now, what's your attitude? This is the array of couples I've worked with:

- Are you both pre-committed?

- Is one of you pre-committed while the other is committed?

- Are both of you committed?

- Are both of you committed, but still holding onto pre-committed attitudes?

- Do both of you have a prematurely committed attitude?

If you are both pre-committed with commitment as your goal, you need to work to achieve the clarity to make a decision to commit or not. It is important that each of you has clarity about your Vision and Requirements. If one of you is pre-committed and the other has a committed attitude, there is incongruence here. I worked with one couple who had been living together for seven years; she was talking about commitment and marriage the entire time, while he continually put her off until he was "sure."

If you are both committed in fact and attitude, the challenges in your relationship are not reasons to think or talk about leaving. This kind of commitment sustains couples through the hard times and strengthens their relationship. As a relationship coach, I love working with couples in this stage!

If you are both committed in action or fact—yet have a pre-committed attitude—you need to ask yourself why you're leaving the door open. Perhaps you're unmarried but have children together, bought property, cohabitate, or have made clear commitments by your actions, but still feel unsure. Or, perhaps you're married and you see divorce as a way to escape the pain and challenges that are overwhelming you.

If both of you have a prematurely committed attitude, you need to look at why it's premature. Are you trying to force this relationship rather than letting it evolve naturally? Are you truly ready and available for commitment? I had a couple seek my help who were both still married to other people when they had an affair with each other and decided they wanted to be together, but were having problems. It was clear that their commitment to each other was premature, as neither was ready and available for the other.

If a committed couple comes in and wants my help to determine whether to stay in the relationship, I explain that if they have made a commitment, my job is to help them make it work. I talk with them about their level of commitment and have them examine their attitudes and choices. While neutral about the outcome of pre-committed relationships, I am not neutral about commitment. I assume that their agenda is to keep their commitment, and we need to discuss and agree on that agenda if we are to work together.

PARTNERS IN LIFE

You remember Cathy, the almost-forty-year-old woman who had divorced and gone back to school to earn her daycare license. Now, joyous children were bouncing around her home, and she was the happiest she'd ever been. She had met Samuel, a forty-five-year-old divorced lawyer with two school-aged children, online. Like Cathy, he had done much soul-searching to figure out his life Vision and Requirements. They'd been dating for six months when they decided to seek a pre-commitment coach.

One of their biggest issues was their religious differences. Cathy, a Christian, went to church every Sunday. Samuel, a Jew, had raised his kids to be Jewish but only went to the synagogue on high holidays. Cathy felt that it was very important for her partner to come to church with her, but Samuel wasn't interested. So, they found a coach through my Partners in Life program to help them evaluate the compatibility of their life Vision together.

For the next three months, they worked on enhancing their communication skills. Cathy did not want to convert Samuel to Christianity, but she really wanted his company in church on Sundays. He did go every once in a while, but begrudgingly. In the end, he was unhappy next to her in the chapel, and she was unsatisfied.

Their coach introduced to them the concept of "Gimme." This is a relationship strategy, which their coach explained as follows:

> *"When you want something from your partner, and he/she is reluctant to do it, you can ask for a Gimme. Essentially, this is a gift you give to your partner, even if you really don't want to it. You do it simply to make your partner happy."*

Over the months, Samuel and Cathy learned how to compromise with their religious differences. Samuel joined Cathy at church a couple of Sundays a month, and she in turn went to baseball games with him on a couple of Saturdays. They worked hard to make their relationship fulfilling, creating a new shared Vision for their life together.

Cathy asked herself: "Am I prepared to live with the fact that Samuel will not go to church with me every Sunday, as I'd like? ... Am I hoping that Samuel will be different one day?"

TO BE SUCCESSFUL PARTNERS FOR LIFE IN TODAY'S WORLD YOU MUST:

- **Be clear about who you are and what you want**

- **Make a good partner choice aligned with what you want**

- **Learn how to get what you want**

CONSCIOUS VERSUS UNCONSCIOUS PRE-COMMITMENT
Pre-committed couples generally fall into two categories:

UNCONSCIOUS: typically following the "mini-marriage" model of trying the relationship out, acting committed without actually making the commitment. A misalignment of fact and attitude.

CONSCIOUS: aware that they are not yet committed, usually have commitment as a goal, asking themselves "Is this the right relationship for me? Should I make a commitment?" An alignment of fact and attitude.

WHAT IS COMMITMENT?
When couples come to counseling or coaching, they usually want the relationship to work and are not aware of the difference between

pre-commitment and commitment. Since I discovered the significance of the pre-commitment stage and the role of fact versus attitude in determining the success of a relationship, I usually begin coaching an unmarried couple by asking about the status of the relationship. Most couples will describe their relationship as committed and are confused about making a distinction between committed or pre-committed. The conversation that follows is often enlightening to all of us!

To help answer the question "What is commitment" when the couple isn't married, I offer the following:

You are NOT in a committed relationship if:

1. Your partner is not aware your relationship is committed

2. You are wondering if this relationship is committed

3. You and your partner have differences of opinion about the status of your relationship

4. Your family and friends have different perceptions about the status of your relationship

5. You and your partner have not acted to explicitly formalize your commitment in some way

6. You are relying on verbal promises of commitment without a significant track record of them being kept

A commitment is explicit and unambiguous. A commitment is a formal event of some kind between two people. A commitment is something you DO over time. A real commitment is usually legally enforceable and there are consequences for breaking it. And, for a relationship to be truly committed, there are no exits—mentally, emotionally, or physically. When the going gets rough, you make it work.

So, when is a relationship committed? When there is an alignment of fact and attitude. What creates the "fact" of commitment?

I propose these three criterion to determine if a relationship is committed:

CRITERIA #1: Promises made to each other about the permanent nature of the relationship that are kept

CRITERIA #2: Explicit, formal, public declaration

CRITERIA #3: Unambiguous to partners and others

In today's world, if all three of the above are met, I would say it is a committed relationship, whether legally married or not.

CONCLUSION

I hope that you recognize that the pre-commitment stage represents an opportunity to gain experience and knowledge about a relationship. I hope you'll have the courage to stay conscious and make a good long-term relationship choice, whether it's to stay together or not. ✿

CONSCIOUS DATING PLAN EXERCISE NO. 16:

Appreciations and Issues

If you are in a pre-committed relationship:

1. Pause for a moment and think about what you appreciate about your relationship with your partner. List the first ten things that come to your mind, without judgment. They can be big or small, important or unimportant. If you run out of ideas, take a break and return to the list.

2. Now list ten issues that you experience with your partner or the relationship. List everything that comes to you, without judgment. They can be big or small, important or unimportant.

3. Review your appreciations and rate each one on a scale from 0 (unimportant) to 10 (very important) on their level of importance to you. A low number means that you could get by without it, and a high number means you would not be happy in a relationship without it.

4. Review your issues and mark each one with "R" if it's a Requirement, "N" if it's a Need and "W" if it's a Want.

- Remember that Requirements are nonnegotiable: they must happen for the relationship to continue.

- Needs must happen for the relationship to work for you, but they are negotiable: you would not break up if they weren't met.

- Wants are pleasurable, changeable, and can be substituted.

5. What challenges do you have in your relationship right now? If you have a coach or therapist, it's best to share your findings with him/her.

It CAN Happen For You!

Congratulations! You have learned the Ten Principles of Conscious Dating and are starting to apply them in your daily life. By doing so, you are not settling for less. You are no longer living in fear that you won't find what you really want.

You are the pioneer of your own life. If you started reading this book with some anxiety or fear about relationships, I hope you now are more confident. You can live anywhere. You can make a living doing just about anything you want. You can start the business you've always dreamed about. You can be a self-made millionaire or a monk. You can have a community of people who support you.

If you were feeling lonely before—or alone, even in a relationship—now you have the tools and strategies to consciously choose to have positive people in your life and be in a loving relationship. It's up to you! You are capable of finding and having the relationship you really want.

It's not too late to have the life and relationship that are genuinely for you.

The truth has been there all along, but you might not have noticed it. You are not too old, overweight, or unattractive. You are not too poor, busy, or uneducated. Now that you're single, you have the opportunity to find or reinvent yourself. It's not too late to have the life and relationship that are genuinely for you. You can create the life that you really want; you can prepare for and find the relationship that you really want.

WHERE ARE THEY NOW?

Did you pick up this book after a recent breakup and realize that you need some time to be on your own and re-create your life? Or, have you worked hard on being a successful single, and now you're ready to dive back into the dating scene? Are you dating recreationally right now, or seeking your life partner?

While reading *Conscious Dating*, you met real singles who were going through situations similar to yours. Like you, they are on their way to becoming the pioneers of their own lives. Perhaps you recognized yourself in at least one of the singles on his or her journey.

Here is what the singles featured in *Conscious Dating* are doing today

Angela

Angela is the forty-year-old single mother of a teenage son who was deserted by her boyfriend. Angela grieved for months; her son also felt abandoned, and gloominess enveloped their household. Angela spoke honestly with her son, explaining to him that although she wanted to find her life partner, she wasn't in a rush. She certainly didn't want to risk hurting him again. She decided that she would be single—by choice for now—while consciously focusing on the positive aspects of her life, such as spending quality time with her son and making positive changes in her community as a social worker. Her friend and coach, Gretchen, supported her in staying true to her Vision.

One day at the gym, forty-five-year-old Jerry approached Angela in the sauna. At first, she was turned off because he didn't have a job, like her ex-boyfriend. But she agreed to go on a date, and learned that Jerry was taking off some time to pursue some lifelong dreams. They've been dating for a few months now, and Angela is very drawn to him. But Angela has made her boundaries very clear (which Jerry respects) and has told him that she's not getting serious with anyone right now and is not available for an exclusive relationship.

This weekend she's throwing a bachelorette party for herself at her condo in Raleigh. Five of her closest girlfriends will show up at her home this Friday with both a tasty appetizer and a (tasty) man!

Mark

After his divorce, thirty-five-year-old Mark fell hard into the Packaging Trap, chasing after young, "hot," beautiful women. Sure, the sex was great, but Mark felt empty. After hitting bottom financially and losing his live-in girlfriend, Mark was down in the dumps.

As he approached forty, he felt old and lost. Even his own daughters were canceling their weekend plans with him to be with their mother instead. It was Mark's cousin who suggested that he join the Peace Corps. At first, Mark resisted: being alone in a foreign country would certainly force him to face himself!

But Mark joined the Corps and found himself in love with the jungles of the Dominican Republic. He also fell in love with Miranda, whom he'd met during their brief orientation. Every week, Mark wrote letters to this lovely thirty-year-old computer consultant from Boston who was making some radical life changes, too. They opened themselves up slowly by mail, talking about their Requirements, boundaries, and life Visions. A year later, Miranda asked for a transfer from Thailand, and moved into Mark's two-room cottage near the beach.

Mark joined the Corps and found himself in love

with the jungles of the Dominican Republic.

He also fell in love with Miranda.

Two years later, back in the United States, Mark invited Miranda to move in with him. She relocated across the country to Mark's big home in the northern California hills. During their first weekend together, the couple attended a workshop on pre-committed relationships. It became clear how aligned their life Visions were, and how much they could support each other's careers. Mark opened his own consulting office a half hour from their home, and Miranda operated her translating business from their home. Just as importantly, Mark's girls adored Miranda—and happily tossed flowers down the aisle when their Dad remarried last summer!

Cathy

Cathy was grieving the end of a ten-year codependent marriage when we met her. At age thirty-eight, she had been battling depression for years, but she saw a psychiatrist to get some support, and decided to move from Denver to Cincinnati to be closer to her father. With her divorce finalized, Cathy signed up for one of my Conscious Dating Relationship Success Training for Singles (RESTS) courses.

Cathy went back to school and became licensed to open a daycare in her own home. Surrounded by children, she was happy for the first time in years! Her next move was putting herself online and dating recreationally while she continued to work on her life with one of the coaches trained by Relationship Coaching Institute.

After a year of dating many men, Cathy met Samuel, a forty-eight-year-old electrical engineer and avid hiker. They were very attracted to each other and after a few months they started going on camping trips together. Every night in the tent they talked and talked, and Cathy saw that Samuel's life Vision was very aligned with hers and he seemed to meet all her Requirements. Like Cathy, he was a loving and joyful person who encouraged compassion in those around him. Also, his ex-wife had been an alcoholic, so he understood Cathy's struggles with codependency. He also had two teenage children whom he saw every weekend, a fact that Cathy loved since she had no children herself.

After nine months of dating, Samuel offered Cathy an engagement ring that had been his grandmother's. The couple announced the news to Cathy's father, who promptly toasted their future. Cathy wanted to be sure that she and Samuel had a sustainable lifelong future together, so she suggested that they sign up for my "Partners in Life" program for premarital couples. He enthusiastically agreed, and a coach helped them evaluate the compatibility of their Vision, Requirements, Needs, and Wants, enhance their communication skills, and explore the possibility of building a successful committed relationship with each other.

One year later, the couple was married alongside a Cincinnati riverbank, and although it rained most of the afternoon, they were too happy to notice. They now live happily in Denver, where Cathy's daycare facility is thriving.

Cathy and Samuel signed up for my "Partners in Life" program for pre-committed couples.

Seth

Seth, age thirty, was on a mission to find the love of his life. He was tired of the one-night stands he'd had for years in New York City, so he set up daily dating "assignments," and was certain that his life partner would be his "degree." He was very aware of his requirements, such as finding a man who was: HIV negative; true to his word; able to support himself financially; and ready to be in a lifelong, monogamous relationship.

After intensely Scouting, Sorting, Screening, and Testing potential partners for over a year, a close friend set up Seth on a blind date with Evan, a forty-year-old entrepreneur with a successful dot.com business. Over time, Evan encouraged Seth to pursue his love of photography: he even offered him some business advice to put his photos on greeting cards and sell them. Within a short time, Seth had a healthy list of freelance photography contracts, and he loved his new career path! He also loved his new boyfriend!

Seth and Evan decided to move in together and they found a lovely West Village apartment where they can join their lives and their dogs. Seth is running his business out of their living room—with Evan's wholehearted support—and his greeting cards are selling like mad.

Dorothy

Dorothy made a bold move to join a video dating service for the first time in her life. She bought herself a new wardrobe, had her hair cut and styled, and signed up for a ballroom dancing class. Her girlfriends said that she looked ten years younger, and she felt it. At age fifty-five she was having the time of her life.

Dorothy also felt she was learning basic dating skills for the first time. At least once a week, she was going out with a different man, practicing Sorting and Screening. Still, she wanted to continue to focus on improving herself and living a fulfilling life, so she joined a reading group. She went to the art store and bought some canvases and oil paints, and turned her spare room at home into a painting studio. She also widened her support system by "promoting" a couple of her acquaintances to intimates.

Two years later, after going out with a variety of men she met through video dating, Dorothy took a break. She was feeling a little disheartened about finding her life partner, but was devoted to focusing on her life and being a successful single. In honor of her fifty-seventh birthday, Dorothy signed up for a relationship workshop in Austin for the weekend, and planned to stay at a girlfriend's house who was out of town.

Just after she lugged her suitcases into her girlfriend's house, the doorbell rang. There was a tall, limber man with salt-and-pepper hair standing in her friend's doorway, with a gas cap in one hand:

"Hi, sorry to bother you—" His name was Nelson, and he was a good friend of her girlfriend. Dorothy's friend had left her gas cap at the station on her way to the airport, and she'd called Nelson to track it down.

Dorothy was exhausted from her trip, but she invited him in for tea. He was very interested in the workshop she was attending, and before he left, they exchanged phone numbers. She found him likable, but did not feel any strong chemistry. One month later, however, sixty-year-old Nelson was in Houston on business—he was very successful in real estate—and he invited Dorothy out to dinner. Nelson surprised her by saying that he'd signed up for the same workshop she'd taken. He told her about his previous marriage of thirty years, his three children, and his last serious relationship. He also read some of his poetry out loud to her.

Nelson and Dorothy spent the next year visiting regularly and Testing each other to see if they were compatible. They took a vacation together in Hawaii, and attended a weeklong relationship workshop in Mexico. Dorothy was ready to have a man like Nelson in her life, someone who shared her life Vision so genuinely, and was so willing to learn new relationship skills.

She and Nelson are getting married this year, and Dorothy says it's a dream come true. Sometimes at night, she's lying in bed in tears, because she's so grateful to have found her life partner. She finds herself wanting to burst out joyfully to every single out there, "Never give up!"

DON'T WASTE A MOMENT MORE

You now have your very own Conscious Dating plan. By reading this book you are much further along in figuring out who you are as a person: your values, traits, skills, deficits, habits, patterns, past influences, judgments, and fears. You are more likely to be successful because you're clear about who you are and what you want. You know what your life Vision is, and this is what guides you to make choices. You know what you want because you've defined your Requirements and Needs.

Now that you have clarity about who you are and what you want, you will be able to choose a good partner and to have a more fulfilling connection with your partner. You are also clearer about whether you're ready for a committed relationship or if you need some time to focus on yourself while you date recreationally for fun. You know how to be The Chooser and get what you want in your life. You are prepared to say "no" to somebody if one of your Requirements is not being met. You take responsibility for getting what you want, and you assert your boundaries proactively.

You have also worked on your communication skills so that you can talk about your relationship issues and resolve them so that your needs are met. You have gained relationship experience with friends, family, coworkers, and others in your life to deepen your understanding of how relationships work. You realize that you are not going to succeed alone, so you have opened up your support system to include others.

I've said many times in this book: if you settle for less, you will get less. You have choices, so why not pursue what you really want in your life, work, and relationships? By choosing to live in alignment with who you are and what you really want, you're going to be more motivated and excited. You will attract the opportunities, resources, and people you need to be successful.

Don't waste a moment more. You can do it! ∕∙

Appendixes

A. FREQUENTLY ASKED QUESTIONS

1. What causes relationship failure?

People want to be happy, but they don't know how. We want a fulfilling relationship, but often choose partners who are not aligned with who we really are and what we really want. Singles fall into "Dating Traps" and make unconscious partner choices, assuming they can "make" a relationship work.

Often, when singles enter a pre-committed relationship, they realize the person they are with is not a good long-term choice, but they stay together because they don't want to be alone. They have a variety of self-sabotaging beliefs such as assuming they can't get what they really want, all the "good ones are taken," they're "too old," "too overweight," etc.

Making a good long-term partner choice starts with taking the trouble to be very clear about who you are and what you really want, and learning how to get what you want in your life and relationships.

2. How can I find my life partner?

If you are ready for a committed relationship (see #6 below) and you are very clear about who you are and what you want, there are many effective strategies for being successful in finding your life partner. For starters, review the "Ten Principles of Conscious Dating" (Chapters 5-15); apply the "Four Steps for Conscious Dating" (Chapter 6); and design your Relationship Plan (Chapter 15), which includes your best "Attraction Venues" (Chapter 6, and #11 below) for who you are and what you are seeking.

3. How do I know if this relationship is right for me?

To be a sustainable Life Partnership, all your Requirements must be met. It's the Requirement you are not aware of that appears later, or the problem you assume is solvable that isn't, that will typically cause relationship failure. When you Sort and Screen, you are gathering information about a prospective partner. Then, make sure to Test the information and get EXPERIENCE and KNOWLEDGE that the relationship meets all your Requirements BEFORE making a commitment.

There's no hurry. Take all the time you need to be very clear that this relationship will really work for you in the long run so you can make a commitment confidently, with your whole heart AND your head.

4. Should I date to have fun, or be serious about finding a partner?

Are you ready for a committed relationship? If you met the person you are looking for TODAY, would you be ready and available for him or her? These are hard questions for many singles who want the benefits of being in a relationship, but who are not really ready or available.

If you are already in an intimate relationship (even a bad one), have unfinished business from a past relationship, are going through divorce, are in a transition of some kind in your life, or have problems you need to work out (emotional, financial, legal, etc.), then you are probably not ready and available to meet your life partner. If this is the case, we recommend recreational dating (preferably nonexclusively) for fun while getting to the place in your life when you are ready.

5. What's wrong with single men/women?

There tends to be a gender difference in the way men and women approach dating. Men generally want to have fun, have sex, and try out the relationship before deciding the future. Women generally focus on the future and are more security-minded when dating. These two polar approaches result in misunderstanding. Many women despair of finding a "commitment-minded" man, and men complain that women are too serious, focused on evaluating and catching them, and that dating isn't fun.

Men and women should be clear and honest with each other about whether they are ready and looking for a committed relationship, or if they just want to have fun in a recreational relationship. If your agendas and goals for dating don't match with theirs, then move on. Don't be afraid to state what you're looking for; if you are rejected, the other person is doing you the favor of deciding for you that there is no future together, which frees you up to find someone more aligned with you.

6. Am I ready for a committed relationship?

Are you clear about your Vision for your life and relationship? Do you know your Life Purpose and ALL your Requirements? Are you emotionally free from your past relationships? Are you successful and happy without being in a relationship? Do you have enough relationship knowledge and experience to bring to a committed relationship and make it work? Do you know how to take responsibility for YOU in a relationship? Can you choose and initiate what you want, and say "no" to what you don't want in a relationship? You are ready when you can answer "Yes" to these questions.

7. Do I have to settle? Can I really find what I want in a relationship?

The fear that you can't find what you really want and the resulting belief that you must settle for less than you really want are self-fulfilling. When people settle in their relationship choices, they don't let go of what they want; they try to fit the round peg in the square hole and make it happen anyway, which is a setup for failure. If you are going to get what you REALLY want, you must say "NO" to what you don't want.

If you can let go of your fear of being alone and strive to be a "successful single," happy without a relationship, and give yourself the time and opportunity to find what you really want, you WILL be successful.

8. Will it really happen for ME?

Many of us tell ourselves we are too old, or too fat, or too poor, or too unattractive to find a Life Partner and have the relationship of our dreams. Of course, if you allow these beliefs to linger, they are self-fulfilling. The first step to finding your life partner is to love and accept yourself as you are, to believe that you deserve to be loved and happy and that you WILL find your life partner if you focus on living the life that you really want. Like the saying from the movie Field of Dreams, "If you build it, they will come." If you build the life that you really want, the people that you want in your life, including your life partner, WILL COME!

9. Should we live together first?

Many people see cohabitation as a necessary stepping-stone to a successful commitment; however, the statistics show that this is not the case. There is a world of difference in the mind-set between a committed relationship and what we call a "pre-committed" relationship.

When you are committed, there are no back doors, no exits; you are in this for the long haul. In a pre-committed relationship, you are trying to decide if this is the right relationship for you. Living together does not help a pre-committed relationship become a successful committed one.

You can get all the information you need by Scouting, Sorting, Screening, and Testing prospective partners and consciously making use of the pre-commitment period so there is no need to live together to test out the relationship. There is a higher risk of entering a "mini-marriage" when you believe you need to try a relationship to see if it fits you.

10. If it feels good, is it love?

People mistake attraction, "chemistry," good sex, attachment, having fun, infatuation, and just about any other romantic or sexual feeling for "love." There seems to be a romantic inside each of us who wants to believe that "love conquers all," "all you need is love," etc. It is tempting to interpret our romantic feelings as "love."

We tend to make our relationship mistakes when choosing and acting unconsciously, using our heart instead of our head. Just using your head might seem pretty unromantic and cold, and that is not desirable either. Conscious Dating advocates using your heart AND your head. To be a sustainable Life Partnership, all your Requirements must be met, and love must grow over time. The normal pattern is for your excitement about the relationship to start high and gradually fall down to earth. We recommend you give a relationship enough time to do this, and then see what you REALLY have and judge more objectively if the relationship is a good long-term choice for you, and if it really is "love."

11. Where do I meet potential partners?

In Chapter 6, we help you identify your "Attraction Venues," which are the places to meet the kind of people you want to meet. Conscious Dating identifies four levels of attraction venues:

Level One: Public places such as the supermarket, post office, art and wine festivals, etc., with a great diversity of people. Finding the Life Partner you are seeking in these settings is possible, but not very likely.

Level Two: Generic singles settings such as singles bars, singles clubs, and events, etc. I would also include personal ads here, because all you really know about the people who advertise or contact you through your ad is that they are single, and you don't really even know that, do you? While your odds increase in these settings because you can meet more singles, these are still low likelihood settings, as many frustrated singles will attest.

Level Three: These are settings in which you share a strong interest with everyone there, such as ski clubs, bike clubs, yoga classes, etc. These are settings where you would go to make friends and have fun, regardless of finding a partner. If you do not meet the kind of potential partners you are looking for, you can still form friendships and network. Your friends are your best scouts, and people whom you would want for friends are more likely to know someone good for you to meet.

Don't just focus on "meet markets" and get discouraged if a setting doesn't have the man or woman you are looking for. Have fun and make friends, and by living a life that is fulfilling and interesting to you, you will attract the people you want in your life. Birds of a feather flock together.

Level Four: These are settings in which you share important values, goals, and/or passions with everyone there, such as your church, service clubs, personal growth venues, etc. These are highly individual and can sometimes be a challenge to find, but the good news is that you can create your own. Remember, "If you build it, they will come!" These settings tend to be communities unto themselves, and have a strong level of mutual support and involvement. These are the people you would invite to your birthday party or wedding, the people who want to see you be happy and succeed in finding your life partner. These settings are the best venues for finding your life partner and/or getting the support you need to find your life partner. ✄

B. CONSCIOUS DATING GLOSSARY

In this book, some common words have very specific meanings. Below are definitions of the terms in this book specific to Conscious Dating:

Committed Relationship:

Closing all doors and exits and staying in the relationship through bad times as well as good. Problems are solved or lived with, and are not reasons for leaving the relationship. The benefits are security, family, companionship, achieving long-term goals, ability to deepen learning, intimacy, and love over time in ways unique to a long-term committed relationship.

Many challenging relationship problems are solved in a relationship only with commitment and perseverance. Breaking up a committed relationship should be an absolute last resort (especially when children are involved) as this choice is typically extremely costly and creates as many problems as it solves. For this reason, a committed relationship should not be entered into before having clarity about who you are, what you want, and the knowledge and experience that this relationship is right for you.

In today's world, couples often think of themselves as committed before actually making a commitment, leading to a difference between fact and attitude that sometimes creates problems. In addition, many couples have alternative lifestyles, and don't or can't embrace traditional forms of commitment such as marriage. We propose the following three criteria to define committed relationships:

CRITERIA #1: Promises made to each other about the permanent nature of the relationship that are kept

CRITERIA #2: Explicit, formal, public declaration

CRITERIA #3: Unambiguous to partners and others

Dating:
The process of socializing and spending time with a variety of people for the purpose of having fun. The practice of dating one person at a time for the purpose of testing if a relationship would work we refer to as "serial monogamy" or the "mini-marriage."

Typically, the sole criterion for dating someone is that he or she is attractive and willing. Conscious Dating is for someone who is ready for a committed relationship and is seeking a Life Partner. Conscious Daters will consciously Scout, Sort, Screen, and Test prospects until they find a high-likelihood candidate, and then enter a "pre-committed" relationship.

Life Partnership:
A long-term, committed relationship, with full intention of being together for the rest of your lives. Both parties are fully committed to the relationship by choice and dissolving the partnership is not considered an option, except as an absolute last resort after much time and good faith effort. A decision to enter into a Life Partnership is best made with the utmost self-awareness and conscious commitment.

Life Purpose:
Practicing your highest values, which give your life meaning and direction. Your Life Purpose is the difference you want to make in the world while you are alive, and the legacy you want to leave behind when you are gone.

Needs:
Events that must occur in your relationship for you to be content or happy. An unmet Need will result in an "issue," and must be addressed for you to successfully function in the relationship. Needs are persistent over time. There are usually many ways to meet a Need. There are two primary kinds of Needs in a relationship: functional needs and emotional needs. Functional Needs are the events

that must happen for you to function on a daily basis with your partner (paying bills, keeping agreements), and Emotional Needs are what you need to feel loved.

Pre-commitment:

An exclusive relationship with the goal of determining if this relationship is a good long-term choice before making a commitment. Making a good long-term relationship choice requires clarity about who you are and what you want, and experiencing that you can get what you really want in this relationship.

Recreational Relationship:

Spending time with someone for the purpose of having fun (see "Dating").

Requirements:

Nonnegotiable events and qualities required for a relationship to work for you. If one is missing, the relationship will not work and you have an unsolvable problem that will most likely result in relationship failure unless solved.

Scouting:

Step #1 of the Four Steps for Conscious Dating. Identifying people you would like to meet, on your own or with the assistance of your support system.

Sorting:

Step #2 of the Four Steps for Conscious Dating. The process of quickly determining if a person you meet aligns enough with your Requirements to engage the screening process and getting to know him or her better.

Screening:

Step #3 of the Four Steps for Conscious Dating. The process of learning enough about a potential partner before entering a relationship to determine whether he or she aligns with your Requirements.

Testing:
Step #4 of the Four Steps for Conscious Dating. The process of gaining the experience of your Requirements being met before becoming an exclusive couple and entering a pre-committed relationship.

Unsolvable Problems:
Requirements or Needs that cannot be met in this relationship. Four alternatives for coping with an unsolvable problem: 1. Live with it 2. Let go of the relationship (common) 3. Let go of the Requirement or Need (rare) 4. Compromise and give up part of what is important to you to meet in the middle (possible, but usually results in unhappiness without outside assistance). Unsolvable Problems are the most common reasons for relationship failure.

Vision:
Inner images about the future life that you really want. Acts as your "inner guidance system" driving you toward certain choices and away from other choices. Often, most of your Vision lies beneath the surface waiting to be discovered.

C. INVITATION TO JOIN
OUR CONSCIOUS DATING ONLINE COMMUNITY

Now that you've finished reading *Conscious Dating*, I invite you to continue your journey to find the love of your life and the life that you love by joining our Conscious Dating Online Community. It's free!

Please visit us at right now at www.consciousdating.org for free:
- audio programs
- e-programs
- live tele-seminars
- online community of like-minded singles
- monthly newsletter with cutting-edge relationship information
- access to our worldwide network of relationship coaches
- and more!

By becoming a member—free—you will have access to our online personal ads and matchmaking service. This is a service like no other matchmaking system. It is designed around our knowledge of what it takes for best success in conscious relationships.

Conscious Dating can be challenging and is not for everyone. You've made the first step by reading this book and completing the exercises. But is Conscious Dating for you? Are you...

- ready and available for a committed relationship?

- clear about who you are and what you want for your life and relationship?

- serious about being authentic, conscious and intentional in finding your life partner?

By signing up at www.consciousdating.org, you will join a community of conscious singles just like you! You will also have access to hundreds of coaches from all over the world.

Lastly, you will be able to listen to free audio programs, and sign up for classes and workshops such as our Conscious Dating Relationship Success Training for Singles (RESTS) program and work directly with a coach to develop your Vision, Life Purpose, Requirements, Needs, and Wants.

I look forward to hearing from you as you begin your journey to find the love of your life. ✐

HOW TO CONTACT THE AUTHOR:

David@RelationshipCoachingInstitute.com

Mailing address:
P.O. Box 111783, Campbell, CA 95011
Telephone: 888-268-4074

Web Sites of the Relationship Coaching Network:

About this book
www.ConsciousDating.com

For singles
www.ConsciousDating.org

For couples
www.PartnersInLife.org

For relationship coaching training
www.RelationshipCoachingInstitute.com

For building a successful private practice
www.BuildingYourIdealPractice.com

Free Conscious Relationship Tele-Seminars
www.ConsciousRelationshipSeminars.com

Free Conscious Relationship Podcast
www.ConsciousRelationshipPodcast.com

RCN Press
www.RCNpress.com

REFERENCES

ENDNOTES

INTRODUCTION
1. Rose M. Kreider and Tavia Simmons, *Marital Status 2000: Census 2000 Brief* (Washington, DC: U.S. Census Bureau, October 2003), 1.

CHAPTER 1
1. Ronald W. Manderscheid and Marilyn J. Henderson, eds., *Mental Health, United States, 2002* (Rockville, MD: U.S. Department of Health and Human Services, Substance Abuse and Mental Health Services Administration, 2002), 21:13.
2. Kreider and Simmons, *Marital Status 2000.*
3. Michael A. Fletcher, "For Better or Worse, Marriage Hits a Low; Study Reports New Lows for Marriage Rates and Wedded Bliss," *Washington Post*, July 2, 1999, A1.
4. Cheryl Wetzstein, "Researchers See Marriage as a Weakening Institution," *The Washington Times*, October 28, 1999.
5. Linda Waite and Maggie Gallagher, *The Case for Marriage: Why Married People Are Happier, Healthier, and Better Off Financially* (New York: Broadway Books, 2001).

CHAPTER 2
1. Shannon, e-mail to Smartmarriages mailing list, June 11, 1999, listarchives.his.com/smart marriages/smartmarriages.9906/msg00016.html.
2. David Popenoe and Barbara Dafoe Whitehead, *The State of Our Unions: The Social Health of Marriage in America, 2005* (Piscataway, NJ: The National Marriage Project, 2005).
3. Popenoe and Whitehead, *The State of Our Unions.*
4. Laurent Belsie, "America's On/Off Relationship with Wedlock," *The Christian Science Monitor*, February 8, 2002.
5. Hedy Schleifer, *The Miracle of Connection* (audio recording). Produced and recorded by David Steele. www.miracleofconnection.com, February 2004.
6. Helen Fisher, *Anatomy of Love: A Natural History of Mating, Marriage, and Why We Stray* (New York: Ballantine Books, 1994), 65.
7. Fisher, *Anatomy of Love*, 293.
8. Dean Ornish, *Love and Survival: The Scientific Basis for the Healing Power of Intimacy* (New York: HarperCollins, 1998), 3.
9. Norval D. Glenn and others, *Why Marriage Matters: Twenty-One Conclusions from the Social Sciences* (Minneapolis: Center of the American Experiment; Washington, DC: Coalition for Marriage, Family, and Couples Education; and New York: Institute for American Values, 2002), 1-28.
10. Waite and Gallagher, *The Case for Marriage*, 155.
11. Nadine F. Marks and James D. Lambert, "Marital Status Continuity and Change among Young and Midlife Adults: Longitudinal Effects on Psychological Well-Being," *The Journal of Family Issues*, 1998, 19:652-86.

12. Walecia Konrad, "The Truth About Women, Men and Money," *Redbook*, October, 2002, 126.

CHAPTER 3
1. Dukcevich, Davide. "Best Cities For Singles," *Forbes*, June 6, 2002.

CHAPTER 4
1. David Bentley, "The Singles Blues," Relationship Coaching Institute Newsletter, March 2001.
2. Ethan Watters, *Urban Tribes: A Generation Redefines Friendship, Family, and Commitment* (London: Bloomsbury, 2003).
3. Sasha Cagen, *Quirkyalone: A Manifesto for Uncompromising Romantics* (San Francisco: Harper Collins, 2004), 4-6.
4. Shakti Gawain, *Relationships as Mirrors* (audio recording) (Novato, CA: New World Library, 1991).
5. Gawain, *Relationships as Mirrors.*

CHAPTER 5
1. John Gottman and Nan Silver, *The Seven Principles for Making Marriage Work* (New York: Crown Books, 1999), 23, 130.
2. Deki Fox, "Philosophy of Requirements," *Relationship Coaching Institute Newsletter*, April 2002.
3. Jackson H. Brown Jr., *Life's Little Instruction Book* (Nashville, TN: Rutledge Hill Press, Deluxe edition, 1991).

CHAPTER 6
1. David Brooks, "Love, Internet Style," *New York Times*, November 8, 2003, A15.

CHAPTER 7
1. Robert F. Bennett, http://bennett.senate.gov/.
2. Rosalind Barnett and Caryl Rivers, *Same Difference: How Gender Myths Are Hurting Our Relationships* (New York: Basic Books, 2004), 1-6.
3. American Society for Aesthetic Plastic Surgery, "8.3 Million Cosmetic Procedures: American Society for Aesthetic Plastic Surgery Reports 20 Percent Increase," news release, February 18, 1004.

CHAPTER 8
1. Fisher, *Anatomy of Love,* 181.

CHAPTER 10
1. Lynn Grabhorn, *Excuse Me, Your Life is Waiting* (Charlottesville, VA: Hampton Roads Publishing Company, 1999), 5.
2. Grabhorn, *Excuse Me, Your Life is Waiting,* 201.
3. Grabhorn, *Excuse Me, Your Life is Waiting,* 202.
4. Grabhorn, *Excuse Me, Your Life is Waiting,* 295.

CHAPTER 11

1. Frank Pittman, *Grow Up! How Taking Responsibility Can Make You a Happy Adult* (New York: St. Martin's, 1999), 278.

CHAPTER 16

1. First Step Family Violence Intervention Center "We Believe in Marriage," http://www.firststepweb.org/marriage.html
2. Waite and Gallagher, *The Case for Marriage*, 155.
3. Diane Sollee, Smartmarriages Web site, http://www.smartmarriages.com/dr.romance.html
4. Popenoe and Whitehead, *The State of Our Unions*.
5. Popenoe and Whitehead, *The State of Our Unions*.

BIBLIOGRAPHY

Barnett, Rosalind, and Caryl Rivers. *Same Difference: How Gender Myths Are Hurting Our Relationships, Our Children, and Our Jobs.* New York: Basic Books, 2004.

Belsie, Laurent. "America's on/off Relationship with wedlock." *The Christian Science Monitor*, February 8, 2002.

Bentley, David. "The Singles Blues." *Relationship Coaching Institute Newsletter*, March 2001.

Bernell, Bonnie. *Bountiful Women: Large Women's Secrets for Living the Life They Desire.* Berkeley: Wildcat Canyon Press, 2000.

Brooks, David. "Love, Internet Style." *New York Times*, November 8, 2003, A15.

Brown, Jackson H. Jr. Life's *Little Instruction Book.* Rutledge Hill Press. Deluxe edition, 1991.

Cagen, Sasha. *Quirkyalone: A Manifesto for Uncompromising Romantics.* San Francisco: HarperCollins, 2004.

Dukcevich, Davide. "Best Cities for Singles." *Forbes*, June 5, 2003.

First Step Family Violence Intervention Center "We Believe in Marriage," http://www.first stepweb.org/marriage.html

Fisher, Bruce. *Rebuilding: When Your Relationship Ends. Atascadero*, CA: Impact Publishers, 1999.

Fisher, Helen. *Anatomy of Love: A Natural History of Mating, Marriage, and Why We Stray.* New York: Ballantine Books, 1994.

Fletcher, Michael A. "For Better or Worse, Marriage Hits a Low; Study Reports New Lows for Marriage Rates and Wedded Bliss." *Washington Post*, July 2, 1999, A1.

Fox, Deki. "Philosophy of Requirements." *Relationship Coaching Institute Newsletter*, April 2002.

Gawain, Shakti. *Relationships as Mirrors* (audio recording). Novato, CA: New World Library, 1991.

Glenn, Norval D., Steven Nock, Linda Waite, William J. Doherty, William A. Glaston, John Gottman, Barbara Markey, et al. *Why Marriage Matters: Twenty-One Conclusions from the*

Social Sciences. Minneapolis: Center of the American Experiment; Washington, DC: Coalition for Marriage, Family, and Couples Education; and New York: Institute for American Values, 2002.

Gottman, John, and Nan Silver. *The Seven Principles for Making Marriage Work*. New York: Crown Books, 1999.

Grabhorn, Lynn. *Excuse Me, Your Life Is Waiting: The Astonishing Power of Feelings*. Charlottesville, VA: Hampton Roads Publishing Company, 2000.

Hendrix, Harville. *Getting the Love You Want*. New York: Owl Books, 2001.

Hendrix, Harville. *Keeping the Love You Find*. New York: Atria Books, 1993.

Hogan, Eve Eschner. *Intellectual Foreplay: Questions for Lovers and Lovers-to-Be*. Alameda, CA: Hunter House, 2000.

Konrad, Walecia. "The Truth About Women, Men and Money." *Redbook*, 2002.

Kreider, Rose M., and Tavia Simmons. *Marital Status 2000: Census 2000 Brief*. Washington, DC: U.S. Census Bureau, October 2003.

Manderscheid, Ronald W., and Marilyn J. Henderson, eds. Mental Health, United States, 2002. Rockville, MD: U.S. Department of Health and Human Services, Substance Abuse and Mental Health Services Administration, 2002.

Marcott, Craig. *Three Minutes of Intimacy: Dance Your Way to a Sensational Social Life*. Northborough, MA: Sundance Publishing, 2000.

Marks, Nadine F., and James D. Lambert. "Marital Status Continuity and Change among Young and Midlife Adults: Longitudinal Effects on Psychological Well-Being." *The Journal of Family Issues*, 1998.

Ornish, Dean. *Love and Survival: The Scientific Basis for the Healing Power of Intimacy*. New York: HarperCollins, 1998.

Pittman, Frank. *Grow Up! How Taking Responsibility Can Make You a Happy Adult*. New York: St. Martin's, 1999.

Popenoe, David, and Barbara Dafoe Whitehead. *The State of Our Unions: The Social Health of Marriage in America 2001*. Piscataway, NJ: The National Marriage Project, 2001.

Schleifer, Hedy. *The Miracle of Connection* (audio recording). Produced and recorded by David Steele. www.miracleofconnection.com, February 2004.

Waite, Linda, and Maggie Gallagher. *The Case for Marriage: Why Married People Are Happier, Healthier, and Better Off Financially*. New York: Broadway Books, 2001.

Watters, Ethan. *Urban Tribes: A Generation Redefines Friendship, Family, and Commitment*. London: Bloomsbury, 2003.

Wetzstein, Cheryl. "Researchers See Marriage as a Weakening Institution." *The Washington Times*, October 28, 1999.